Cambridge Studies in French

TASTE AND IDEOLOGY IN
SEVENTEENTH-CENTURY FRANCE

Cambridge Studies in French

General editor: MALCOLM BOWIE

Recent titles in this series include:

MITCHELL GREENBERG
Corneille, Classicism, and the Ruses of Symmetry

HOWARD DAVIES
Sartre and 'Les Temps Modernes'

ROBERT GREER COHN
Mallarmé's Prose Poems: A Critical Study

CELIA BRITTON
Claude Simon: Writing the Visible

DAVID SCOTT
*Pictorialist Poetics: Poetry and the
Visual Arts in Nineteenth-Century France*

ANN JEFFERSON
Reading Realism in Stendhal

DALIA JUDOVITZ
*Subjectivity and Representation in Descartes
The Origins of Modernity*

RICHARD D. E. BURTON
*Baudelaire in 1859
A Study in the Sources of Poetic Creativity*

For a full list of books in the series, see p. 231

TASTE AND IDEOLOGY IN SEVENTEENTH-CENTURY FRANCE

MICHAEL MORIARTY

Fellow of Gonville and Caius College, Cambridge

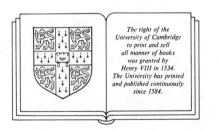

The right of the
University of Cambridge
to print and sell
all manner of books
was granted by
Henry VIII in 1534.
The University has printed
and published continuously
since 1584.

CAMBRIDGE UNIVERSITY PRESS

CAMBRIDGE

NEW YORK NEW ROCHELLE

MELBOURNE SYDNEY

Published by the Press Syndicate of the University of Cambridge
The Pitt Building, Trumpington Street, Cambridge CB2 1RP
32 East 57th Street, New York, NY 10022, USA
10 Stamford Road, Oakleigh, Melbourne 3166, Australia

First published 1988

Printed in Great Britain at
the University Press, Cambridge

British Library cataloguing in publication data
Moriarty, Michael
Taste and ideology in seventeenth-century
France. − (Cambridge studies in French).
1. France. Society. Role of ideologies,
1600−1700
I. Title
306'.42'0944

Library of Congress cataloguing in publication data
Moriarty, Michael, 1956−
Taste and ideology in seventeenth-century France / Michael
Moriarty.
p. cm. − (Cambridge studies in French)
Bibliography.
Includes index.
ISBN 0 521 30686 8
1. French literature − 17th century − History and criticism.
2. Aesthetics, French − 17th century. 3. Social ethics in
literature. 4. Etiquette − France − History − 17th century.
I. Title. II. Series
PQ245.M74 1988
840'.9'004 − dc 19   88-2856 CIP

ISBN 0 521 30686 8

WS

And therefore in reasoning, a man must take heed of words; which besides the signification of what we imagine of their nature, have a signification also of the nature, disposition, and interest of the speaker.

Thomas Hobbes, *Leviathan*, Part I, chapter 4

All rulers are the heirs of those who conquered before them. Hence, empathy with the victor invariably benefits the rulers. Historical materialists know what that means. Whoever has emerged victorious participates to this day in the triumphal procession in which the present rulers step over those who are lying prostrate. According to traditional practice, the spoils are carried along in the procession. They are called cultural treasures, and a historical materialist views them with cautious detachment. For without exception the cultural treasures he surveys have an origin which he cannot contemplate without horror. They owe their existence not only to the efforts of the great minds and talents who have created them, but also to the anonymous toil of their contemporaries. There is no document of civilization which is not at the same time a document of barbarism. And just as such a document is not free of barbarism, barbarism taints also the manner in which it was transmitted from one owner to another. A historical materialist therefore dissociates himself from it as far as possible. He regards it as his task to brush history against the grain.

Walter Benjamin, 'Theses on the Philosophy of History', VII

With this defiance, Mr Weller buttoned up his change in his side pocket, and, with many confirmatory nods and gestures by the way, proceeded in search of the subject of discourse.

Charles Dickens, *The Pickwick Papers*, chapter 45

To the memory of my father,
Martin Moriarty,
1904—83

CONTENTS

PREFACE

This book started life as a Ph.D. dissertation in the Faculty of Modern and Medieval Languages of Cambridge University. Two terms' grant from the College Council of St John's College made it possible for me to continue research on the project at a crucial stage, and by electing me into a Research Fellowship the College Council of Gonville and Caius College enabled me to complete the dissertation and to embark on the process of turning it into a book. To those two bodies, therefore, my first thanks are due.

After the economic base, the intellectual and personal super-structure: but the theoretical terms are an ungracious mode of acknowledgment of the many people who have helped over the years in the eventual production of this book. My former supervisor, Professor Odette de Mourgues, has provided constant guidance, support, and encouragement, and much salutary criticism too. This book has benefited incalculably from her insight into seventeenth-century French literature and literary ideas. I should like to thank the General Editor of this series, Malcolm Bowie, for his painstaking reading of the manuscript. It is a great pleasure, also, to be able to thank here the following people, who have all contributed, directly or indirectly, to this undertaking: Peter Bayley, Terence Cave, Dorothy Coleman, Peter France, Liz Guild, Edward James, Lisa Jardine, Gillian Jondorf, Paddy O'Donovan. There is another debt, not a personal one, that I should like to record, to the work of Raymond Williams, whose influence on this book is much greater than the mere endnote references suggest. And finally I want to thank Morag Shiach.

ABBREVIATIONS

CAIEF   *Cahiers de l'Association Internationale des Etudes Françaises*
L   *Lettres* (Méré, Saint-Evremond)
MLR   *Modern Language Review*
OC   *Œuvres complètes* (Méré, Boileau)
OP   *Œuvres en prose* (Saint-Evremond)
PFSCL   *Papers in French Seventeenth-Century Literature*
RBPH   *Revue belge de philologie et d'histoire*
RHL   *Revue d'histoire littéraire de la France*

1

'TASTE' AND HISTORY

The object of this book is 'taste' in seventeenth-century France, as a unit of discourse within a field of ideological struggle. The writing of the book, and its publication, belong to Britain in the 1980s. The initial problem is that of the relationship between these two historical moments.

It is, of course, often denied that there is any such problem; it is asserted that the historian's duty is to steer clear of involvement in the present, to deal with the past for its own sake and in its own terms, on pain of anachronism. There is some value in this claim as a working assumption: it helps to preserve the past in its difference, to keep facile contemporary judgments at bay. But in another sense the risk of anachronism is greatest where the links between past and present, act of study and object of study are repressed; where the history-writing forgets that it is itself part of history. To 'study the past in its own terms' can then be tantamount to denying real connexions between past and present. And this is perhaps particularly clear in the present context. For there are many things that separate us from seventeenth-century France, France of the *ancien régime*, but 'taste' is one of those that do not: our culture still commits us − as, through a process of ideological struggle, the privileged classes of seventeenth-century France were committed − to making judgments of taste, and to having them passed upon us.

To take account of this fact, it is not necessary to postulate a universal human nature, which is simply reproduced through different stages of history. This assumption, indeed, would be of scant assistance here, since, while it is undoubtedly true that all cultures deem some things preferable to others, the object of this study is, specifically, the referral of these preferences, many of them dealing with intangible, and certainly inedible objects, to a criterion derived metaphorically from the action of eating; and there is no evidence that this is a universal phenomenon. Even if it were, the fact remains that the consecration of certain preferences in speech, dress, and literature (to name but

1

three possible spheres of 'taste') in Western Europe over the last three or four centuries has a particular significance for us different from that of whatever normative processes hold sway in other cultures.

But this significance can be viewed from many different historical perspectives. In seventeenth-century France, the imposition of certain cultural norms in the name of 'taste' was viewed, not only as the re-enactment of timeless standards, but, in particular, as the revival of great ages of the past: the reign of Augustus especially. Being still habituated to a view of history inherited from the Enlightenment, linear rather than cyclical, we may feel more comfortable with the idea that our ideals are related to those of seventeenth-century France as two moments in a single 'civilizing process' (using these words in their everyday sense, rather than in specific relation to the theories of Norbert Elias).

But it is precisely the use of 'we' there, and the sense of historical solidarity with the people of the past that it tends to foster, that is the problem. For this comfortable sense of belonging, in this sphere at any rate, to one and the same order of values as they, even the gratitude we may feel to them for this inheritance, conceals the problem of who, in fact, is making these judgments, and on behalf of whom, now and in the seventeenth century.

There is an element of parody, of course (but is it a matter of course?) in my use of the term 'inheritance'; but it does encapsulate one way of thinking about the past and our relationship to it: that is, in the figurative as in the material context, to identify ourselves with the people in possession, the people in power.

For power indeed, as I shall be arguing, is what is at stake in all the talk about 'taste' in seventeenth-century France, the talk through which a measure of sociocultural control is negotiated, in which hegemonic struggles between classes and class fractions are fought out. One of the aspects of victory, in such cultural conflicts, is to be able to impose the terms in which the conflict is subsequently represented. In that case, the historian who reads and writes 'with the grain', that is to say, viewing the history as the field in which the values are sown that nourish our culture (whose culture?) today, is simply consecrating the interests asserted in those values.

One could of course argue that, for all their implication in cultural debates and preoccupations of the past, the values are no less relevant today; that they have, over time, precisely become liberated from their original matrix. This detachment of 'ideologemes' from their original context of operation is a frequent enough phenomenon − 'freedom' didn't mean the same to a Negro slave as it does to a privatizing Tory

2

minister – but one is not thereby given access to 'the thing itself', simply to its relation to a new set of elements in discourse. And this is the second factor affecting the subject-position of the contemporary analyst: the subsequent fortunes and associations of the notion under investigation. As I said at the outset, we are still, like it or not, under the sway of discourse of 'taste' – whether we consciously pass 'taste'-judgments or not, we cannot escape their being passed on us – and, in the 1980s Britain in which I am writing, these cannot be separated from consciousness of class, from the class struggle in ideology. It is not just that, in these recent years of recrudescent and thriving re-action, 'taste' has been one of the fields of struggle, with the emergence and valorization of cultural types – Sloane Rangers, Young Fogeys – who symbolize the enforcement of norms of appearance, preference, behaviour to which access is restricted to those from traditionally privileged backgrounds. The whole notion of a spontaneous sense of what is right and proper in a whole field of practices and situations (which is what, I take it, most people would understand by 'taste') is premised on an early and wide-ranging acculturation; and since it is in practice middle-, or more precisely upper-middle-class definitions of 'taste' that prevail, then the discourse of 'taste' postulates a subject from these class-origins.

This state of affairs can hardly fail to affect the significance of a study of earlier notions of 'taste'. For if that study accepts the 'taste'-utterances it deals with at their face-value, from within the perspective of 'taste', then it is helping to legitimize that perspective and hence reproducing, consciously or not, the contemporary ideological effects of 'taste'-discourse. On the other hand, an awareness of these effects is methodologically salutary, inviting a healthy suspicion of the utterances dealt with that, instead of merely glossing and evaluating them in terms akin to their own, asks what they meant at the time, what interests they advanced, whom they privileged, whom excluded.

In espousing the return of the discourse to its historical conditions of production and operation, I am not saying that those writers who have used it to nourish their own views about (contemporary) culture (Naves on Voltaire is a good example) are *mistaken*.[1] On the contrary, their doing so simply bears out the point I have just been making: the potential continuities of a perspective of 'taste'. It is, from my own point of view, precisely the existence of these continuities, with their characteristic ideological effects as mentioned above, that calls for the denaturalization of that perspective as a worthwhile intellectual and political task.

This denaturalization can of course be achieved within the contemporary frame of reference, and this is what Bourdieu has attempted with his formidable *La Distinction*, in which 'aesthetic' preferences and cultural attitudes in contemporary France are meticulously correlated with social position and 'cultural capital'. It is none the less noteworthy how often Bourdieu resorts to the *ancien régime* (quoting Méré, for instance, who is studied here) to provide categories and illustrations for his enterprise.[2] In fact, to demonstrate historical filiations and discontinuities, returning familiar concepts to a possibly unfamiliar history − a history of difference − can exert a certain denaturalizing effect in terms of contemporary ideology. I hope that this book, which is also and in a sense primarily a contribution to the academic discipline of studies of seventeenth-century France, may achieve something on this other level as well.

A sociological study of seventeenth-century French 'taste', investigating, *à la* Bourdieu, the distribution of particular preferences and practices among different social groups would be invaluable, but it is not what I am attempting here.[3] I shall be looking at some contemporary statements as to this distribution, but in doing so, I shall remain on the level of discourse, not attempting, on the whole, to correlate them with established fact. This distinction between the sociological reality and its representation in discourse is in itself obvious enough and throughout this book it should be clear enough from the context. But I am making a further claim, namely, that the whole notion of 'taste' as a faculty of discernment is implicitly defined and manipulated by some of the authors studied so as to privilege certain social groups, while excluding others − so that without having to find distinctions in practice between the 'taste' of the subordinate groups and that of the dominant groups, one could know *a priori* that the former was bad. In other words, it is not just that certain specific tastes can be valorized because they are imputed to the dominant class, while certain others are proscribed by being represented as socially inferior. The very notion of 'taste' as a faculty can already exert ideological effects prior to those of any specific comment on people's actual tastes, by virtue of the social criteria operative in its definition. If this is so, we can say that the dominant and the subordinate classes are distinguished both by their tastes (concrete preferences, real or supposed) and by 'taste' (a cognitive faculty so defined as to be attributable only or mainly to the dominant classes). The faculty of 'taste', that is, vouches for the superiority of the dominant class's concrete preferences, and moreover, that faculty is characteristically

4

to be found in members, though not necessarily all members, of the dominant class. Usually, the distinction between the actual preferences and the general faculty is sufficiently clear from the context: but when I want to emphasize that the faculty of 'taste' is not an objective reality but a key term in a language of social distinction I place the word in quotation marks. The result is inelegant, but the point at issue is important.

Reverting to a more concrete level, we should note one major difference between seventeenth-century attitudes to taste and those of modern Europe: a difference in the range and form of distinctions. Thus, the type of house one inhabits and how it is furnished are nowadays highly indicative of one's 'taste' and suggestive of one's social position. It would appear, from Jean Alter's account of anti-bourgeois satire, that this was not so in the seventeenth century. The condemnation of bourgeois luxury does not encompass the objects in which it is manifested: the shame is, simply, that they should have fallen into bourgeois hands.[4] The palace built by La Bruyère's anonymous bourgeois features on the tourist trail alongside the Palais-Royal, the Luxembourg, and the palatial *hôtel* of the parvenu courtier Langlée; buildings are silent as to the rank of their owner, but there is nevertheless an absurd disproportion between the splendour of this one and the anonymity of its occupant, as if that silence were in fact regrettable.[5] The bourgeois banquet attacked by satirists is characterized by excessively rich dishes and ridiculous or vulgar behaviour; sometimes, however, the food itself is bad as well, as in Boileau's *Le Repas ridicule* (satire III).[6] Clothes were another area of class-tension: Montchrétien complained it was no longer possible to class people by their external appearance: 'l'homme de boutique est vestu comme le gentilhomme'.[7] This complaint was doubtless exaggerated, but it does bear out the point that taste as such is not an index of class-distinction; otherwise the assertion of possible confusion would be incredible. In point of fact, it would appear that the clothes of the middle bourgeoisie were held to be ridiculous in themselves, but the upper bourgeoisie dressed in the same way as the nobility, to the indignation of those who would have wished them to externalize their social inferiority in their appearance. No doubt the discreet and tasteful luxury, eschewing vulgar ostentation, of the dress of the *honnête homme* is to be viewed as a response to competition from rich *roturiers*.[8] Even so, the point seems to remain that in the material culture of everyday life distinctions of rank were less legible than conservative moralists and satirists would wish.

Another historical difference throws its shadow across the seventeenth-century French discourse of 'taste'. This is is the construction of 'the aesthetic' as a mode or domain of experience and of 'aesthetics' as the science that deals with it.

I take this construction to be essentially an eighteenth-century phenomenon, closely associated with the selective identification of 'the arts' (alias the 'fine' or the 'creative' arts) as a separate realm.[9] It seems to me that the very proximity of this development to the period under discussion here creates serious problems in the use of these terms.

It is, of course, true that questions of beauty and pleasure were discussed long before Baumgarten coined the term 'aesthetics' and thus baptized the new area of discourse. The familiar seventeenth-century insistence on the need to give pleasure (*plaire*) bears out the point. To recite the familiar litany:

Je voudrois bien savoir si la grande règle de toutes les règles n'est pas de
plaire.   (Molière)

La principale règle est de plaire et de toucher.   (Racine)

Le secret est d'abord de plaire et de toucher.   (Boileau)

Voulez-vous long-temps plaire, et jamais ne lasser?   (Boileau)

not to mention Méré's expatiations on *les agréments*, or La Bruyère's subtle analysis of the different effects of Racine and Corneille.[10]

All these references − bar the example from Méré − come from an explicitly literary context; and there are plenty of other utterances from literary contexts, or that can be given a literary significance, that can contribute to a plausible reconstruction of the classical literary aesthetic, as something more elusive and flexible, more oriented towards practice and less towards precept, than 'la doctrine classique'. 'Taste' can easily find its place in this construction.[11]

Two things are, however, invisible in this perspective: first of all, discursive context, and secondly, the subject.[12] They are indeed in some sense superfluous from the point of view of the institution of literary criticism. For the requirements of that institution themselves determine context, make it possible to abstract from past discourses whatever contributes to the project of expounding and appreciating literary texts, whatever helps the constitution of Literature. The subject of the pleasure these texts speak of, the value-judgments they pass, is absent because the critic is there to take its place, to appropriate the meaning of the utterances in order to inhabit the perspective of their speaker, the better to apply them to his or her own subsequent reading of the literature of the period.

6

However, these absences are not unimportant. Literary practice doubtless has its own, historically variable, specificity, and thus to abstract literary from other references is compatible with the preservation of a kind of coherence. But it dissolves the actual and historically variable social relationships of literary with other practices, the articulation of literary with other discourses. This articulation, moreover, helps to determine the range of subjects addressed by the discourse, its capacity for excluding some and privileging others, and hence its general ideological effect.

In response to these problems, which may appear more clearly and more concretely as we proceed, the method adopted here has been to let the signifier *goût*, within a limited number of chosen texts (more about this choice presently), determine the contexts of its operation, whether literary or not. From this a picture of the subject-positions constructed by the various discourses begins to emerge. It will be seen, I think, that these discourses and their effects range far beyond the field generally identified as aesthetic.

There is nothing particularly novel in emphasizing the articulation of literary with other practices. Mornet's important chapter on the *art de plaire* in his *Histoire de la littérature française classique* contains the observation that in this context 'il est souvent fort difficile de faire le départ entre ce qui ne concerne que la vie, ce qui ne touche que la littérature et ce qui importe à la fois à l'une et à l'autre'.[13] J.-P. Dens's study of *L'Honnête Homme et la critique du goût* similarly stresses the interaction between literary standards and those applied to social life, and Christoph Strosetzski's important study of conversation draws attention to the social grounding of the literary *bienséances*.[14]

These writers all make use of the technique of assembling a large corpus of utterances, from a variety of authors, bearing on the matter in hand. The approach adopted here is a different and, as it may appear, more old-fashioned one, in which the object of study (with the exception of a chapter on dictionaries) is the *œuvre* of individual authors. Moreover, there is nothing particularly recondite in the choice of authors: Méré, Saint-Evremond, La Rochefoucauld, La Bruyère, Boileau. The last three are securely in the seventeenth-century literary 'canon', the first two known to all specialists of the period.

There are various objections to this procedure. The first, and to my mind most serious, is its male-centredness. This particular choice of authors permits, it may be, certain conclusions to be drawn about the class ideology of taste-discourse and about the position of women

7

in male taste-discourse. It does not permit discussion of the position of women as active subjects – speakers – of the discourse of taste; the few remarks about Anne Le Fèvre (Mme Dacier) here scarcely deal adequately with issues of gender. I can at this stage only apologize to women readers for this lack.

Secondly, it might be contended that to concentrate on such a narrow range of authors can only give rise to rash generalizations and muttered quotations from Blake in response. But the point of this work is not, as the objection supposes, to produce generalizations about taste-discourse in seventeenth-century France from the work of a handful of authors. The terms 'taste-discourse' and 'the discourse of taste' are used here to designate the body of potential utterances – potential, that is, in seventeenth-century France – in which the signifier 'taste' contributes to strong normative judgments. But this corpus is evidently a purely abstract construct, and it would be improper to credit it as such with a characteristic ideological effect. The bulk of this work is devoted rather to analyses of certain actual discourses of taste (i.e. subsets of the corpus of taste-discourse), centred on an author and constituting a certain ideological position: the interest is in the specific articulations of judgments of taste with other judgments, other ideological positions. It is argued that each of these authorial corpuses contributes, consciously or unconsciously, to the class struggle in ideology in seventeenth-century France.

The differences between individual taste-discourses militate against any attempt to make general statements about taste-discourse, considered as the sum of all *actual* discourses in which 'taste' operates as a signifier. The sample here studied is big enough to reveal these differences. It is not big enough (it would have of course to be exhaustive) to permit of positive assertions about hypothetical common features of all actual seventeenth-century French taste-discourse. The presence, however, of certain common features uniting otherwise contradictory discourses does, I think, permit *probable hypotheses* about the prevailing ideological effect of actual discourse about taste in general; especially when these hypotheses agree with and bear out a general picture of seventeenth-century French society that is not derived from the limited range of texts studied here but from a body of historical work and social theory. This may indeed have been misapplied here; but that is another question. What I claim to derive from the analysis of the texts themselves is a profile of some of the various ideological positions that particular taste-utterances help to constitute. What this means is that the findings of this work could not simply

8

be taken over and applied to authors not covered within it, who would each require individual treatment.

There is, then, a problem of selection. But before I attempt to justify the solution to it offered here, there are other problems, more basic, to consider. Firstly, it might seem that the method adopted by the authors mentioned above — Mornet, Strosetzski, Dens — of illustrating a series of pertinent topics by quotations taken from a wide variety of authors would have been preferable here, expanding as it does the range of texts brought into consideration. And certainly there is a sacrifice of range in the approach adopted here. None the less, it has its distinctive advantages. For the other approach depends on the characterization of a set of topics to which the texts studied are held to be pertinent. Thus Dens writes that his objective is to illustrate the passage from 'la critique érudite' to 'la critique mondaine', and for this the approach he adopts is ideally suited.[15] But I am interested in this transition, and in 'l'esthétique classique', only in relation to a much larger ideological struggle within French society. With the author-centred approach, one observes the play of 'taste', the signifier, over a wide range of contexts: one doesn't select the contexts oneself; one observes the articulation of 'taste'-judgments about 'literature' with similar judgments about quite other fields of activity, and one tries to relate this articulation to the historical study of ideology. If 'il n'est d'idéologie que par le sujet et que pour des sujets', then the author, as subject, provides the richest field for a study of the operations of ideology.[16] Of course, criticism, or rather literary theory — or 'theory' *tout court* — has been notorious in recent years for proclaiming the death of the author, and the last thing I want to do is to resurrect that venerable old figure, source of meaning and value. But if not the source of meaning, the author, as the utterer of a discourse, is the place where meanings gather to exert their effects.

From this viewpoint, the author is a privileged subject of discourse, of ideology, simply in that we have access to his or her discourse, while that of other contemporaries has vanished. An insecure subject, in that discourse escapes his or her control: not the least interesting type of moment in the texts here studied is when the author is not himself, so to speak, but the site of a quotation from a taste-discourse to which he wishes to express his opposition (I revert to using the male pronoun only because of the selection of authors). When thus quoting, however, and thus for a moment not himself, the author is still a subject occupying a certain position in ideology, determined on one level by his place in the network of social and cultural relations, and on another by the interweaving or juxtaposition in 'his' texts of certain determinate discourses that he upholds and that uphold him.

As to the choice of authors, the selection adopted here may seem both dully conservative and aberrant at the same time: solid canonical figures, no minor master who 'deserves to be better known'. At the same time, the choice may seem not canonical enough: where is Bouhours, where Rapin, who one might think should figure in any treatment of the theme of 'taste' in seventeenth-century French writing?

They should, of course, if that treatment were devoted to exploring the history of literary ideas. (I should mention here a good, if brief, treatment of the use of 'taste' in Guez de Balzac by H. Frank Brooks.)[17] But, as I say, this study has other priorities, and one of these is frankly political.

In the institution of humanist literary criticism, authors are prized according to their power to speak to the human condition, to illuminate, broaden, deepen, and intensify our experience of living. The institution itself works to promote this kind of reading. It goes beyond, of course, the institutions of higher education, in which indeed quite different practices of reading are also in operation. Literary humanism is the prevailing philosophy of the book reviews of the so-called quality papers, of literary programmes on television or radio. It largely depends on the notion of a canon, first of texts that are 'literature', as distinct from all those that are not, secondly of literary texts (thus defined) that rank as 'great', as particularly capable of addressing us as human beings across the centuries. This kind of canon stands in an uneasy relationship to the kind of canon required by the academic institution of literature as a historical discipline (the body of texts that must be studied to ensure an understanding of a certain period in the history of literature). One way of negotiating this unease is to operate as a scholar *and* a humanist, to sign off each work of scholarship with a humanist flourish. And how better to signal humanism than by a placing judgment, that acknowledges that as a specialist of a certain period you have a good reason to study X, and to claim for your study the attention of other specialists, but that at bottom X is less interesting than Racine or Milton, say, for the sake of whom he or she is being studied? In explorations of the attitudes and consciousness of a particular epoch, what more common than to find that minor authors are completely enslaved to them, while the major ones transcend them in their capacity to address us in the here and now?

To show that Bouhours, say, operates within an ideological framework dedicated to the reproduction of the dominant cultural and social relations will leave most withers unwrung. The argument has more force if it can be shown to apply to the 'great' figures as well, those who are read as 'literature', who have a place in the humanist as well as the scholarly canon. It is true that the focus on the 'great' authors risks reproducing their existing privilege. The aim is, however, to call into question the humanist grounds of that privileging, by showing their texts as no less implicated in ideology than any 'minor' text; by arguing that the sensibility ('taste') that they exhibit and celebrate is a class sensibility, reflecting certain social determinants and reproducing the dominance of certain social relations; that it is the field wherein rival social forces clash and, equally importantly, negotiate.

The point applies even to authors not counted as great, not read as literature, but who can also be brought within a humanist canon of values. La Bruyère has always been praised for his independence and detachment, but Saint-Evremond too can be so praised. Méré's hierarchy of values seems to pay no respect to merely social hierarchies. If, however, we read their explicit utterances against the presuppositions of their discourses, a rather different picture emerges; and this is true of all three authors.

Of course, wherever reading is going on, there is a selection of interests and priorities that constitutes a *de facto* hierarchy of value. This applies both in the seventeenth-century French context and in the twentieth-century context in which I am discussing it. As Raymond Williams has said, the process of judgment is itself inevitable: the problem arises when the judgment is passed in oblivion of the actual conditions of its production.[18] The present work attempts to return seventeenth-century French taste-judgments to their own conditions; this does not mean arguing that La Bruyère is no more intrinsically interesting or worthwhile than Méré. It is the notion of 'intrinsic' interest that is at fault. In certain determinate situations, for certain purposes, it might well be justifiable to put La Bruyère above Méré; in others, the reverse might be true. The particular claim here is that, in the matter of 'taste', the 'major' writers are no less time- and class-bound than the 'minor' ones.

I have used certain terms here such as 'ideology' and 'discourse' without defining them, although the particular sense in which they are used is implicit in what I have written above. More explicit definitions are, however, called for.

Discourse, as defined by Benveniste, covers 'toute énonciation supposant un locuteur et un auditeur, et chez le premier l'intention d'influencer l'autre en quelque manière'. It is thus distinguished from *histoire*, the mode of utterance pertaining to the narration of past events in an impersonal fashion without the intervention of a speaker.[19] The notions of subjectivity and influence are crucial here. What is in question in the following analyses, however, is not primarily concrete interpersonal transactions, between a particular letter-writer, say, and a correspondent, or, indeed conscious subjective intentions. What constitutes a given utterance as discourse, for the purposes of this study, is its capacity to function, irrespective of the speaker or writer's intention, as a message to those who happen to receive it to take some action or, more usually, to adopt some pragmatic attitude. The message need not be interpreted as coming from an individual; it will perhaps be more powerful if perceived as impersonal in origin, as coming from the culture, or from *les honnêtes gens*, or from religion. The specifically linguistic characteristics of discourse as defined by Benveniste (such as the use of first- and second-person forms as well as, and in opposition to, those of the third person, p. 242) can be dispensed with here. La Rochefoucauld's *Maximes* can count as discourse, even when the first-person forms *nous*, *notre*, and *nos* are absent: even their most impersonal formulations can be recognized by the reader as addressing a message to him or her of the type described. This is perfectly compatible with the fact that, formally, the *Maximes* are descriptive rather than prescriptive, in keeping with the preoccupations of the *moraliste*.[20] They are discursive in the sense pertinent here in that they allude to, albeit frequently in order to criticize, a moral language and a set of social and moral values that the reader can recognize in his or her experience. Indeed, the critique of the language works precisely by addressing areas of the reader's experience that the language obscures.

An example from La Bruyère will indicate how abstract formulations can operate discursively in this sense, so as to influence the receiver: 'Entre le bon sens et le bon goût, il y a la différence de la cause à son effet' ('Des jugements', 56). Encountering a definition of 'good taste' prompts the reader to ask 'Am I, on this showing, a person of taste?' Now, good sense is a very minimal requirement, and to suppose oneself to possess 'la chose du monde la mieux partagée' is to make no great claim.[21] The definition proposed by La Bruyère thus normalizes good taste, puts it well within the reader's grasp, encourages a feeling of complicity with and respect for this admirably sensible and generous author. It is true that other contexts of judgment may be involved here: the simple term *bon sens*, as in Boileau, may carry along with it all sorts of hidden implications about cultural values. Even so, to place these values under the sign of 'good sense' is to give them an air of accessibility.

But other definitions of taste can work entirely differently. Take this one, from Méré:

Le bon goût ne vient que d'une connoissance exquise & juste à juger du bien & du mal pour toute sorte de bien-seance & d'agrément, & qui que ce soit ne peut avoir cette connoissance bien parfaite sans se l'estre acquise avec beaucoup de soins & de reflexions.[22]

'Good taste' here is a remote and enigmatic reality, access to which can come only as the reward of long and painstaking effort. Whereas La Bruyère attaches 'taste' simply to a normal human property of rationality, Méré associates it with the whole life of a culture ('bien-seance' and 'agrément'), considered as a mystery requiring prolonged initiation. He thus *places* 'taste', if not precisely, then still rather more definitely than La Bruyère. One of these definitions clearly opens up 'taste', the other closes it off. Although formally akin, as definitions, they operate on the reader in quite different ways and produce quite antithetical images of the subject of 'taste' whose place the reader desires to occupy, one as a normal human being, the other as an exceptional individual. Discursively, then, their effect belies their common status as definitions.

When discussing the methodological issue of the focus on the author, I referred to the articulations of judgments of taste with other judgments, or judgments of taste about literature with other judgments of taste (above, pp. 7–9). Articulation is an important characteristic of discourse. A statement occurring in more than one text can belong to more than one discursive ensemble. It thus becomes as many different statements as there are discursive ensembles within which it operates, and to represent it as expressing one and the same opinion shared by all its utterers is to endow it with a false self-identity.

Thus, it is true that Anne Le Fèvre (Mme Dacier), Bouhours, and Frain du Tremblay all characterize good taste as a harmony or accord between the mind (*esprit*) and reason. But the consensus involved is merely apparent.

The first of the three authors to use the phrase is Anne Le Fèvre, in the preface to her translation of Aristophanes's *Plutus* and *Clouds*.[23] The analysis of 'taste' here comes after an introduction to the life and writings of Aristophanes. Despite his outstanding excellence, she is aware that public reception of the translations is unlikely to be rapturous because 'l'autorité & l'exemple des temps les plus éclairez & les plus polis ne nous touchent point'. This matter needs further analysis. She divides the public into three categories, each with its own distinctive level of response: those with good, mediocre, and bad taste respectively. Taking them in reverse order to her own, those in the third category appear as entirely bound up in their own world of self: anything that does not reflect it back to them is rejected out of hand. She has nothing but scorn for the complacency with which 'ils donneront hardiment un démenty à toute l'antiquité'. They will reject Aristophanes out of hand because they think his subjects silly, and because his plays lack the familiar apparatus of young lovers, cunning servants, and old men waiting to be duped.

Those with mediocre taste do not in general judge of anything for themselves: 'ils sont renfermez dans certaines bornes qu'ils ne sçauroient passer'. They are not incapable of sentiment or perception, but their judgments are often topsy-turvy, and they never react with intensity. These will be less struck by the beauties they perceive than by the supposed defects.

The judgment of those with 'good taste', however, is unhampered by temporal limitations, and they are capable of clear perception and vigorous response. They will be delighted with Aristophanes, even in translation, confirming the judgment of great men of past centuries that he is the supreme writer of comedy.

It is only people of this type whom Anne Le Fèvre wants to please. None the less, she attempts to remove some of the difficulties faced by the other two types. If most people nowadays do not appreciate the ancients, this is due to a prevalent cast of mind, a systematic repression of difference: 'on ne veut jamais perdre de vûë son siecle, &... on veut le reconnoistre en tout'. The latter phrase exactly parallels what was said about people of 'bad' taste: 'ils veulent se reconnoistre en tout'. Bad taste is thus identified with the application of the standards of one's own time to the products of other ages. Le Fèvre counters this with an affirmation of difference: 'les siecles se suivent sans se ressembler'. This sounds relativistic, but should probably not be taken that way, since people with taste were said to judge 'comme s'ils avoient été de tous les temps'. What is probably implied, then, is that there are eternal values that survive the accidental variations between one period and another. But the formulations are far from unambiguous.

What is needed in order to dispel this hostility or indifference to Aristophanes is an account of the operations of judgment and 'taste' that people can apply to their own responses, so as to determine whether the reason for a particular response lies in the object itself or merely in their own mind. This Le Fèvre undertakes to provide.

As she observes, most writing on 'taste' involves an infinite regress from one validating principle (such as, for example, *raison* or *bon sens*) to another, as new difficulties crop up with each formulation. The chief criterion of truth, on the other hand, is when 'un mesme principe sert à expliquer toutes les difficultez'. Her principle, then, is that 'taste' is 'une harmonie, un accord de l'esprit & de la raison'. The individual's taste is greater or less according as the harmony is more or less perfect. Objects give off a kind of sonority that affects the imagination (an acoustic image akin to a visual image). When this sound is in harmony with the inner harmony between the mind and reason, the object is inevitably approved. But there are cases where the opposite takes place, where dissonance prevails. This dissonance, however, may originate in the mind or in the object, or indeed in both. When the sonority of an object clashes with the above-mentioned inner harmony, the object is rightly rejected as defective. But if the mind is not attuned to reason, then the best of objects will produce a dissonance, and will thus be wrongly rejected; for familiarity prevents our perceiving our own mental disharmony. By the same token, the object that harmonizes with a mind ill-attuned to reason is bound to be bad, although it will be perceived as good.

It is perhaps a pity that the discussion is not taken further: but as Le Fèvre herself observes, she is writing a preface to Aristophanes, not a dissertation on taste, and further discussion on a general level is out of place. She has, however, cleared the ground for an account of the plays that anticipates possible criticisms on the part of a reader now convinced, at any rate, that his or her own reactions are not in themselves an infallible guide to the intrinsic nature of the object, but may be due to ignorance or insensitivity. The former, at least, can be remedied by the information Le Fèvre provides in her commentary.

The definition of 'taste' presented in Le Fèvre's preface is thus linked to a certain conception of the contemporary public and contemporary culture, as well as, more specifically, to the vindication of a particular pair of classical texts. It calls into question the adequacy of subjective response, which may fail to reflect the real qualities of the object, especially the object overlaid with the deposit of the centuries. Le Fèvre is implicitly criticizing certain elements in contemporary culture as complacent and blinkered. Since good taste means not being confined to one's own temporal perspective but being at home in all historical periods, it implicitly presupposes learning. In other words, the attack on the Moderns here is linked to a vindica-tion of learned humanism against the strictures of the *honnête homme* who goes by his own sense of what is right and proper. This rather summary statement of the issues at stake in Le Fèvre's preface will be borne out by analysis of texts by Méré, who takes the opposite side on certain crucial points, and by La Bruyère and Boileau, whose position is closely related to Le Fèvre's. All the great men of past cen-turies, says Le Fèvre, held Aristophanes supreme in comedy: this kind of appeal to a cumulative consensus across the centuries will recur in Boileau. In another, more famous, work, *Des Causes de la cor-ruption du goût*, Le Fèvre/Mme Dacier insists on the imitation of the ancients as a precondition of any worthwhile achievement in literature; La Bruyère is of the same opinion, which is also implied in several passages of Boileau's *Art poétique*. Again, like Boileau, Le Fèvre tends to present certain passages from the classics as veritable touchstones of taste: those who fail to appreciate them must be seen as lacking in the quality. Her image of the person of taste does not associate him or her with courtly *honnête* culture, but does presuppose associations with learned humanism: another point of contact with Boileau and La Bruyère.[24]

There are discrepancies as well. Although Le Fèvre represents taste as a rare quality, she does not specifically deny it to the popular masses as such, as the other two do.[25] Indeed, the celebration of ancient culture in the preface to Aristophanes seems to have critical political overtones, as when she praises the love of liberty that both inspired the comic poet to denounce the leaders of Athens and earned him the gratitude of the people he had enlightened. As she rightly says, both the criticism and the response would be impossible in her own day. Again, she notes, in connexion with Act II, scene i of the *Plutus*, that the comedy was for all the Athenians, magistrates and people alike, and that the peasants of Attica were part and parcel of the intelligent and discriminating Athenian public.

It is not simply a matter of observing the coexistence in Anne Le Fèvre's text of a certain conception of taste in general with certain theses about ancient and contemporary culture. The latter can in fact be persuasive only if the former is accepted. The aim of the *Préface* is to vindicate Aristophanes against a potentially hostile or indifferent contemporary reaction. To avert this reaction, Le Fèvre has to explain this or that feature of the representation which might strike the seventeenth-century reader as rebarbative. But the explanation can only take effect if the reader is already convinced that his or her sub-jective reaction is a doubtful guide, being determined not necessarily by some intrinsic quality in the object but possibly by a defect in his or her own inner harmony that sets up a faulty relation to the object. In other words, the account of taste contributes to a critique of the 'spontaneous' cultural reactions of a seventeenth-century French reader faced with an unfamiliar representation – a critique which is itself a necessary preliminary to the rehabilitation of Aristophanes.

It is worth noting that her gender puts pressure on Anne Le Fèvre's capacity to occupy this position, with its implicit commitment to humanist learning. As we shall see, the learned culture tended for various reasons to misogyny, one of the reasons being its perception of the salons, centred on and animated by women, as rival cultural institutions. The exclusion of women from the learned culture reflected the lack of educational opportunities for women in seventeenth-century France. Anne Le Fèvre's own background was exceptional: she was the daughter of the great humanist scholar Tanneguy Le Fèvre, professor of Greek at the Protestant Academy of Saumur, and her relationship with him undoubtedly facilitated not only her remarkable acquisition of learning but also her acceptance in the community of the learned. Her husband, André Dacier, had also studied at Saumur (the son of an *avocat*, he came from the legal background so often associated with humanist learning), and after her marriage Anne Le Fèvre not only collaborated in his scholarly career but pursued her own (that her contribution to the joint effort was the greater is implied by a scabrous epigram by the abbé Tallemant mentioned in one of Boileau's letters to Brossette).[26] All the same, there are frequent asides in her work that testify to a sense of difficulty in attempting, as a women, to speak in the name of learning (this despite an erudition which her most learned contemporaries, like Ménage, could regard as formidable). The following may serve as an example:

Quelqu'un a fort bien dit que *le Savant est le Dieu de l'Ignorant.* Qu'on ne m'accuse point de parler ainsi pour moi; je n'ai jamais prétendu à ce savoir qui rend respectable, je ne me suis jamais amusée à lire ou à écrire que pour me délasser des occupations que les femmes doivent regarder comme leur principal & leur plus indispensable devoir. Mais j'honore, je respecte les veritables Savans, ces grands personnages qui par leurs lumieres éclairent tous les hommes dans tous les temps.[27]

But, whatever difficulty Anne Le Fèvre may have had in gaining acceptance as an equal within the learned community, she could not, like other women of the time, have found in the salons a congenial cultural environment, since, with its bias against erudition, salon culture could never have provided a platform for her to put forward the kind of arguments she upholds in the preface to Aristophanes and elsewhere.

The echo of her definition of taste in Bouhours's *La Manière de bien penser dans les ouvrages d'esprit* sounds within a very different context. The work in question is a dialogue in which the two speakers Eudoxe and Philanthe quote and discuss passages from a wide variety of literary works. This structure, and the frequent anonymity of the authors quoted, have the effect of subordinating the quotations, and still more the authors, to the discursive process in which they are caught up. Thus, the definition of taste as 'une harmonie, un accord de l'esprit et de la raison' is attributed simply to 'une Personne sçavante bien audessus de son sexe', and the work it comes from is not named. It is quoted not, in the first instance at any rate, to throw light on the nature of taste but in order to exemplify the risk of obscurity in the multiplication of metaphors: for to define 'taste', itself used in a metaphorical sense, by the metaphor of harmony is, according to the speakers, to offend against clarity, even though the underlying idea is sound. Eudoxe, however, points out that the (non-metaphorical) explanation of the definition clarifies the obscurity of the metaphors, thought this is perhaps to underestimate the role of the metaphor in shaping the concept it is adduced to illustrate.[28]

Philanthe then produces another definition of taste, from 'une très-belle Lettre', which this time is intended to 'nous aider à en avoir des notions nettes & distinctes'. In other words, the subject of the conversation has shifted from the perils of obscurity to the nature of taste, a shift that tends to suggest that what the conversation is about is really conversation itself, and its power to range from theme to theme (it has in fact a definite direction beneath this appearance of fluidity). The definition quoted is as follows (we shall meet it again, in an abbreviated form, in the entry *goust* in the second edition of Furetière's *Dictionnaire universel*):[29]

Le goust ... est un sentiment naturel qui tient à l'ame, & qui est indépendant de toutes les sciences qu'on peut acquérir; le goust n'est autre chose qu'un certain rapport qui se trouve entre l'esprit & les objets qu'on luy présente; enfin le bon goust est le premier mouvement, ou, pour ainsi dire, une espéce d'instinct de la droite raison qui l'entraisne avec rapidité, & qui la conduit plus seûrement que tous les raisonnemens qu'elle pourroit faire.

(pp. 516–17)

Eudoxe applauds, but does not comment on this definition, except to say that it bears out the truth of the assertion, credited to the author of the *Réflexions morales*, that 'le bon goust vient plus du jugement que de l'esprit' (the author is of course La Rochefoucauld, and the quotation his maxim 258); whereas the same author's statement that 'quand notre mérite baisse, notre goût baisse aussi' (maxim 379) is pronounced unclear, or excessively subtle.

These further displacements of the topic of conversation confirm the supposition that the discourse's commitment, at one level, is to its own mobility and to the multiplication and celebration of the act of judging. The elucidation of the nature of taste is strictly subordinated to this movement. If it were not, if the discourse were committed to the establishment of truth, the relationship between the successive quotations would be more problematic; as it is, they simply succeed one another on the conveyor belt of discourse under the unwinking eye of the quality controllers. Concern for overall conceptual coherence is slight. It is by no means evident that the definition 'le bon goût vient plus du jugement que de l'esprit' simply confirms, as Eudoxe suggests, the earlier and more prolix definition, which carries no reference to *jugement* and which uses *esprit* in a different sense from the La Rochefoucauld maxim (discussed below, pp. 128–9). Again, the assertion, in the long quotation, that taste consists in a certain relationship between the mind and objects is rather at odds with the Le Fèvre definition (which was after all deemed to be basically sound, though badly expressed); for in Le Fèvre's schema the cognitive value of the relationship between the mind and the object was determined by the degree of harmony between the mind and reason. In other words, the relationship is a ternary one in Le Fèvre, binary in the apparently corresponding passage in Bouhours.

I am not saying that all these difficulties couldn't be tidied up and a more coherent formulation produced. But even so it seems reasonable to suppose that if Bouhours's prime concern were with conceptual coherence and truth, he would seek to bring the various utterances about taste into a different kind of relation. This is not of course intended as a criticism: Bouhours has his priorities and they are elsewhere. He is seeking not to define taste but to represent the judgment of taste in action, and thereby to establish certain literary values through what appears to be the play of freely moving discourse. During the course of the dialogue, Philanthe (the lover of flowers or ornaments, as his name suggests) is converted to the views of Eudoxe, the 'right thinker', who upholds Latin, Greek, and contemporary French models against Spanish and Italian ones, and, among Latin writers, prefers those of the Golden Age to those of the Silver. To use the inevitable simplifications, a national classicism triumphs, politely but firmly, over an alien baroque.[30]

The definition of taste as a harmony of the mind and reason appears in a third author, Jean Frain du Tremblay. His approach and priorities are different again. Unlike Bouhours, he names names, gives chapter and verse. The definition is credited to Mme Dacier, and the work it comes from is identified, by means of marginal notes.[31] The longer Bouhours definition just discusssed is also mentioned, and here too the work it comes from is named, although the author is not, perhaps out of politeness, since Du Tremblay is going to criticize him somewhat severely (p. 124). This precision suggests a work intended for scholars, or at any rate one aiming at a certain seriousness of treatment; to name authors and works implies a certain moral economy, in which the individual subject is held responsible for discourse. Like Anne Le Fèvre, Frain du Tremblay is actuated by a desire to clarify, to do away with the rash of mutual accusations of bad taste. But although he accepts her definition as theoretically unimpeachable, he points out that it is not of practical assistance in deciding, say, between *Anciens* and *Modernes*, or between partisans of Horace and those of Plautus. The terms of the definition (*esprit, raison*) are unstable: for everyone thinks that his or her mind is perfectly attuned to reason (pp. 128–9). Some more concrete criterion of good taste is required.

Du Tremblay accordingly interrogates the metaphor. Physical taste (a person's appetites) is a sure guide to his or her health, and similarly for 'le goût de l'esprit'. It should be possible, then, to identify spiritually and mentally healthy people by the quality of their appetites. 'Good taste' may be predicated of one whose habitual nourishment is of the right sort: conducive, that is, to enlightening and strengthening the soul in its progress towards its sovereign good, the possession of God (pp. 130–4). Like Anne Le Fèvre, Du Tremblay thus invokes an external basis for the 'taste'-judgment: for him, it is the truth of the Christian religion, for her the intrinsic and timeless value of ancient literature.

If Anne Le Fèvre has failed, according to Du Tremblay, to follow up the concrete implications of a basically sound abstract definition, Bouhours has fobbed off his readers with a mass of verbiage. The definition of taste as 'un sentiment naturel qui tient à l'ame', which Eudoxe and Philanthe had passed to and fro with such complacency, is declared by Du Tremblay to be riddled with confusion and inaccuracy, although it does contain a kernel of truth in the statement that good taste results from a certain relationship between the mind and the objects presented to it (pp. 124–6).

There are obviously problems in Du Tremblay's own definition, the most evident being the assumption of the truth of Christianity as axiomatic. But this assumption, or an analogous one, is itself premised on the more basic presupposition that the metaphorical equation between taste in books and physical appetite reflects a fundamental alignment on the plan of the real, so that cultural 'health' must be as objective and as readily determinable as physical health. Even so, the basic contrast between Du Tremblay's discursive stake in the definition of taste and that of Bouhours is clear enough. Du Tremblay wants to solve a theoretical problem about taste-discourse − how, given the variety of empirical tastes, it can none the less be normative − and to use the notion of taste, properly understood, to bring literary preferences and practices within the sphere of religious discourse. Bouhours pays lip-service to the idea of producing clear and distinct ideas about taste (p. 516), but his main commitment, as I have argued above, is to the vindication of a classical as against a baroque stylistics, and, more generally, to the celebration of literary conversation and the production of a harmonious discursive spectacle.

From the study of this particular case, the general point emerges that the significance of utterances about 'taste' is determined by the discursive ensembles to which they belong. These ensembles should therefore be maintained as units of analysis. The argument might then be that one should endeavour to constitute a map of the field of taste-discourse, within which the articulations of different utterances about taste would appear as delimiting so many 'regional' taste-discourses. But for this project to be viable, it is, I think, first of all necessary to study these articulations as determining the position within ideology of the concrete subject: in this case, the author; and I mean by 'the author', not the human being, the biographical object, but, as I have said above, the place of utterance of discourse, the place, within the general ideological field, where different utterances are articulated. In other words, I am studying taste-discourse in its subjective dimension, in line with the definition of discourse offered by Stephen Heath:

A discourse is a social organization of the elements − the signifiers − of language into the relation of an order of meanings and a subject posed as such in that order, a positioning, a certain representation to the individual of the place of his or her sense, his or her desire.[32]

In other words, the notion of *discourse*, as put into operation here, is inseparable from that of the *subject*; and the notion of the *subject* brings in the further notion of *ideology*.

21

In common parlance, 'ideology' usually has pejorative connotations, suggesting ideas, usually political ones, that are mere abstract dogmas, perhaps no more than slogans, in contrast to the practical realities of experience. I use the term here, however, in the sense mapped out by Althusser, according to which lived experience itself is, to use Terry Eagleton's phrase, 'the homeland of ideology'.[33] The argument is that lived experience is itself a product of the inexorable insertion of individuals into the space of discourse: discourse that addresses them, and that obliges them to respond, as *subjects*; so that they learn to recognize themselves, in their response, as positioned, by the consent implied by that response, within a certain order. (What child can say to what it is consenting when it first learns to recognize itself as 'he' or 'she'?) That order appears, to experience, as the condition of all experience, since one has never heard anything outside it, never spoken outside it.

But if experience appears to the individual as a seamless whole, unified by his or her presence to his or her self as subject, its wholeness in reality is not its own, but that of the social formation that constitutes it. For discourse does not come from nowhere, though it may feel as if it does, but from the institutions into which the individual is inserted as subject: the family, first of all; the school system (and one does not learn only school subjects at school, one learns to place oneself among one's contemporaries); the Church, in many cases; and so on. There is some problem with the designation of such institutions as, in Althusser's phrase, so many Ideological State Apparatuses (ISAs), but the general point remains, that it is through one's lifelong and incessant subjection, through institutions, to the interpellations of discourse, or ideology, that one learns to do things and to want things without compulsion. To the extent that a given set of production relations reproduces itself through consent as well as force, these institutions, ideological apparatuses, perform a key role in that reproduction.

The different discourses are not always harmonious; as Althusser puts it:

Ce concert [of ideological discourses] est dominé par une partition unique, troublée à l'occasion par des contradictions (celles des restes des anciennes classes dominantes, celles des prolétaires et de leurs organisations): la partition de l'Idéologie de la classe actuellement dominante. (p. 107)

It is these discordances that appear to make the label 'Ideological *State* Apparatus' problematic, and it may be surprising that Althusser includes the Trade Union apparatus and the party political apparatus among his list of Ideological State Apparatuses. He certainly admits that the ISAs may be areas of class struggle (pp. 100, 102), but holds that this does not impair their character as State Apparatuses: there is a very difficult point here in the Marxist theory of the state, which I shall not here attempt to solve. What one can advance with more confidence is that the so-called ISAs are sites of class hegemony: that is, institutions through which the dominant class wins consent to its system of representations, and within which, at the same time, the subordinate class can struggle for power.

What, at any rate, the Althusserian theory of ideology offers – and to offer this much is a very significant achievement – is a way of linking the operations of 'civil society', considered as the institutional continuation of class power by non-violent means, and individual experience as constructed within the institutions of civil society. If this link is accepted, then one's assent to the dictates of experience is, objectively speaking, an assent to the institutions that produce that experience, and to the dominance of the dominant class over and within these institutions.

It will be seen that this theory does not in fact consign experience to the realm of sheer illusion, even if experience is the field within which ideology (and thus in the last analysis class power) both operates and occludes its operations. The dictates of experience have a relative reality: they reflect, in the sense that they are a product of, our objective conditions, our objective relation to certain institutions. Hence one can 'learn from experience': in other words, one learns to manipulate discourse, and find one's way about the institutions.

There is no room here to do more than set out these arguments, but I have done so at some length because certain aspects of them are highly germane to the topic of this book. For taste-judgment is precisely, for the subject who passes it, a matter of experience: and, as we shall find, certain seventeenth-century writers on taste emphasize and celebrate its nature as an instinctive response, rather than a learned conformity to rule. Modern criticism frequently mirrors this response; it is very tempting, when reading seventeenth-century taste-judgments, to try to make sense of them by agreeing with them, to look to one's experience to confirm them – to call 'un chat un chat' and a 'pédant' a pedant, without interrogating the ideological investments in such labelling. Of course, one doesn't have to interrogate these investments if one assumes that seventeenth-century critics were right (or at least that some of them were) in ways that our own experience can vindicate. And this isn't really an unreasonable assumption, in that our experience can easily be made to vindicate theirs. It is always easy to side with the dominant representation. It is perhaps less easy to do so once that representation has been returned to the institutional and ideological conditions of its production.

But, whatever the merits of the Althusserian theory of ideology as an interpellation – of emphasizing the role of discourse in the constitution of subjectivity – it might be argued that I have omitted one crucial problem: I have automatically identified power-through-institutions, the solicitation of consent, with class power; and the case might be made – has indeed frequently been made – that this notion is simply not applicable to the *ancien régime* because the *ancien régime* was not a class society. To this argument we must now turn.

Social relations (i): class

If ideology is conceived not simply as ideas in people's heads, but as the reproduction of social relations in experience through institutions and discourses, it becomes necessary to distinguish what forms of social relations are pertinent to my examination of seventeenth-century notions of 'taste'. The key concepts in this study are those of class and gender. But to speak of 'class' in the *ancien régime* is to arouse protest from many quarters. Carefully defined, however, the notion seems to me to be extremely pertinent, indeed indispensable. It might be thought that writings on 'taste' could be adequately studied without a generalized discussion of the social relations of the *ancien régime*, these being better left to historians and sociologists. Passing references to the social order as 'background' or in order to gloss particular passages might be felt sufficient. But this *ad hoc* approach yields unsatisfactory results. To base one's discussion of social relations on the representations of them given in a text is to espouse the text's perspective on these relations, and thus to obscure its position within them (including the positions of the author, the implied reader, and actual categories of reader). The issue is particularly serious where the texts in question are, as here, interventions in a struggle for cultural power, in which, moreover, the majority of them are fighting on the eventually victorious side. To accept their representations as in some sense accurate is to align oneself with the victors, and thus, as Walter Benjamin has it, with their successors.[34]

The present work, on the contrary, follows E. P. Thompson's injunction to scrutinize 'everything transmitted to us through the polite culture ... upside-down'.[35] The (materialist) inversion in question here consists in reading the representations of the polite culture in relation to what they obscure: the social conditions of their production.

24

But these cannot be sketched in (as 'background') by a few cursory remarks.

Thus, when J.-P. Dens remarks that 'une haute naissance, ou à défaut, de la fortune, sont des conditions indispensables pour être honnête', he is, I think, right: but the texts he adduces, though apposite, are not in themselves conclusive. They need, as Dens perceives, to be referred to social relations, but allusions to 'fortune' and 'naissance', or to 'la Cour et la Ville', are inadequate to characterize these relations.[36] Again, Domna C. Stanton mars an otherwise perceptive, and even rigorous, analysis of the semiotics of *honnêteté* by references to social relations of a breathtaking arbitrariness.[37]

Of course, the problem of correctly identifying the relevant social relations is far from easy. In what follows, I attempt to relate Marxist definitions of class to descriptions of seventeenth-century French society proposed by various historians, many of whom are not Marxists. In other words, I am working with secondary sources rather than primary historical research, and using them to build up an overall interpretation to which many of the authors drawn on would be loath to subscribe. Again, from a literary-historical point of view, it might seem that the debates that are the object of this book are too far removed from the brute realities of agrarian social relations for consideration of the latter to be relevant. But to call that separation into question is precisely the aim of what follows: an aim impossible of fulfilment without a scrutiny of fundamental social divisions in seventeenth-century France.

One of the most widespread objections to a class analysis of the *ancien régime* is that it fails to correspond with contemporaries' perceptions of their social relationships. This view has been argued at length by Roland Mousnier; it is neatly summarized by Robin Briggs in his excellent *Early Modern France*:

The whole notion of social class fits rather badly with the realities of life in seventeenth-century France, since it is difficult to find any 'class' – even the inevitable bourgeoisie – which can be said to have possessed a genuine class-consciousness. As a result there is little sign of people's behaviour being influenced by ideas about their class interest, beyond the natural inclination of the propertied to unite when threatened by popular violence and disorder. It is disconcerting, in this context, to find that most of the identifiable social conflicts of the period cut across any reasonable divisions by social class, with vertical solidarities proving at least as strong as horizontal ones.[38]

As a description of contemporary attitudes, this may be accepted as accurate. But the inference Briggs draws from it, which presupposes that class implies class-consciousness, is unwarranted. It is in fact possible to construct a concept of class that does not involve consciousness, and that is therefore applicable to societies where consciousness of shared social and economic position is absent or intermittent. (The general Marxist tendency is to argue that class-consciousness emerges only with industrial capitalism.)[39]

In the article cited above, which deals with class struggle in eighteenth-century English society, E. P. Thompson insists that class cannot be conceived independently of historical relationship and struggle (p. 149). The notions of relationship and struggle are central to the theory of class elaborated by the historian of antiquity G. E. M. de Ste.-Croix, a theory all the more valuable for the present purpose because developed to deal with a pre-capitalist society.

Class, Ste.-Croix argues, is essentially a relationship: 'the collective social expression of the fact of exploitation, the way in which exploitation is embodied in a social structure'. Exploitation, following Marx, is defined as the appropriation of part of the product of the labour of others. A class is 'a group of persons in a community identified by their position in the whole system of social production, defined above all according to their relationship (primarily in terms of the degree of ownership or control) to the conditions of production (that is to say, the means and labour of production) and to other classes.'[40] 'It is of the essence of a *class society*', Ste.-Croix goes on,

that one or more of the smaller classes, in virtue of their control over the conditions of production (most commonly exercised through ownership of the means of production), will be able to exploit – that is, to appropriate a surplus at the expense of – the larger classes, and thus constitute an economically and socially (and therefore probably also politically) superior class or classes. (p. 44: Ste.-Croix's italics)

I have quoted from Ste.-Croix at length because it seems to me that he gives a particularly clear statement of the necessary concepts for a materialist understanding of historical social formations. What determines the character of a given social formation, is, according to the materialist thesis, in the last analysis the 'specific economic form in which unpaid surplus labour is pumped out of the direct producers', and the corresponding relationship between the direct producers and the owners of the conditions of production.[41] But surplus labour can be extracted in many ways, and it is frequently far from easy to identify those that operate in a given case.

Marxists have generally classified the society of seventeenth-century France as feudal, thus frequently arousing the ire of historians, often the same ones who object to the terminology of 'class'. P. J. Coveney, for instance, who also prefers the term 'order' for the social divisions of the *ancien régime*, writes that 'to use the word "feudal" to describe either the seventeenth-century monarchy or its attendant aristocracy is to discount centuries of economic, social and political transformation and development'.[42] Roland Mousnier reserves the term 'feudal' for the society that operated from the eighth to the eleventh century between the Loire and the Meuse:

le régime des grands domaines, cultivés par des serfs tenanciers, astreints à acquitter des redevances seigneuriales illimitées surtout sous forme de travail, des domaines vivant en économie presque fermée, avec leurs ateliers de serfs artisans; tous ces serfs soumis au seigneur dont ils sont les 'hommes', et qui exerce sur eux la plupart des pouvoirs de l'Etat.[43]

And Mousnier goes on to observe that the French society of the seventeenth century presented a very different appearance. This is true; and yet there is still a sense in which the term 'feudal' can be applied to its social relations, even though they cannot be fully described in feudal terms. In the Marxist sense, in which I shall be using the word here, 'feudal' social relations are those involving landowners and subordinated peasants, in which 'the surplus beyond subsistence of the latter, whether in direct labour or in rent in kind or in money, is transferred under coercive sanction to the former'.[44] Here, the direct producers do not fully own their labour-power, although they may own means of production; compare the case of the slave, whose labour-power belongs entirely to his or her owner, and that of the wage-labourer, whose labour-power belongs to himself or herself as a commodity, but who does not own means of production.[45]

In this sense, feudal social relations were still a major feature of seventeenth-century France, even though the juridical relation of serfdom, which had earlier secured them, was a thing of the past. It is true that Mousnier urges the freedom of the peasant proprietor as an argument against interpreting the society of the period as feudal. But he is using 'feudal' in a different sense, as we have seen, and it is important, moreover, not to overestimate the 'freedom' of the peasant. Except in those parts of the Midi where the proportion of allodial (totally free) property was significant, peasant ownership was always 'tenure' rather than outright possession: it was circumscribed by the rights of the seigneur, which were both juridical and financial in nature. Thus, the peasant could sell or exchange land: but the transaction had to be registered in the seigneurial court, at a price (the *saisine*), and was almost always liable to the further charge of *lods et ventes*, which might amount to a fifth or sixth of the price. The seigneur was also entitled to step in and purchase the property for sale himself, at the price agreed (the right of *retrait*). A further tax, also frequently heavy, the *relief* was payable when property changed hands by inheritance. All these charges served to confirm seigneurial authority as well as to nourish the seigneurial coffers.[46]

Moreover, seigneurial financial pressure was also exerted on a constant basis: the product of the peasant household's labour was subject to all kinds of dues: *cens*, *surcens*, *rentes*, *champarts*, *banalités*, and so on. There was considerable variation here, both in the types of dues exacted and in their magnitude, from region to region: in general, the Midi was an area of lower seigneurial pressure than the North.[47] All the same, according to Robert Mandrou, ninety per cent of the French population in this period was involved in the seigneurial relation.[48]

But this bald statistical assertion may suggest too simple a picture, not simply because we must also take ecclesiastical and state taxation into account but because the basic pattern of a seigneurial class extracting a surplus from a class of dependent peasants, more or less proprietors of the means of production, is insufficient to describe the agrarian social relations of the period. For Mousnier is right to speak of these relations as being modified under the influence of emergent capitalism.

In order to chart this process it will be helpful to examine the social distribution of land ownership in the France of the period. Only approximate proportions are obtainable here, but they will serve for the purposes of the present analysis. We must distinguish, as did contemporary jurists, between two modes of ownership: *utile* and *éminent*. The latter is the ultimate ownership, the ownership in the last instance, enjoyed by the seigneur. The former is effective immediate ownership, like that of the 'free' peasant (other than the proprietor of an allodial holding) whose situation has been described above. If we look at this kind of ownership first, we find, using Goubert's estimates, that peasants owned in this sense about half of the soil of France, perhaps less. The rest belonged to the various privileged categories. The nobility owned more than a quarter; the Church approximately a tenth; various bourgeois categories about a fifth. If we look at the distribution of 'eminent' ownership, that is, of seigneuries, the proportions of the various privileged groups have to be approximately doubled. (The tendency of bourgeois landlords to turn into nobles, which I shall discuss shortly, is not directly relevant here.)[49]

The privileged groups thus appear in two guises. They are the ultimate owners, the seigneurs, of most of the land owned, in the immediate sense, by the peasantry. But they are also the direct owners of about half the land of France, the half that does not come under peasant ownership, and that consequently does not conform to the feudal pattern as set out above: peasants performing unpaid surplus labour for a landlord on land owned in the immediate sense by themselves. To put it another way, two to three peasants out of five did not own the land on which they worked. Instead, this land was governed by very different types of tenure: for the most part, either *métayage* (sharecropping) or *fermage*.[50]

The development of these forms of tenure was promoted by a change in seigneurial strategy going back to the fifteenth and sixteenth centuries. Earlier, in the Middle Ages, seigneurs had abandoned the direct exploitation of their demesnes (or *réserves*), parcelling them out instead among peasant smallholders.[51] Now they were attempting to regroup them, mainly by gradual purchase, often by the exercise of the right of *retrait*, so as to produce larger, more coherent farming units to be leased out to tenants on new principles.[52]

In certain regions of France – the West, the Centre, the Midi – *métayage* became the dominant form.[53] Under this system, the landowner provides not only land, but other forms of capital as well: livestock, and perhaps seed. The tenant farmer contributes his labour-power, but also another portion of capital: a few cattle, some equipment. The product is usually split down the middle, but may be divided in different proportions, depending on custom or contract. Marx identifies sharecropping as a stage in the evolution of capitalist rent, since it presupposes a tenant lacking sufficient capital to undertake full-scale capitalist cultivation. And in fact the areas of France where it prevailed were the poorer ones, where livestock and equipment were scarce among the peasantry. What differentiates sharecropping from feudal rent is that

the sharecropper ... has a claim to a share of the product not in his capacity as worker but as owner of a part of his tools, as his own capitalist. On the other hand the landowner claims his share not exclusively on the basis of his ownership of the land but also as the lender of capital.[54]

None of the less, *métayage* often contained a feudal element, although to some extent it cut across the pattern of feudal relations, since the lessor might be a seigneurial tenant rather than the actual seigneur. Be that as it may, the lessee had to pay, not only state taxes, but any traditional (seigneurial or ecclesiastical) dues to which the land was liable. The share-out took place on the basis of what remained after these had been settled.[55]

The system of *fermage* was similarly hybrid in nature. Like other forms of leasing, it spared the landowner the trouble of directly supervising his property, therefore liberating him for other activities: and this benefited all kinds of property-owners with outside interests, from merchants and shopkeepers to great noblemen. But it was the larger landowners who profited most from the system: the most reliable and straightforward method of extracting income from their estates, often scattered all over the country, was to lease them out to tenant farmers for an annual rent fixed by contract. The estate was usually leased as a whole, with or without the corresponding seigneurie. As with *métayage* agreements, *fermages* might be partly feudal in character, but the social relations they fostered were very different from the pattern set out earlier, of peasant proprietors working part of the time to produce their own subsistence and part to maintain the seigneur. The lessee would still be obliged to pay traditional charges like the *cens*; he might have to perform services or keep the seigneur in capons. But the bulk of his contribution would be rent on the actual land, the rate of which varied from region to region, in line with the productivity of the soil.[56] In this and in other respects, his possession approximates to that of the capitalist tenant: the *fermier*, as Jean Jacquart points out, is essentially a cultivator of the land rather than a possessor.[57] But he must possess more capital than the sharecropper, livestock and equipment enough to run a sizeable holding: in the Paris basin and in the North thirty hectares would be the minimum, and a hundred or more not out of the question.[58] So large a farm would be out of the grasp of all but a few peasants, who would be obliged to work it with the help of hired labourers, a few full-time but most seasonal; their status as employers would enhance their prestige. So would the additional position, which certain of these farmers enjoyed, of seigneurial *receveurs*. The seigneur would frequently save himself the trouble of collecting his various dues by farming them out to an intermediary in return for a regular lump sum. It was not uncommon to farm out an estate and the surrounding seigneurie to one and the same person, who could then use the latter source of income to nourish the former.[59]

Fermage operated at more than one level in the social structure. Goubert cites two cases in point: the wealthy *fermier-receveur*-cum-village money-lender, both cultivator and *rentier* of the soil, and the urban bourgeois, an officer or a merchant, with large landed estates of his own, farming the dues of other people's, and lending money on a large scale (often expanding his estates in this way, by means of *rentes constituées*, loans on the security of the borrower's property, which could then be seized by the creditor in case of default).[60] This latter type is one stage further removed from direct production than the former: his activity in the countryside is essentially as an investor and accumulator of capital.[61]

Patricia Croot and David Parker sound an important note of caution here. It is always tempting to shout 'Eureka' prematurely when the object of search is embryonic capitalism. But as they remind us,

Though the development of large consolidated holdings, in France ruthlessly exploited, has been seen perhaps rightly as a transitional form between feudal and capitalist farming their exploitation never managed to break out of the old seigneurial/*rentier* framework, despite the existence of a potential labour force and despite the way in which they cut across old jurisdictions: large estates did not necessarily lead to capitalist farming.[62]

None the less, as the above passage acknowledges, the systems of *fermage* and, to a lesser extent, *métayage* helped to bring about a crucial shift in the pattern of agrarian social relations, fundamental in the *ancien régime*: the articulation of direct production with peasant possession and the transfer of a surplus to the seigneur, characteristic of the existing stage of development of feudalism, was being dissolved over much of France by the operations of capital as the middle term between land ownership and direct production. The tenant farmer might himself remain to some extent a direct producer, employing wage labour only periodically and in no great quantities, but the scale and pattern of his operations certainly widened the scope for capitalist development in agriculture. Moreover, in certain areas such as Picardy, this upsurge of agrarian capitalism must be considered in relation to the penetration into the countryside of manufacturing capitalism. The rural household in these areas not only had to resort to seasonal agricultural wage-labour, but also to domestic manufacturing work such as spinning or weaving, using raw materials and equipment supplied by the manufacturer.[63] But this latter process concerns us less here than the mechanisms for the extraction of the agricultural rent by which the privileged classes were chiefly supported.

For it is with these henceforth that I shall be chiefly concerned. The direct producers, the families of small peasants and wage-labourers by whose efforts the privileged classes and their culture were maintained, will disappear from view. But, although not themselves directly visible, they continue to be present in the social conditions of the production of the discourses here studied, and as negative terms in the system of values these propound.

Invisible also are the 'village aristocracy' or 'rural bourgeoisie' of peasants with resources enough to run a large-scale farm leased out to them by a landowner. They formed a distinct social class, within which they tended to remain, consolidating and expanding their fortunes. But they were not − not yet, at any rate − rivals of the dominant class of landowners, on whom they largely depended and whose needs had in a sense called them into existence.[64]

One can speak of landowners in general as forming a class, since they stand in the same relation to production, living on a surplus extracted from their tenants in various forms of rent. But this should not obscure the substantive differences between them: differences in wealth, for one thing, but also the differences in rank perceived by contemporary society. Rank of course did not depend on wealth in the sense of automatically reflecting it; but it was impossible to maintain rank without the requisite degree of wealth, while at the same time rank offered many opportunities to maintain and enhance wealth, as we shall see. And by the same token, in the long term, wealth gave access to rank. The relationship between the two factors, which could also be expressed as a relationship between 'order' and class, needs further scrutiny.

As has been seen, the landowners of the *ancien régime* lived as a group off two kinds of rent: feudal rent levied on land immediately owned by peasant cultivators, and rent of a proto-capitalist type from *fermiers* and sharecroppers. At the level of production emergent agrarian capitalism generated a new class of capitalist tenant farmers and expanded the importance of wage-labour. At the level of rent-extraction, however, it largely left traditional social relations intact. For, to a very great extent, it arose within and from the existing agrarian social relations: from the need of the seigneurial landowners to extract rents. They used their existing economic, social and juridical position, their ownership of *réserves* and their right to levy dues and so forth, to introduce new patterns of exploitation (in both senses of the word) which reinforced that position. Jean Jacquart's study of the Hurepoix region, south of Paris, important because of its nearness to the capital, shows that in that area profits from the *réserve*, leased out to proto-capitalist farmers, far outstripped the yield in dues from the *censives*.[65] Elsewhere, this might not be the case: thus, even in the late eighteenth century 60 per cent of the income from the duchy of Penthièvre in Brittany was made up of various kinds of feudal dues.[66]

But where agrarian capitalism had taken root, one of its effects was to strengthen, even to revitalize, the seigneurial institution, in all its social, economic and ideological complexity.

That ideological factors operated with a relative autonomy in this context is clear from the tendency of seigneurs to exclude from farming-out arrangements certain dues, privileges and properties that particularly symbolized their traditional social privileges and over which they therefore wished to retain direct control. Labatut shows the *ducs et pairs* acting in this way, retaining rights of provision to offices and excluding their châteaux from leases of their estates.[67] But these 'feudal' motivations have to be seen in a changing context of socio-economic relationships.

The continuing pull of the seigneurial institution is legible in the effects it exerted on upward social mobility. In his discussion of the sixteenth-century bourgeoisie's rush into land ownership, Jacquart points out that, from the strictly economic point of view, the purchase of a seigneurie was sufficiently problematic to deter some aspiring members of that class: the privileges had their price, and it might make more financial sense to purchase a *censive* and lease it out to a tenant who would pay the dues on it. But the title of seigneur would hold irresistible attractions for the *officier*, as a final canonization of his social status.[68] For the purchase of a seigneurie was a tried and trusted mode of ascent into the nobility. Goubert shows how it worked: having acquired his seigneurie, the *roturier* exercises seigneurial rights, privileges and justice; he purchases an office conferring exemption from the *taille*, the tax that effectively served as a sign of non-nobility; he takes the name of his seigneurie, like Monsieur de la Souche, *ci-devant* Arnolphe, but with better justification; he adopts the lifestyle of a nobleman, albeit perhaps encountering the same problems as La Bruyère's Sannions; within a couple of generations his family will be accepted as belonging to the surrounding *noblesse*.[69]

Office-holding in itself could provide an alternative route to nobility; but nobility through office didn't cut as much ice as the real thing. Better to back it up with a more traditional title, such as land ownership could provide. Over half of the sample of officers studied by Roland Mousnier derived half or more of their income from land. Among the great officers of the sovereign courts, however, it was slightly more common for income from land, office, and *rentes* to be approximately equal.[70] This picture appears to be borne out by the case of Chancellor Séguier, who left four million *livres* at his death. Of the three million whose source can be traced, slightly more than a third came from his *terres et seigneuries*. However, the *rentes sur les particuliers* (*rentes constituées*) that accounted for another third of a million were essentially interest-bearing loans on the security of the borrower's property, which could be taken over by the creditor in case of default; they were promises of future annexations of land. As Goubert puts it, 'les rentes de tous les Séguier et de leurs émules sont des revenus de la terre française, et bientôt la terre elle-même'.[71] (Although these figures about officers' landowning give no indication as to how much of the land in question was seigneurial, much of it presumably was, for the seigneurie, as we have seen, was a key nexus between the economic condition of owning land and the social condition of the nobleman.)

There were in fact a variety of pressures on the *roturier* who was in a position to make the upward move into the nobility to do so. Firstly, the dominance of nobiliary ideology, the prestige and privileges of the nobility, whether material or symbolic: exemption from the *taille*, entitlement to deference from *roturiers*. Secondly, the accompanying prestige of landowning as such, prized above other sources of income; but then this has to do with the third factor, the relative lack of alternative sources of income and profit, due to France's lagging behind its competitors, Holland and England, in economic development.[72] 'Less than 10 per cent of the working population was seriously engaged in any kind of industrial activity'; and many of these were chiefly employed in meeting the needs of the rural world.[73] Although the role of French mercantile capitalism expanded markedly from 1680 on, it was still constrained by the limited size of its potential consumer market: one to two million people. At the beginning of the eighteenth century, the value of foreign trade was only a sixth of that of total agricultural production.[74] In these circumstances, the scope for large profits from mercantile activity was restricted, except in a few big towns like Lyons, Marseilles, La Rochelle, Bordeaux, and Nantes. The only really big profits were to be made through tax-farming or lending money to the Crown, or both, although the risks here were enormous.[75] This of course had the effect of harnessing available capital to the royal financial system, as did the venality of offices, which provided both greater security and higher social prestige than trade. But, as has been said, the tendency was wherever possible to combine office-holding and landowning.

With these considerations in mind, we can see how 'class', defined in terms of social patterns of exploitation, interacted with 'order', the hierarchy of ranks recognized in the consciousness of contemporaries.

There was no automatic correspondence between class-position and order-membership. Rather, class-position acted upon order-membership in the sense of determining it in the long run, not at the individual level, but over a succession of generations; while the whole ideology of orders tended to conserve existing hierarchies of dominance and subordination, and thus channel the effects of changes in production relations along the well-worn paths of the feudal/seigneurial structure.

The advent of capitalist production relations in certain areas of the French countryside did cut across traditional social structures to some extent, especially at the level of the direct producers, turning the poorer peasants increasingly into semi-proletarians, while their better-off counterparts flourished in their new guise as capitalist tenants. But, as we saw, it made far less difference at the level of the *rentier*, since it had so largely been generated within the existing seigneurial framework, which continued to constrain its scope.[76] This can be seen in the preservation of earlier feudal forms of rent alongside the proto-capitalist *fermage*, but it appears above all in the survival of an ideological structure, the hierarchy of estates, originally derived from feudal production relations of a classic type, but now supporting and supported by an embryonic agrarian capitalism. The 'relative autonomy' of ideology is not a talismanic formula here but a crucial tool for the understanding of the *ancien régime*.

Within this contradictory situation, certain ideological and social tensions were inevitable. The tendency of *robins* to move into land ownership had the long-term effect of making the higher echelons of the *robe* and the *noblesse d'épée* in many ways hard to distinguish. Indeed, by Louis XIV's time, one could frequently find, within a single family, some members in the army, others in the judicial-administrative apparatus, others with posts at court.[77] But behind this effective fusion of interests and assimilation of statuses, the old hierarchical attitudes could remain, so that Saint-Simon could denounce as 'vile bourgeoisie' a body of royal ministers noble to a man.[78]

Which raises the matter of the state apparatus and its effect on the social relations of the period. They cannot indeed be understood without the state. For the surplus labour of the countryside was by no means entirely absorbed by lay and ecclesiastical landowners and *rentiers*. A great proportion of it went in taxes to the Crown, which thus acted, as Robert Brenner puts it, as a 'class-like' surplus-extractor.[79] But this formula raises problems, for it leaves the class dimension of state fiscality unclear.

Like so many seigneurs, the Crown farmed out its revenues, to the *partisans* or *traitants* who contracted to supply the state with loans which they recouped by collecting its taxes. In this way, a new group of land *rentiers* came into being (since it was agricultural production that bore the brunt of royal fiscality), operating outside the traditional seigneurial framework, and capable of amassing enormous fortunes, but at the same time particularly vulnerable precisely because un-supported by the solid institution of the seigneurie, and thus totally dependent on their continuing ability to supply the Crown, an often unreliable but a very persuasive debtor, with credit. The interaction of class and ideology (order-membership) is particularly noteworthy here: the tax-farmer was frequently of fairly humble origin (that La Bruyère takes this for granted doesn't mean it wasn't true), and therefore lacked the intrinsic 'dignity' (in the juridical sense) conferred by birth and secure order-membership. He was thus particularly at risk in an extremely risky career: a ruined financier was just 'un bourgeois, un homme de rien, un malotru', a ruined nobleman was entitled to concern, even assistance.[80]

This brings us to the question of the second social group to which the absolutist state was organically linked: the fraction of land *rentiers* corresponding to the high nobility. It is of course commonplace to identify the policy of the absolutist state under Richelieu and again under Louis XIV as anti-nobiliary; and so, in political terms, it was. Or to be more precise, the magnates of the *noblesse d'épée* found themselves excluded from political activity, and superseded by a new 'political nobility' recruited from the *robe*.[81] But the often-asserted class-independence of the monarchy is most clearly called into question by its enormous financial investment in the court nobility. Their political passivity was only partly secured by force or terror (the execution of duellists and conspirators). It was also purchased at an enormous price: that of securing the nobility's social dominance. This transaction needs to be studied. It reveals on the whole that the objective distinction between the great aristocrat and the parvenu *partisan* was less than might appear.

J.-P. Labatut's study of the highest aristocracy, the *ducs et pairs*, shows them as deeply concerned to preserve their fortunes, in particular the great ancestral fiefs from which their rank and title derived. Land was the most important element in their capital assets, which in general they showed themselves well capable of conserving in good shape. (The traditional stereotype of the insouciant aristocratic landowner is somewhat removed from the reality.) That they could do so in the face of their often staggering expenditure (for luxury and liberality were key nobiliary values) was due to financial support from the Crown. This took various forms: grants of office, which could be highly lucrative (the capital value of a great office might equal or surpass that of a great estate) or pensions. Half to two-thirds of the income of the *ducs et pairs* studied by Labatut came from these sources.[82] In 1655, the vast estates of the prince de Conti brought him in under 200000 *livres*; he had spent over five times that amount in the year. The deficit was made up by a royal pension of nearly half a million *livres*, and by the sale of capital in the form of the governor-ship of Berry, which went for 400000 *livres*.[83] On a much smaller scale, the same composite structure reappears in the income of the duc de Montausier, known to the student of seventeenth-century French culture for his real relation to the Hôtel de Rambouillet, as the husband of Julie d'Angennes, and for his imaginary relation to *Le Misanthrope*, as the supposed model of Alceste. In 1664, his income was 100943 *livres*. 38950 came from the *fermages* of his lands (the resort to *fermage* is significant), 47493 came from royal offices, chiefly the government of Angoumois and Saintonge, and 14500 from his interests in the tax farms on the river Charente and in taxes on paper.[84] Tallemant mentions his negotiating with the King over the income from his *gouvernement*, and observes drily that 'tous gouverneurs, mais luy moins que les autres, sont tous partisans'. The Rambouillet family into which Montausier married had earlier been faced with problems getting hold of their share of the *aides* (indirect taxes).[85]

In this way, although the state's extraction of wealth from the countryside modified traditional social structures and hierarchies by promoting the rise of the *partisans*, it also served to maintain the social and political compromise on which the absolutist régime was based: it financed the hand-outs to the court nobility that kept them economically dependent and politically subservient, but at the same time preserved their status and resources. It thus consolidated the traditional links between large-scale land ownership and high nobiliary rank, and in so doing helped to preserve the residual feudal framework of emergent agrarian capitalism.[86]

The above account, it should be clear, is not intended as even a summary description of seventeenth-century French society as a whole. In conformity with the theoretical premises set out above, it seeks to identify the social and material foundations of the dominant culture: by which I mean the culture of the class whose position within the system of production relations enables it to live off the labour of other classes in such a way as to reproduce that position. Culture plays a vital role in this reproduction. But before opening the discussion of the role of culture, which in effect is the concern of the rest of this work, there is more to be said about social relations, which have so far only been partially characterized. For it is becoming increasingly clear nowadays that any attempt to analyse a social formation without taking into account the relations between men and women that help to produce it and that it tends to promote must be defective.

Social relations (ii): gender

To bring gender into the discussion of the social relations of taste-discourse is not simply a political and theoretical choice. For taste-discourse is gendered in a variety of ways, which it may be useful to summarize here.

First of all, it can be produced by women and by men. Whether this makes a difference, and to what extent, depends on the field of cultural relations in which it is produced: a field divided along gender lines. Secondly, taste-discourse can reinforce this division by assigning men and women different places within its representations. It can represent them as subjects of taste: generalizing, for instance, about women's taste as such. It can also represent them as objects: a woman can be appraised, within the discourse of taste, by the discriminating eye of the man of taste, who, beyond registering a purely individual attraction or aversion, can decree 'types' of women pleasing or unpleasing in general.[87] This example adopts the male perspective: man as subject of taste, woman as object, but we have representations, in Saint-Evremond and La Bruyère, of the converse process, where the woman is the subject of taste, the man the object.[88] Here, however, the man is patently in control of the representation: women are being blamed for their attachment to unworthy objects; for their 'bad taste', in short. I do not have examples of women actually voicing taste-judgments about men, whether because I have not looked in the right places, or because such assertions would be intrinsically hard to find, perhaps even to make.

To place this gender dimension of taste-discourse within its context, we have to look at the specific place of women in various seventeenth-century elite cultures.[89] In the first place, the ecclesiastical-university culture: its key sources – Aristotle, the Bible, the Church Fathers – were all deeply hostile to women. For Aristotle, woman is an inherently inferior creature, an imperfect male. For the Christian tradition, she was responsible for the Fall and continues to perform the role of temptress and obstacle to salvation. The abandonment of the 'imperfect male' theory by the early seventeenth century was in itself insufficient to sap the powerful legacy of philosophical and theological misogyny. Obviously, women had no place in this culture from which to challenge its prevailing representation of them.[90]

The same is true − in France, at any rate − of the tradition of secular humanism that flourished from the Renaissance onwards, and whose heartland, as Fumaroli has shown, was the 'Gallican Republic of Letters', based in the *robe* milieu: lawyers, magistrates, *parlementaires*.[91] For one thing, this kind of learning, though distinct from the more purely ecclesiastical culture of scholastic philosophy and theology, was not uninfluenced by the traditions mentioned, with their misogynistic dimensions. Then again, the level of education available to women at this period scarcely enabled them to participate in a culture founded on learning, and they were of course excluded from the public and professional functions associated with it. Lacking an appropriate institutional and professional position, those women who did become learned inevitably appeared as marginal: as prodigies or freaks, depending on one's point of view. On the whole, then, the learned cultures of the period, both ecclesiastical and secular, must be seen as operating to exclude and to subordinate women.

But, both in theory and in practice, women had an essential place within another culture: that of the court and the salons. That place is charted in the following passage from Castiglione's *The Courtier*:

A worthie gentlewoman spake pleasantly unto one ... whom she to shew him a good countenance, desired to daunce with her, and hee refusing it, and to heare musick, and many other entertainments offered him, alwaies affirming such trifles not to be his profession, at last the gentlewoman demaunding him, what is then your profession? he answered with a frowning look, to fight. Then saide the Gentlewoman: seeing you are not now at the warre nor in place to fight, I would think it best for you to be well besmered and set up in an armory with other implements of warre till time were that you should be occupied, least you waxe more rustier than you are. Thus with much laughing of the standers by, she left him with a mocke in his foolish presumption.[92]

The woman here is a spearhead in a confrontation between a new ideal of nobility − courtiership − and an old one, from which the elements of chivalry and courtesy have vanished, leaving only a military *machismo*. Elsewhere in *The Courtier*, when one of the participants in the symposium objects to the mention of women in connexion with the ideal courtier, he is sharply rebuked:

Like as no Court, how great soever it be, can have any sightlinesse or brightnesse in it, or mirth without women, nor any Courtier can bee gracious, pleasant or hardie, nor at any time undertake any galant enterprise of Chivalrie, unlesse he be stirred with the conversation and with the love and contentation of women, even so in like case, the Courtiers talke is most unperfect evermore, if the entercourse of women give them not a part of the grace wherewithall they make perfect and decke out their playing the Courtier.

(p. 188)

This emphasis on the socializing and refining qualities of women was echoed by the French followers of Castiglione, such as Faret, in their definition of the *honnête homme*. Thus Faret writes that it is 'bien rustique' not to treat virtuous women with reverence: submissiveness is the proper response to their imperious humour (itself an effect of their natural weakness).[93] This last point testifies to the sense of male superiority that underlies the ethos of chivalry; as does the celebration of women's conversation:

Comme elle [la conversation des femmes] est la plus douce et la plus agreable, elle est aussi la plus difficile et la plus delicate de toutes les autres. Celle des hommes est plus vigoureuse et plus libre; et pource qu'elle est ordinairement remplie de matieres plus solides et plus serieuses, ils prennent moins garde aux fautes qui s'y commettent que les femmes, qui ayant l'esprit plus prompt, et ne l'ayant pas chargé de tant de choses qu'eux, s'aperçoivent aussi plutost de ces petits manquements, et sont plus prontes à les relever.   (p. 89)

This passage eloquently describes the place of women in the discourse of *honnêteté*. The 'solid' and 'serious' matters discussed by men are, presumably, political and intellectual. But women are debarred from both of these spheres. Having less to communicate, they live a different relationship to language; they are more sensitive to what men overlook in their preoccupation with subject-matter: language as a quasi-autonomous rule-governed system. Yet language as such, as Faret is busy arguing, is crucial to the art of *honnêteté*. If women, then, have a privileged cultural role — being indispensable to the formation of the ideal cultural type, the *honnête homme* — that role is predicated on the marginality and inferiority of their position: their exclusion from the 'serious' and 'solid' world of men. This dialectic between centre and margin is reproduced elsewhere in the discourse of *honnêteté*.[94]

The position of women in *honnête* discourse will be discussed below in more detail, with particular reference to Méré. But their position in discourse cannot be adequately gauged without reference to their position in the institutions of civil society and to the relation of these institutions to the state.

The key institution here is of course the salon, through which the impact of women on the privileged culture chiefly made itself felt. It may seem odd to think of the salon as related to the state; the tendency has always been to stress its autonomy. I shall come to this problem presently. What I want to look at for the moment is the class profile of salon society.

This has been most amply and valuably studied by Carolyn C. Lougee. The basis of her investigation is Somaize's *Dictionnaire des précieuses* (1660), a list of salon women disguised under pseudonyms, with potted biographies and some brief disquisitions on aspects of *précieuse* culture. Much of Somaize's work is fanciful, but nearly three quarters of the characters in his repertory are identifiable, largely through the keys provided by himself. Lougee methodically analyses their backgrounds and marriages according to several criteria. She finds evidence against the view that they represented a traditional aristocratic elite, drawn from old families of the *noblesse d'épée*. The great majority of them were legally noble; but a significant minority of the 171 who can be identified were not (24 women, or 14 per cent of the total). Then again, at least a quarter of salon women came from newly noble families (with fewer than four generations of nobility). Only 48 per cent of the identifiable salon women are known to come from 'old' noble families, with four or more generations of nobility, as against the 39.7 per cent whose families were either newly noble or not noble at all.[95] A study of fathers' titles of nobility confirms the impression that the salons were not the preserve of a traditional nobiliary elite. For although nearly half the salon women in Lougee's sampel (44.4 per cent) had titled fathers, the titles in question were by no means always old ones, and the titled families in question were frequently newly noble. Rather than reproducing Lougee's statistics, I shall merely quote the conclusion to this part of her analysis:

The most striking characteristic of salon women which emerges from this investigation is the diversity of their origins: the salons did mix nobles and nonnobles [sic], daughters of old and new noble families, titled and untitled families, those who acquired titles with those who inherited them.   (p. 122)

Nor, again, were the fathers of salon women uniquely recruited from the military profession traditional among the old nobility. Many held offices in the sovereign courts, the central state administration, or the state financial apparatus. But they tended to come from the top end of these various professional hierarchies (Lougee, pp. 123–5). And this merger of diverse occupational groups can be assimilated, for the seventeenth century at any rate, to the other merger studied above, between old and newly powerful families: since 'certain types of occupation (military, *maisons royales*) were filled by old nobles, while other types (bureaucracy, sovereign courts, finance) were filled by new nobles or nonnobles' (Lougee, p. 126).

Up to now, the keynote of this study of the salon population seems to have been social heterogeneity, within of course a general context of privilege. But there was one powerful homogenizing element among families of salon women: wealth. To assess this, Lougee makes use of the capitation table devised by Louis XIV's ministers in 1695, and based on the assumption that the office or offices held by an individual reflected his general economic position. Lougee finds that half of the fathers of salon women who can be placed in the table come into the top five categories (out of twenty-two), while nearly 80 per cent come into the top seven. Fewer than 5 per cent lie in the bottom seven categories. Again, Lougee's conclusion is worth quoting:

Heterogeneity of lineage and occupation combined with relative homogeneity of wealth suggests that polite society was a vehicle of class fusion within a larger society which was still, legally at least, a society of orders. Members of traditional status groups mingled with members of newly powerful families in an elaborate form of social activity which ensured that acquirers of economic status could also acquire social status.   (pp. 129–30)

This view is confirmed by a study of the marriages of salon women. Among their husbands, Lougee finds the same kinds of social mix as among the fathers. But the husbands, by all the indicators (nobility, age of nobility, title, age of title), tend to rank higher than the fathers: the offices they hold are more likely to be military, less likely to be in the sovereign courts or the bureaucracy (administrative or financial), and they tend to be wealthier (pp. 138–49). Although substantial fusion of different social categories remains, there is, then, a tendency towards female hypergamy. Women born into the world of the sovereign courts or the bureaucracy frequently moved up in status by marrying officers in the army or the royal household, or noblemen of high rank without office. In so doing, they were frequently marrying into families whose nobility was older than that of their own. This is one kind of social fusion within salon society. But there is another kind as well. For many women from non-military families married into other non-military families:

In the salon itself alongside the daughters of the old nobility and women who had married into the old nobility were women who belonged both by birth and by marriage to new families. Their inclusion in the salons ... suggests that the salon itself functioned to integrate old families and new through common participation in a cultural activity. (Lougee, p. 158)

The integration of different social groups within the salon points to an emergent community of interests between them; and it should, I think, be seen as part of a general transformation of both the conditions of existence and the membership of the French dominant class. Differences of status ('order') between families of the old nobility, the sovereign courts, and the world of finance should not be allowed to obscure the similarities in their economic positions. As we saw, the great aristocrats of the *noblesse d'épée*, like the magistrates and bureaucrats, depended largely on Crown offices – and even tax-farms – for their revenue, while there were strong pressures on the other two groups to convert the gains of office or finance into landed capital. When they did so, moreover, it was within the seigneurial framework that upheld traditional noble authority in the countryside – a framework, however, now responsive to, and supporting, in many regions, an emergent agrarian capitalism. In the process of establishing himself as a seigneur, whether or not he continued to exercise his official functions, the magistrate or bureaucrat could acquire a more 'authentic' type of nobility than he could derive simply from office-holding. Hence it is possible to speak of these various groups – the old nobility, the *robe*, and the financiers – as cohering to form a dominant class based on a double relationship to the surplus extracted from the rural masses: firstly, through rent (of various kinds) levied on one's own property; secondly, through various forms of economic dependence on the Crown (pensions, the revenue from office, tax-farms), itself financed by surplus-extraction in the form of taxation. This class tended to cut across traditional order-demarcations, but, as I have argued, it also tended to adjust to them; and the salons, as analysed by Lougee, were a major site of that adjustment. For they compelled the new nobles they incorporated 'to adopt the ideology and behaviour which earlier had been the preserve of the old nobility', and thus 'French culture remained aristocratic even as the character of its formulators changed' (Lougee, pp. 212–13).

The salons, then, were a site of class, as well as gender, politics. Indeed, Lougee suggests that this is the main reason why they came in for so much contemporary criticism (though other reasons are not difficult to find). For the salons were perceived as blurring the social distinctions instituted by birth, through mixing together men and women from different backgrounds, and as leading in this way to misalliances. In allowing rich bourgeois or their daughters to mix with the traditional nobility, the salons jeopardized the status of the latter by obliging them to compete in luxury and display with the former; in general, they represented a morally corrupting and enervating feminine influence (Lougee, pp. 70–84). (In other words, criticism of the salons' adverse influence on traditional social hierarchies is linked with a certain phallic insecurity.) Moreover, the salons enabled the disturbance of an asymmetry noted by Ruth Kelso in Renaissance thinking about women: an opposition between the gentleman, distinguished from the common herd by his individual qualities – birth, breeding, virtue – and the lady, who shared in a general female nature and was bound by a general female ethic, and whose superiority was not personal but conferred purely by her relationships to men: the father who gave her her original rank, and the husband whose rank she assumed on marriage.[96] In the salon, however, we find women *distinguishing themselves* from other women (outside the salon). The *précieuses* marked themselves off from the rest of their sex by rejecting traditional female (i.e. domestic) roles, and by appealing to an exclusive rather than a general set of ethical standards. What they wanted, according to Lougee, was 'the freedom long enjoyed by aristocratic men either not to marry or to engage in a marriage which did not claim the sum total of their affections' (p. 25).

But salon women were also demanding knowledge, and this had its effect on the social composition of the salon. As was argued above, women were for the most part excluded from the dominant learned culture, both by its mechanisms and by its representations. They responded, on one level, by 'relexicalization' – rebaptizing the learned culture 'pedantic', and appropriating the term *savante* to designate a woman versed in their own valorized forms of knowledge.[97] This devaluation of traditional learning ricocheted on the few women who did succeed in acquiring it: thus, the learned Françoise de Diodé appeared to Madeleine de Scudéry regrettably pedantic and provincial (she came from Marseilles).[98] (Somaize, however, includes Anna Maria van Schurman, the celebrated scholar, in his list of *précieuses*, as if, contrary to what has just been suggested, she was recognized by women in Parisian polite society as a spiritual kinswoman. But why he lists her is not completely clear.)[99]

There were two options, then, for women desirous of knowledge: to assimilate the knowledges provided by the learned culture, but from outside that culture's institutions, or to valorize different and more easily accessible knowledges. Both were realized in practice. Women's cultural situation at this period reflected, but as in a magnifying mirror, that of the *noblesse d'épée*: which, to anticipate, helps to explain the symbolic position of women in *honnête* discourse. For if women – all women – were culturally deprived by their gender, then so, albeit to a lesser extent, were the men of that class fraction. Their access to the institutions of education was also problematic. The best educated among them, those scions of the richer nobility who were sent to the Jesuit *collèges*, acquired a good education there, but tended to leave early to begin their military career, while their former classmates of *robe* origins stayed on to receive the full humanist educational treatment.[100] Works that made knowledges from the learned culture – philosophy, theology, rhetoric – available to those outside it thus performed a double function. They enabled male aristocrats to preserve and perhaps extend the culture they had acquired through formal education, while for women of a wider range of social backgrounds they provided a remedy for the lack of it. Some works indeed – by writers like Louis de Lesclache and René Bary – were addressed to a specifically female audience, but the scope of cultural popularization was broader than this.[101]

Published works, however, were probably less important as mediating agencies between the learned culture and polite society than personal contacts. In the salon, as is well known, men of letters of bourgeois origin, Voiture being the inevitable example, made a major contribution. Again, this incorporation of the man of letters into polite society was part of a larger trend: between 1610 and 1630, according to Marc Fumaroli, a steady stream of young men of letters left the legal world for which they had been educated to take service with great lords. Théophile de Viau, son of an *avocat*, helped to set the trend, attaching himself to the duc de Montmorency. It was through the literature produced by such cultural refugees (in the theatre, after 1630, especially) that the court asserted itself over the *robe* as the dominant public.[102]

But polite society was not wholly dependent on such mediation for its literary culture: both women and male aristocrats had a literary culture of their own, based on works in the vernacular and in the modern languages (Italian and Spanish: necessary accomplishments for an international aristocracy, less so in the more nationalistic milieu of the *robe*). Poetry and prose romance were the favoured genres.[103]

In other words, although salon women were effectively excluded from learning in the sense recognized by the masculine learned culture, the salons could foster cultural knowledges of a different type. The kind of woman who embodied them was the so-called *précieuse*. I say 'so-called' because the referential value of the term has been radically called into question by Domna C. Stanton. Her incisive article 'The Fiction of *Préciosité* and the Fear of Women' analyses the *précieuse* as a fiction in various phallocratic discourses: a traditional anti-feminist satirical discourse going back to Juvenal, and its contemporary embodiment in the conservative contribution to the *querelle des femmes*, with its typical stress on women's inherent moral and intellectual shortcomings. (*Précieuse*, one might suggest, is the concept by which the upholders of patriarchy ward off the threat posed by contemporary women who seem difficult to accommodate in this traditional stereotype.) Most of all, Stanton argues, the *précieuse* is at the discursive antipodes of the ideal woman of *honnêteté* who both forms and recognizes the *honnête homme*.[104] Stanton deprecates the appeal to the real as a guarantee of the worth and pertinence of discourse (one cannot say 'there must have been *précieuses* because Molière satirized them'). Yet her deconstruction of the discourse of (anti-) *préciosité* does throw important light on 'real' gender and class relations in seventeenth-century culture. In particular, the opposition she identifies between the *précieuse* ('the castrating female who denies man's primacy' (p. 126)) and the ideal female type who helps to constitute the *honnête homme* is eloquent of the ambiguous status of the salon as an institution. For it was a new place in which women could assert their moral and intellectual emancipation, their power to recreate language and relationships. As such, it was, and was perceived as, a threat to the patriarchal order: hence the fear of women gave birth to the fiction of *préciosité*. Yet at the same time it was a place in which, through the status of daughters and wives conferred on them by patriarchy, women formed relationships with men that contributed to the realignment of class forces, and thus, within patriarchy, to a certain redistribution of power between men.

The notion was touched on earlier that court and salon culture assigned women a specific task of education, in a broad sense, and refinement. Stanton, as we have seen, mentions the image of women as initiating men into the social graces ('The Fiction of *Préciosité*', p. 126); elsewhere she speaks of them as essential instruments in the self-realization of the *honnête homme*.[105] According to Lougee, 'ladies made gentlemen ... in an existential sense. This was the social mission of women in seventeenth-century France' (p. 54). The salon was, among other things, the institutionalization of this mission. But the full significance of this woman-sponsored process of refinement emerges only in the light of the salon's articulation with other institutions. For Faret, indeed, the importance of the salon to the aspriring *honnête homme* lay precisely in this articulation. Let us return to his discussion of women's conversation.

To experience it at its best, one must go to the Louvre, 'lorsque les Reynes tiennent le Cercle' (p. 89). The spectacle of the court ladies all assembled is an inspiring one, but none the less problematic. For the company, paradoxically, is less select than it might be: the would-be *honnête homme* is at the mercy of bores, court spies, and people of high rank. One might have thought that the presence of these last was an attraction rather than a drawback; but there is an ambivalence here intrinsic to the relationship of the *honnête homme* to the court. For the court is attractive to the ambitious *honnête homme*, or would-be *honnête homme*, precisely because it is a site of power (hence, though, that other drawback, the spies); but the kind of power involved (monarchical-aristocratic) means that rank commands respect independently of merit. Thus a fool of a *duc et pair* can bore the company rigid with impunity; while even an intelligent *duc et pair* cannot but disturb the participation of the *honnête homme* in a cultural experience to which his merit seems to entitle him, but where, in relation to a magnate, he can occupy only a subordinate position. (Faret's *honnête homme*, like Castiglione's, is presumed to be of noble birth, but it is presupposed that he has his way to make in the world.)[106] In other words, the nature of the court itself, as represented in different ways by spies and *grands seigneurs*, interferes with its nature as a repository of the cultural values embodied in the circle of ladies. Since these ladies are themselves, by their rank and by their presence at court, in a political position, there is no generalized opposition between political and cultural values here; simply, from the point of view of the *honnête homme*, there is a contradiction between his cultural and his political relationships to one and the same politico-cultural institution. The *art de plaire à la cour* is the art of overcoming this contradiction; but it involves, in this case, temporarily bypassing the court, in order to gain access to the noble ladies that embody the desiderated values without the interference of spies and magnates. So Faret advises his reader to 'descendre à la ville, et regarder qui sont celles d'entre les Dames de condition que l'on estime les plus honnestes Femmes, et chez qui se font les plus belles assemblées' (p. 90). The aim is to 'se mettre dans leur intrigue, afin qu'elles s'intéressent à nous rendre de bons offices aupres de tous ceux qui les visitent' (ibid.) Faret doesn't name names, but the passage shows clearly enough how the relationship between the court and the city salon could be envisaged within the perspective of *honnêteté*. The salon is not set over against the court: it is centred on women of rank, it is a 'belle assemblée', if less magnificent than the circle of ladies at court. The crucial difference, from Faret's point of view, is that the salon offers the *honnête homme* readier unimpeded access to the influence of ladies. If there are men of rank in the picture, it would seem that rank as such counts for less in such groupings than at court, and merit unvarnished by title for more. But if the influence of female well-wishers is significant for the *honnête homme*, this can only be because of their contacts with the world of power. (Lougee notes that the defenders of women frequently stress their capacity to do good by intrigue (pp. 48–9).) The dialectic noted earlier in the discursive construction of *honnêteté* between centre and margin is operative again here.[107]

It is, then, the continuities between the world of the salon and the world of the court that enable women to act as mediators between the merit of the *honnête homme* and the great men's favour that he seeks: continuities, moreover, that we should expect from the class composition of the salon, with its fusion of the traditional aristocracy and newer financial and bureaucratic elites. In general, however, historians have tended to emphasize the separateness of court and salon, and to contrast the refinement fostered by the latter with the crudity of the former in the early part of the seventeenth century. Thus Magendie locates the revival of social life at this period, after the disorders stemming from the Wars of Religion, outside the court, and points to the specific role of the Hôtel de Rambouillet as an autonomous cultural institution. He is echoed by Stanton and, to some extent, but with qualifications, by Fumaroli.[108] Other historians, however, point to continuities between court and salon. Lougee sees the salon as an extension of the sixteenth-century Valois courts; Adam observes that 'c'est à l'Hôtel de Rambouillet que Vaugelas observait, bien plus qu'au Louvre, le bon usage de la Cour'.[109] It is of course true that the marquise de Rambouillet herself kept away from court, preferring the more select company she assembled in her *chambre bleue*. But this company itself was largely recruited from the court: 'c'estoit le rendez-vous', says Tallemant, 'de ce qu'il y avoit de plus galant à la Cour, et de plus poly parmy les beaux-esprits du siècle' (*Historiettes*, I, 443).

Fumaroli's treatment of the matter is particularly suggestive. He sees the Hôtel de Rambouillet as in some sense a marginal institution, a place where the best elements of the court and the *robe* could mingle, away from Richelieu and his political-rhetorical calculations; where the art of living and conversing together could be fostered independently of official pressures (p. 658):

L'Hôtel de Rambouillet apparaît ainsi en pleine monarchie absolue, comme une République des honnêtes gens qui, ayant accompli leur devoir d'état, donne par surcroît au reste du royaume une leçon d'élégance et de haute culture libérale.   (p. 660)

Yet, on this showing, the 'République des honnêtes gens' appears as something of a client state, tributary to the larger state outside. Firstly, even if its *habitués* are off duty, 'ayant accompli leur devoir d'état', it appears that they still have a 'devoir d'état' to accomplish: autonomous in their leisure hours, they are not, for all that, independent of the state apparatus.

Then again, the Hôtel's national cultural role, stressed by Fumaroli, as a model of good language and good behaviour is actually reinforcing, consciously or not, a state-sponsored 'civilizing process'. This process, in seventeenth-century France, should be seen as both imposed and self-imposed: as, in the first place, part of a process of struggle and negotiation between the *noblesse d'épée* and the state. During the Wars of Religion, the state had come close to destruction at the hands of warring magnates. When the monarchy was stabilized, these had their wings clipped. The state sought, and largely achieved, a monopoly of force. It weakened the scope for destructive rivalry among the magnates by weakening the magnates as a group. Yet it preserved, as we saw, their economic and ideological pre-eminence. To this new relationship of the nobility to the Crown – less autonomy, greater dependence – corresponded a transformed nobiliary ideal: that of the courtier or *honnête homme*. I want to examine in this light some of the strands that went to make up this ideal.

While respecting nobiliary ideological privilege, the state transformed it. It prevented its being represented, for example, in military terms: as in fortified châteaux. The edicts against duelling (far from completely successful as they were) struck at a central aspect of aristocratic consciousness: the nobleman's sense of his superiority grounded on his readiness to expose his life at any moment in defence of his and his family's honour. Collectively, the aristocracy retained its traditional military role, but now as a breeding ground of officers for the royal army. Otherwise, the state aimed to demilitarize noble life: and with this enforced demilitarization went, as Norbert Elias has argued, a gradual change in personality structure: an increasing restraint of behaviour that inhibited the now problematic resort to violence.[110] On one level, this process is the origin of the spread of 'polite' behaviour among the male *noblesse d'épée*.

49

In the sphere of language, cultural developments can be seen as similarly prompted by the state's attempt to weaken the social forces that had fuelled the Wars of Religion, one of these being regional particularism. The association of magnates with particular regions in which they held land, and where they could count on the loyalty of the local gentry and their followers, themselves attracted by the prospect of patronage, was a fact of life in early modern France, although one that gradually decreased in importance during the seventeenth century, and it could make, indeed, for a certain stability (it was institutionalized in the system of provincial governorships).[111] But its centrifugal potential was manifest. The demilitarization of the countryside (the razing of noble fortresses and so forth) was only part of the state's response to this peril: another was the deliberate promotion of linguistic homogeneity among the court nobility. The systematic purge, in the name of good usage, of provincialisms in Vaugelas's *Remarques sur la langue française* tended towards the dissolution, among the court nobility, of the sense of belonging to a particular region, and thus towards dissociating them from the provincial gentry.[112] The process of dissociation on the cultural level can be seen in Tallemant's anecdotes of the Montausiers' visit to Angoumois in the company of the duchesse's sister Mlle de Rambouillet:

Il y eut un gentilhomme qui dit hautement qu'il n'iroit point voir M. de Montausier tandis que Mlle de Rambouillet y seroit, et qu'elle s'esvanouissoit quand elle entendoit un meschant mot. Un autre, en parlant à elle, hesita long-temps sur le mot d'avoine, *avoine, aveine, avene.* 'A *voine, avoine,*' dit-il, 'de par tous les diables! on ne sçait comment parler céans.'   (I, 467)

Despite Mlle de Rambouillet's amused indulgence, these anecdotes suggest an important political dimension of the mission of linguistic refinement attributed to itself by the Hôtel de Rambouillet. The manifest differences between the mixed society of the Hôtel which blended aristocratic romance and playfulness with conscious refinement, and the male scholarly world of the state-appropriated *Académie française* should not blind us to their joint involvement in this process of imposing a new homogeneous good usage, 'good' because formed in and near the national centres of power.

Politeness and correct speech were only two of the attainments that went to make up the *honnête homme*, but all of his attainments could be summed up in the notion of the *art de plaire* (pleasing the right people according to the established norms for his position).[113] But we can see from Faret's *L'Honnête Homme* that, however much, in other texts, the art of pleasing might cut itself adrift from utilitarian considerations, its original goal was the conquest of the favour of the great. The *art de plaire* functioned on two levels: firstly, that of the relationship between the monarch and the magnate who required his favour; secondly, that of the homologous relationship between the *grand seigneur* and his dependant or would-be dependant, noble or otherwise. (One should consider separately relationships founded on specific professional qualities − financial or administrative ability − not covered by the discourse of *honnêteté*.) But with the relative demilitarization of the traditional aristocracy, mere physical prowess or skill in arms, let alone the ability to put a number of armed men in the field, ceased to be sufficient recommendation to a superior. What were required were skills appropriate to the world of the court, with its singular mixture of business and pleasure, 'l'ambition et la galanterie' (in Mme de Lafayette's phrase), public and private concerns (as later cultures have distinguished them). The *grand seigneur* needed people to divert him, people to flatter him, people to further his interests and keep his secrets. Best if one person could fulfil all four roles: the person thereby constituted as the *honnête homme*.

Again, the role of women in court society and in the milieux outside it but related to it comes into play here: their favours (political, erotic, or both) being desirable, the skills were needed to earn them: comparable skills to those needed to win over the *grand seigneur*, with perhaps more accent on the social graces and pleasure as ends in themselves, and less on tangible services. But this gender division of labour does not imply any real separability of male and female spheres of practice. For a court, also, has the function, among others, of producing pleasure: by its magnificence, by the quality and distinction of its denizens and of their lifestyle as perceived by the courtly eye. All this contributes to the glory of the monarch. In its national mission of refinement and enlightenment, the Hôtel de Rambouillet was producing, away from the court, and even in conscious separation from it, models for the courtier, as giver and receiver of pleasure.

There was more, however, to *honnêteté* than this. The literary element in *honnête* culture came to it from more than one source. The continuing interest in romance literature derived from a residual aristocratic chivalric tradition, revitalized during the Renaissance by Ariosto and Tasso. But *honnêteté* also drew on the classical literary and rhetorical tradition, made available partly (to men) by the humanist education provided by the Jesuits and other orders, partly, also, by the *robe* refugees mentioned above (p. 45). So there was a *robe* input too into *honnêteté*, though it was not the ideal of the *robe* as a self-conscious formation. As we shall see, *honnêteté* was accessible to the *robin*, but only when he was off duty and in mufti. But through its recourse, however limited and critical, to the humanist tradition, *honnêteté* excluded the possibility of constructing itself as an integrally aristocratic ideal.

Honnêteté, in short, was a complex cultural formation, not a simple expression of class position. It was open to those from outside the traditional dominant class. But so was the dominant class. *Honnêteté* was the name of an ideal, a set of valorized practices, with which the traditional aristocracy could redefine its identity, come to terms with its increasing dependence on the state. But the ideal could also be appropriated by groups outside the traditional aristocracy. It could provide a means for the new recruit to the dominant class (or the scion of a newly-recruited family) to complete, on the cultural level, his social integration. It was also a means for individuals outside the dominant class but whose lifestyle brought them into contact with it (such as men of letters of bourgeois origins) to lubricate that relationship. If *honnêteté* has appeared to some as essentially a classless ideal, this is because it was the site of a class's renegotiation of its position, a renegotiation that took account of new recruitment to the class and a new relationship of the class to other social groups. Inseparably from this, the ideology of *honnêteté* was also the sign and vehicle of a transformation in the relationship between men and women of the dominant class, in which the latter succeeded in asserting a more favourable image of themselves.

At the same time, it is certain that the state power had an interest in transforming the lifestyle and values of the traditional aristocracy in the direction of greater restraint and docility, while it was obviously in the interest of the dominant class and its aspirant members to adjust their behaviour to the norms asserted by the state. But the absolutist state stood to gain in another way from a more refined and educated dominant class: for such a class would be more permeable to the cultural representations (literary and artistic) on which the state, throughout the seventeenth century, was laying increasing ideological stress. To some extent, we are dealing here with a revival of the vigorous cultural life of the late Valois court, with its blend of aristocratic and *robe*-humanist elements.[114] But the simultaneous control and promotion of literary and artistic activity was more systematic under Richelieu and, later, Colbert than ever before. The object of all this was clearly to glorify the monarchy through the abundance and excellence of these literary and artistic achievements.

'Taste' and history

To point to the actual autonomy of such key cultural institutions as the Hôtel de Rambouillet is, then, a useful corrective to a monolithic view of seventeenth-century culture, as if nothing happened in that sphere without a specific warrant from Richelieu or Colbert. Again, the *Académie française* itself started very much as an unofficial group, reluctant to be nationalized by the Cardinal. But the very fact of its appropriation is evidence of the profound connexion between the apparently autonomous project of fostering literary production in a newly-refined French language and the self-reproduction of the absolutist state. And this is simply a special case of a general relationship between the increasing 'refinement' of speech and behaviour in seventeenth-century French society and the increasing discipline and enforced self-discipline of the dominant class, in its relation to the state.

All this, and we have not yet got to the texts. But now at last I want to move on to the analysis of a quite specific type of text — the dictionary entry — with the aim of mapping out the field of taste-discourse in general. I shall then move on to the analysis of individual bodies of text occupying different, though sometimes overlapping, spaces within that field. It will be argued that these texts construct and are constructed by an order of meanings enmeshed in an order of power which it has been the business of the present chapter to reconstruct.

2

DEFINING *GOÛT*:
THE DICTIONARIES

The entries on *goût* in the great dictionaries of the late seventeenth century provide an excellent starting-point. Not that dictionaries will tell us the 'meaning' of *goût* − to discover which, as I have said, is not the object of the present exercise. They are valuable, however, because they insert *goût* into a different discursive framework from that of the text produced by an individual author. They seek to mediate a common culture rather than to express individual options within it, or to attach its proclaimed values to sectional interests. As Richelet put it in his *Avertissement*, 'Un Dictionnaire est l'Ouvrage de tout le Monde.'[1] The lexicographer is not of course disinterested, Olympian, in reality. The 'common culture' his work embodies is a sectional one: no less than the individual author he is socially, culturally, ideologically positioned. But part of this positioning is a conscious subjection to discourse in general rather than to the particular and competing discourses that seek to purvey a certain truth not universally recognized. He must incorporate, in his individual position, the sum of all the other individual positions deemed to merit consideration (although it is he who does the deeming). For example, one dictionary quotes two definitions of good taste that manifestly contradict each other, one stating that taste is something you have to be born with, the other that it may be, albeit painstakingly, acquired. But it is not for the lexicographer to say which is right: they are simply presented as examples of the sort of thing that can be said about taste. The discourse of the dictionary is thus more obviously heterogeneous than that of other genres: it postpones the foreclosure of the true/false opposition; it gives one a fuller idea of the system of taste-discourse, or, to borrow the Saussurean terms, the *langue* of taste, to which individual utterances stand in the relation of *parole*. The linguistic analogy, though, is misleading in that it may suggest that these utterances are compatible within an overall system: what the dictionary conceals, and what individual texts reveal, is the extent to which the signification of the particular utterance, and its

54

compatibility with other utterances, are determined by the connotations it acquires from its original discursive and ideological context. Two utterances superficially similar in their terms may thus belong to antagonistic ideological formations, as we have seen in connexion with Mme Dacier, Bouhours, and Frain du Tremblay.

The dictionaries to be considered here are four in number: that of Richelet (first edition, 1680), Furetière's *Dictionnaire universel* (1690), the *Dictionnaire de l'Académie françoise* (1694), and the revised edition of Furetière produced by Basnage de Bauval in 1701. For brevity's sake, I shall refer to these as R, F1, A, and F2 respectively. Where F1 and F2 coincide the reference is simply to F. This has the further advantage of diverting attention away from the author (as he himself would have wished) and on to the dictionary itself as a more or less coherent text. This perspective governs the treatment of the anomalies, contradictions, and lacunae sometimes observable within a dictionary entry. It seems foolish to blame these on the lexicographer or the rigours of lexicography: although as Basnage complains in the preface to F2, 'en raisonnant trop avec soi-même sur les mots, & en cherchant à en fixer la signification avec trop de justesse, l'esprit se fatigue, le goût s'émousse, & la difficulté s'évanouït'. The mistakes one can make are obviously limited by the nature of the subject-matter; the worst hangover in the world would hardly cause one to define *goût* as 'the knee of a horse'. The point is to see whether these apparent slips on the part of the lexicographer follow any coherent pattern.

These dictionaries are all French–French, the earliest of their kind. The appearance of monolingual dictionaries in France reflects the growing independence of French 'elite' culture from the Renaissance humanist tradition. The formation and dissemination of notions such as *goût* and *honnêteté* are part of the same process. If one looks at Latin–French dictionaries of the seventeenth century (for instance, those of Nicot, Monet, or Père Pomey) one finds a few figurative uses of *goûter*, but no attempt is made to give a Latin equivalent of *goût* or *bon goût* in the metaphorical sense. This suggests that the notion of 'taste' was not a native growth of the scholarly culture of the seventeenth century: when, towards the end of the century, it appears in writers like Mme Dacier, Boileau and Rapin, who were scholars, it is arguable that they had appropriated it from a *mondain* non-scholarly culture. Although some 'taste'-discourse, as in Mme Dacier, La Bruyère, or Boileau, does identify 'good taste' with the 'taste' of the Ancients, other writers (Méré, Saint-Evremond, Morvan de Bellegarde) invoke 'taste' to sanction a more critical attitude to

55

antiquity. Méré admits that the word *honnête* is derived from Latin, but asserts that it has been given a broader signification in French.[2] It is interesting that Latin should have made a comeback in two early eighteenth-century dictionaries, the *Dictionnaire de Trévoux* (1704) and Père Fabre's edition of Richelet (1709). But here it was largely intended to help educated foreigners understand the definitions.[3] This is merely a logical extension of the progress of French towards autonomy; having taken over the role of Latin as a literary language, French was now using Latin in order to usurp its function as an international language.

The absence of Latin from the dictionaries to be studied here serves to constitute the culture whose language they record as self-sufficient, and to ratify its constitutive exclusions. What they exclude, apart from cases of sheer oversight, is defined as linguistically marginal, if not non-existent. For R and A, this is true of all words deemed unfit for the consumption of the *honnêtes gens* at whom these dictionaries are aimed.[4] This restrictiveness is precluded by the intentions which a bilingual dictionary was supposed to fulfil: Pomey justifies his indifference to norms of purity and good usage in French by pointing out that however unfashionable a word may be one may still on occasion need to know its Latin equivalent.[5] Unlike its monolingual counterpart, the bilingual dictionary cannot equate a temporary state of the language as spoken by the hegemonic social groups with the essential language itself. The normative monolingual dictionary, like R, A and to a certain extent F2, thus carries out the same operations of censoring and censuring linguistic usage as 'taste' itself and *honnêteté*.

This is not the case with F1. Furetière repudiated the separation of 'les termes des Arts et des Sciences' from 'les mots communs de la langue' as chimerical.[6] Bayle's preface to F1, written after Furetière's death, which preceded the publication of the dictionary by two years, underscores the technological and in some sense democratic trend of the work. The comprehensiveness of F1 is somewhat offset by the inadequacy, pointed to by Matoré, of its definitions of 'termes de civilisation' (he cites *air*, *mérite*, *galant*, *sensible*, *honnête*, *gloire*, and *commerce* as examples).[7] *Goût* of course falls into this category. F2's treatment of it, however, is very ample and instructive. This may be connected with F2's reintroduction of a normative intention alongside the universalist one: 'On a crû', says the Preface, 'que pour bien remplir le titre de *Dictionaire universel*, il faloit qu'on y pût apprendre à parler poliment, aussi bien qu'à parler juste, & dans les termes propres à chaque Art.' Concern with the requirements of polite speech may be the reason for the more thorough treatment of *goût*.

A proclaims itself in its Preface as addressed to *les honnêtes gens* alone. Consequently it omits 'les termes des Arts et des Sciences' except those which have passed into everyday speech. Other technical terms were relegated to the *Supplément* edited by Thomas Corneille which also appeared in 1694. *Goût*, however, as a term in the discourse of painting (equivalent to 'style'), does not appear in the *Supplément* but in the main dictionary: painting is obviously supposed to come within the purview of *les honnêtes gens*. Unlike F2, which provides illustrative quotations from named authors, A offers specially constructed specimens of each usage it lists. Its lexicographical standards, as evidenced in the entry on *goût*, are high. It gives synonymic equivalents of the various meanings, whereas F is content with vague descriptions of the headword's fields of reference. The different senses of *goût* are particularly well demarcated by A. (Not that this resolves all the problems, as we shall see.) R is referred to much less frequently in what follows than either A or F. Some of its specimen sentences are interesting, but the definitions suffer from an insufficiently methodical approach — not a surprising failure in a pioneering work.

Literal senses

Obviously the chief concern of the present work is with figurative senses of *goût*. But it will not do simply to assume that the use of these is self-explanatory. The status and function of *goût* as a metaphor can only be gauged by collating the figurative with the literal uses. The homology between them is by no means perfect.

Here, even more than in the section on figurative uses, the treatment of dictionary entries has, for reasons of space, to be rigorously selective, confining itself to a handful of salient points. First of these is the definition of *goût* as one of the five senses, its task being, as both A and F have it, to 'discerner les saveurs'. There are problems here with the word *discerner*. If we look at the definitions of it in F and A, and particularly at the illustrative examples, we shall find that it has two senses: to distinguish something from its opposite (as in 'Discerner l'ami de l'ennemi, le bon du mauvais, le vray du faux', A), and to perceive some particular thing, to isolate it from a general background of sensations ('cet homme estoit trop esloigné, je ne l'ay pû discerner de si loin', A). In the first sense, the perception often seems to carry a value-judgement along with it: thus, to discern something as true or false, good or bad, is simultaneously to pass a judgment on it. Yet this is not necessarily the case with the taste-discernment, as is indicated by an exemplary quotation from F1: 'les gousts sont différents, les uns ayment le doux, les autres le salé'. To distinguish sweet from savoury carries no *inbuilt* value-judgment: and any judgment premised on this perception is relative to the individual's preference, as the quotation suggests, or to his or her idea of what is appropriate to the dish under consideration. This is all the more true when the perception does not involve locating the object with reference to a binary opposition; when it merely registers the presence or absence of some element or quality. To discern the flavour of garlic in a dish is not in itself to pass a judgment on it: that depends on the individual and on the dish. So the definition of taste as a form of discernment is by no means free of ambiguity. When, if at all, are taste-discernments to be taken as involving a value-judgment, and when do these value-judgments claim objective status? The implications of these ambiguities will surface more clearly later.

That taste-reactions in the literal sense are not subject to normative judgment is of course the meaning of the proverb 'il ne faut pas disputer des goûts'. This is listed by A, along with other expressions of the variety of tastes; but only under the literal sense of *goût*, as if figurative tastes were allowed no such freedom. It is not simply that A is avoiding repetition, for many expressions are listed under both literal and figurative senses, as we shall see. F also has 'il ne faut pas disputer des gousts', but lists it separately, as a proverb, and this in itself is significant. As Natalie Zemon Davis notes, the status of the proverb declined in seventeenth-century France: from being a repository of collective wisdom, it came to be identified by the elite culture as a definitely 'popular' speech-form.[8] To cite it, therefore, in defence of the variety of tastes, or of one's right to one's own taste, would be, in polite society, to jeopardize one's status as a speaker.

Of the expressions that appear in A under both literal and figurative senses, the most interesting are 'avoir le goust delicat, le goust exquis'. The use of these expressions in the figurative sense posits a wide variety of cultural practices as analogues of *luxury* eating and drinking. The ideal subject of these practices is therefore postulated as analogous to, if not identical with, a member of the privileged classes whose lifestyle makes possible such fine discriminations about food and drink. Along with language (a field for the exercise of figurative taste), eating- and drinking-habits play a crucial role in the socialization of the individual. Norbert Elias has pointed to the close parallel between the 'civilizing' of eating and drinking and that of speech: a parallel to which the dictionary here bears witness. In either realm, the establishment of standards presupposes, as Elias says, a system of socio-cultural relations, more particularly the existence of 'model-forming' circles.[9] The social foundations of such hegemonic groups have been discussed in chapter 1.

Language, as recorded in the dictionary, goes further towards constituting a system of ideological relations focused on 'taste'. It may be said of a subject of taste that 'il a le goust exquis' or 'le goust delicat', and of an object that it is 'd'un goust exquis' or 'd'un goust delicat' (A). The two may not always coincide: good food may be wasted on the undiscerning, while the epicure struggles with food of poor quality. Nevertheless, language here helps to produce an ideal assimilation of the exquisite taste of the object to the exquisite taste of the subject, each reflecting the other's perfection. It thus fosters the possibility of a collective euphoria that excludes the inferior subject along with the inferior object from the charmed circle of those who find their own perfect taste mirrored in the fare before them.

Figurative senses

We can distinguish between five figurative senses of *goût* on the basis of the entry in A, the fullest and most precise. F2's entry, however, is also fairly substantial, having been expanded from F1's, itself much more ample than R's. F2 gives one meaning absent from its predecessor, tries to make the definitions more accurate and comprehensive, and adds a host of illustrative quotations. This is a far cry from R's airy remark that 'ce mot au figuré a un sens fort étendu', backed up by a few examples with glosses. R, however, does single out a special use of *goût* as a 'terme de peinture', which corresponds to the fifth of the meanings listed below. While the expansion of entries on *goût* from earlier to later dictionaries is no doubt partly an effect of rising lexicographical standards in general, it perhaps also reflects a particular concern on the part of lexicographers to come to terms with increasingly widespread and varied uses of the word.

The five senses are as follows:

1. 'Le discernement, la finesse du jugement' (A).
   'GOUST, se dit figurément en Morale des jugemens de l'esprit' (F1).
   F2 adds 'du choix, & du discernement' after 'des jugemens de l'esprit'.

2. 'Sensibilité' (A).
   'GOUST, se dit aussi pour marquer qu'un homme n'aime point quelque chose' (F).
3. 'Le sentiment agréable ou avantageux qu'on a de quelque chose' (A).
   'Sentiment, plaisir' (F2).
4. 'Maniere dont une chose est faite, caractere particulier de quelque ouvrage' (A).
5. 'Caractere d'un Autheur, d'un Peintre, d'un Sculpteur, ou mesme, Caractere general d'un siecle' (A).
   'GOUST, se dit aussi des bastimens, des statuës, des tableaux' (F1). F2 adds 'et de tout ce qui est bien inventé et bien travaillé'.

Sense (1) receives the fullest attention. F2 illustrates it with no fewer than sixteen examples. That it should be assigned by F to the domain of 'Morale' is an indication of the absence of a category of the 'aesthetic' from the discourse of French classicism.

The definition of this sense of *goût* raises certain problems in relation to the terms *esprit* and *jugement*. Is *jugement* a self-subsistent faculty, or, as F implies, a function of *esprit*? La Rochefoucauld's maxim 258, 'Le bon goût vient plus du jugement que de l'esprit', which is quoted by F2, implies that *jugement* and *esprit* are not identical, but in maxim 97 La Rochefoucauld asserts that 'le jugement n'est que la grandeur de la lumière de l'esprit'. From such ambiguities it results that the relationship of *goût* with other mental qualities or activities remains uncertain.

A further problem is with the definition of *goût* as *discernement*. The word's ambiguities have been touched on already. If taste, in the figurative sense, is a *discernement*, what kind of discernment is it? Does it simply register certain features or qualities (analogous to the garlic in the dish discussed above) that may inhere in the object but that do not compel a particular attitude on the part of the subject? Or does it operate within a system of polarities, distinguishing qualities from their opposites? If the latter, does the taste-discernment involve an *inbuilt* value-judgment, like the discernment of true from false, which needs to invoke no criterion outside the judgment itself? Or is the value attached to the opposing qualities in some way relative — to a subject's individual preferences or interests, or to some general notion about the kind of object under consideration? It is certain that a perfectly accurate discernment may yet be accurate only in relation to a particular subject or category of subjects. Looking again at the illustrative examples of *discerner* from A, we see 'Discerner l'ami de l'ennemi, le bon du mauvais, le vray du faux'. The last two may be held to relate to a universal and objective order of values, whereas the values presupposed by the first are totally relative to a subject or category of subjects: I may rightly perceive X as my enemy, but he may be on the best of terms with everyone else. The matter is even clearer if one thinks of two collective subjects, in the form of two warring armies, for whom perceptions of friend and foe are strictly reversible. So what kind of subject does the taste-discernment presuppose: a universal human subject, or one defined in some more restrictive way?

In short, the definition of taste as *discernement*, which might seem to favour a normative discourse of taste by imparting a certain cognitive quality to the taste-judgment, raises formidable problems. Yet, if conceptually problematic, it has certain discursive advantages. Firstly, it permits the discourse of taste to shuttle back and forth between the appeal to universal standards of truth and rightness and the more exclusive appeal to a certain category of subjects whose preferences enjoy authoritative status. This kind of movement will be studied repeatedly below. Secondly, it obscures the complexity of the process of forming value-judgments. If taste is a discernment, and certain discernments (for instance, that of true from false) carry with them an inbuilt evaluation, then it becomes possible to represent particular taste-judgments as incorporating their own criteria of value in similarly unmediated fashion, as needing no reference to any outside criterion. The extent to which such judgments may be relative, to a subject, singular or plural, to a situation, to a set of attitudes and assumptions, is thereby obscured. These indeterminacies in the definition of taste are thus profoundly suggestive of the capacity of taste-discourse to give partial and contingent judgments the status of universal and self-evident truths.

The expression 'finesse du jugement', proposed by A as an equivalent to *goût*, inevitably evokes Pascal's *esprit de finesse*. Such associations, however seductive, should be treated with caution. There is a tendency, in writers such as Borgerhoff, to lump together the *je ne sais quoi*, the *esprit de finesse*, *goût*, *sentiment* and the rest into a great jumble of perceptions all dealing with some mysterious realm of the ineffable. I agree that this polymorphous proliferation of discursive elements is in itself a fact of great importance, but each of these terms has its own determinate articulations within discourses which should not be blurred by the application of a single totalizing perspective. It is true, for instance, that Pascal's *esprit de géométrie/ esprit de finesse* distinction is homologous with Méré's separation of

61

the two *justesses*, one of which is declared to be a function of *goût* or *sentiment*.[10] The fact is, however, that the zone of application of Pascal's two *esprits*, epistemological concepts concerned with investigating the truth-value of discourses, is far removed from that of the two *justesses*, chiefly focused on literary, rhetorical, and other proprieties. Of *goût* as such Pascal has very little to say. The fact that the word *finesse* occurs in A's definition of *goût* is not really a reason for going off at a Pascalian tangent.

After the definitions, the examples. Of these the most interesting are the quotations listed in F2, several of which indeed attempt to provide further definitions of *goût*, supplements to that provided by Basnage himself. It is true that these sentences originally figure in the total discourse of the work from which they come; to discuss them here seems to be taking them out of context. But this is not so; for here they enter into, and are partially constituted by, the discourse of the dictionary; they are specimens of the kind of thing that can be said and implied using the term *goût*.

Here are the quotations that count more or less as definitions of *goût*:[11]

1. 'Le bon *goût* en matiere d'esprit est une harmonie, ou un accord de l'esprit avec la raison' (Mlle de Scudéry).
2. 'Le bon *goût* est un sentiment naturel qui tient à l'ame; c'est une espece d'instinct de la droite raison' (Bouhours).
3. 'Le *goût* est un sentiment qu'on ne sçauroit apprendre, ni enseigner; il faut qu'il soit né avec nous. Ainsi il ne faut pas traitter de haut en bas ceux qui ne l'ont point; on n'a pas de pièces en main pour [les] convaincre qu'ils ont tort' ('Saint-Evremond').
4. 'Le bon *goût* ne vient que d'une connoissance exquise, & juste à bien juger du bien, & du mal, pour toute sorte de bienseance & d'agrémens: on ne l'acquiert qu'avec beaucoup de soins, & de reflexions' (Méré).
5. 'Le bon *goût* vient plus du jugement, que de l'esprit' (La Rochefoucauld).

These definitions have shared and unshared, indeed contradictory, qualities. Several of them seek to express the essence of *goût* in dualistic formulas. The first invokes *esprit* and *raison*, the second *instinct* and *droite raison*, the fifth *jugement* and *esprit*. But the terms are linked or dissociated in different ways: in the first by addition $(X + Y)$, in the second by a genitive (X as a function, quality, or mode of Y), in the fifth by an ordering (X rather than, although not excluding, Y). The fourth defines *goût* as an effect of knowledge:

to that extent it is unitary in nature, but the passage contains several double-barrelled formulations, 'exquise' and 'juste' describing the mode of the knowledge, 'bienseance' and 'agrémens' specifying its object, 'soins' and 'reflexions' the mode of its acquisition. These have the effect of constituting *goût* as complex and highly valuable because of the multiplicity of its necessary conditions.

There are two types of definition. The first (examples 1, 2, 4, 5) identifies *goût* in terms of relationships between abstract qualities or mental faculties: *esprit, jugement, raison, sentiment*. It deals, that is, with the internal relations of *goût*: its constituents, its place in a certain psychical economy. The second (examples 3 and 4) treats it as an asset, and specifies the terms of its possession: it can be acquired (Méré), you must be born with it ('Saint-Evremond'). This second type focuses on *goût*'s external relations: the subject's relations with others, which are discussed by 'Saint-Evremond', and with the object of his or her reflexions (Méré). The objects of *goût* (*agrémens* and *bienséance*) are qualities attached, though not exclusively, to persons and to that extent *goût* locates its subject in sets of personal − that is, ultimately, social − relations.

The relationships between these two types of definition are problematic. The focus on external relations produces a notion of 'taste' as a *distinctive* possession (since only some people are born with it or because you have to work hard to acquire it), whereas the internal relations seem at first sight to presuppose a *universal* psychology ('un sentiment naturel qui tient à l'ame'). This suggests the possibility that 'taste' is as much a normal human faculty as the physical sense of taste. But this must be checked by a more rigorous interrogation of these abstract concepts. In fact, they are the site of a chronic ambiguity. Are terms like *raison, esprit, jugement* to be taken topographically, as regions or elements of the psyche? or are they realities external to it? *Raison*, for instance, might refer to the individual's personal allowance of the (human) ability to reason, but it might also designate 'what is reasonable', even a transcendental Platonic archetype of Reason.

This ambiguity can be pursued through several of the definitions. Take the one attributed to Mlle de Scudéry: 'good taste' is a harmony of *esprit* and *raison*. Read without a definite context, this could mean several things. If we take *esprit* and *raison* as personal qualities, the definition becomes an instruction: 'In order to conform to good taste, temper your *esprit* with *raison*, eschew intellectual self-indulgence.' The *harmonie* here is produced on the level of the subject. But what if *esprit* and *raison* are taken to be external realities existing independently of the subject? How in that case does the harmony come about? Is it given in advance or is it the effect of a deliberate activity of harmonization? The suggestion could be that some people's minds are naturally attuned to reason, but not all people's; just as some, but not all, people have perfect pitch. (Compare this to the 'Saint-Evremond' quotation.) Or it could mean that one must bring one's mind into line with the dictates of reason, as a source of authority external to the self (here the affinity is with Méré).

Trying to attain harmony with reason is all very well: what if one's ear is playing one false? The standard of harmony cannot be the individual as such, which would make normative judgments like that conveyed in *bon goût* impossible. It is necessary, then, to posit either a privileged subject who will set the tone or some kind of authoritative ear existing outside the subject (it all sounds rather surrealist). Why not the 'normal human ear'? This would give us a 'humanist', universalist, taste-discourse, in which, as in Boileau, the *consensus gentium* provides the criterion of 'good taste'. There is of course the problem that, as the article on harmony in the *Oxford Companion to Music* points out (1955 edn, p. 445), 'the combinations, or chords, which the human ear (i.e. the European ear, for with small exceptions only European races have yet developed harmony) has respectively enjoyed, tolerated, and allowed have varied greatly at different periods'. Be that as it may, the point remains that 'good taste' cannot adequately be defined by juggling with abstract values: in practice, these have to be associated to a particular image of the subject of good taste, whether represented as a normal or as a distinguished individual.

The second quotation, from Bouhours, bristles with problems. It provides the best example of an ambiguity or instability common to several of these passages, indeed to the whole discourse of taste. It will be noted that all of these quotations except the third refer not to plain *goût* but to *bon goût*. The two terms are used interchangeably, notes Dens,[12] but he does not investigate the reasons for this duplication. It is at first sight bizarre, for if *goût* actually means 'le discernement, la finesse du jugement' (A), and if *discernement* is the ability to distinguish good from bad, true from false, then it apparently contains its own inbuilt validations: there is no need further to specify it as *bon*. If you have 'taste' you'll get things right; if you get them wrong you have no 'taste'.

The existence, however, of the locution *bon goût* is no mere linguistic superfluity; it corresponds to a structural necessity of taste-discourse: that of integrating 'taste' in the sense of 'what one likes' with 'taste' as a cognitive faculty within a normative discourse of 'taste'. The cognitive faculty, being in some sense rational, as most writers agree, should carry its own validation. Yet people obviously differ in what they like; and at the same time human beings are by definition rational. In order to safeguard the normative discourse, then, it is necessary to postulate, as I have argued, a privileged category of subject whose reason shall count as authoritative, whose taste shall count as good; and alternatively, or simultaneously, an external and objective order of values. R defines *avoir le goût bon* in this way, as 'aimer ce qui est bon'; the problem then is how to know what is good.

This is particularly clear with the Bouhours definition. Suppose he had said 'le goût est un instinct de la raison'. This would be to locate *goût* within a general human psychical economy. It would suggest that one's instinctive reactions can often be subsequently backed up by rational argument. To this extent, any taste which could advance reasons in its support would be a good taste. But this is not sufficient to constitute particular preferences as good, as the discourse of taste seeks to do. Thus Bouhours invokes not *raison* simply but *droite raison*: a reason whose 'rightness' is somehow given in advance and/or validated by the (exceptional) individual subject. Not necessarily, one might argue: the goodness of the taste might be held to depend on the validity of the reasons. The objection would be sound if it came from within the rationalizing 'geometric' discourse of taste of certain eighteenth-century writers.[13] However, Bouhours himself does not reduce questions of taste to questions of logic. (Nor does Méré: his second type of *justesse*, which deals with what he takes to be logical entailments, is specifically distinguished from the first type, which is a matter of *goût* and *sentiment*.)[14] In part of the original passage omitted from the quotation given in the dictionary, Bouhours alleges that taste directs reason 'plus seûrement que tous les raisonnemens qu'elle pourroit faire' (p. 517). In other words, the rationality of good taste is beyond the scope of the rational activity of the individual; 'right reason' is divorced from the actual process of reasoning. It is both a transcendental value external to the subject and the mysterious prerogative of a certain kind of subject (since presumably not all human reason is right). The questions then arise, where is 'right reason' located? how is the privileged subject recognized?

This transgression of the limits of the dictionary entry may be justified inasmuch as it makes the point that the dictionary, by its very nature, gestures outwards to other discourses; and these give the ambiguous terms in the definition greater precision, a keener ideological edge. But there is more to say about this passage. Its verbal texture is persistently loose, vague, 'un sentiment qui *tient à* l'ame', 'une *espece* d'instinct'. This serves to obfuscate the essence of 'taste', to postulate it as something exceeding the resources of discourse: the resources of psychology in particular, since the locations and relationships in question are so imprecise. The word 'naturel' is another locus of uncertainty. It could suggest that the *sentiment* in question is a universal human attribute, like the soul, like reason. Alternatively, it could suggest, with specific ideological implications, that 'taste' is natural to the privileged individual, not the result of some process of education or acculturation. This indeterminacy allows 'taste' to combine the privileges of the 'natural' both as a universal order and as the source and justification of inequality and elitism. (These implications will be discussed more fully below in connexion with the opposition established between 'taste' and 'pedantry'. They emerge rather more fully in another omitted section of the original passage, where 'good taste' is declared to be 'indépendant de toutes les sciences qu'on peut acquérir' (Bouhours, p. 516). The effect of this is to displace 'good taste' from academic-humanist culture to the extra-academic culture of the salons and *honnêteté*.)

'Saint-Evremond' at any rate is perfectly frank about all this. Like Bouhours, he calls 'taste' a *sentiment*, and quite explicitly denies it to all but the lucky few who happen to be born with it. These, however, are counselled not to treat the less fortunate 'de haut en bas'. This is a revealing indication that lack of 'taste' is commonly held to mark someone as an object of contempt, while its possession is regarded as a considerable advantage. It is also just the kind of thing that a class-conscious but broad-minded aristocrat would say about noble descent: the more so if 'taste', like rank, is something you just happen to be born with. (The sentiments are benignly aristocratic, even though Mitton, the real author of the definition, was not himself of noble birth.) Not only is 'taste' itself an exclusive order, so is taste-discourse: 'on n'a pas de pièces en main pour convaincre [those without taste] qu'ils ont tort'. But the authority of taste is no less valid for being unable to justify itself by reason: one must simply submit to the order one cannot participate in. The similarity of this kind of logic to that of the discourse of aristocracy is evident. Assent to the aristocratic order invoked acceptance of a mysterious privilege conferred on certain people by birth in accordance with the will of God; a privilege, therefore, analogous to 'Saint-Evremond''s concept of taste.

With becoming nonchalance, 'Saint-Evremond' gestures towards 'taste' as an inherited property; Méré, however, acts as its estate agent, crying up its value, showing off its good points, explaining how it is to be acquired. As with the Bouhours passage, there is a saturation of abstract nouns: again, these serve to celebrate the richness, many-sidedness and omnicompetence of taste. Every form of linguistic valorization is brought into play, qualitative ('exquise') and quantitative ('*beaucoup* de soins', '*toute* sorte de bienseance', my italics), restrictive (the double 'ne ... que ...'). Méré differs from Bouhours in making individual effort a means of access to good taste, but he agrees with him in another way: it is produced by 'soins' and 'reflexions' rather than knowledge of any definite and formal kind.

The sphere of taste is extensive: 'toute sorte de bienseance & d'agrémens'. It is of course to be noted that this does not associate taste particularly with the sphere of 'the arts' or 'literature'. *Agrémens*, as we shall see, are qualities as much associated with persons as with books, if not more so: the term is often used of female attractions. *Bienséance* governs all forms of social practice, including linguistic ones. The term features an ambiguity precisely akin to that of *goût*. As we saw, 'taste' can denote the individual's (correct) evaluation of certain relationships of value. But it is also a set of values already established: those that are agreed to count as good taste. *Bienséance* likewise could be the real relationships of appropriateness perceived by the good taste of certain individuals, or simply the mass of established proprieties and decorums. It depends on whether one moves outwards from the subject to the external order of values or inwards from the values, practices, ideologies to the subject as constituted by them. In the former case, we are left with the privileged subject of taste, here identified as the possessor of a certain knowledge, but elsewhere in Méré defined by other kinds of criteria as well. In the latter 'taste' appears as a mechanism for internalizing established social and cultural codes of propriety. These perspectives are largely complementary. It is true that Méré stigmatizes assent to 'false' *bienséances* as want of taste, as if the business of taste were precisely to distinguish those proprieties, customs, and so on that one should assent to from those that one should not (*OC* III, 94). Nevertheless, the point remains that it is 'taste' that conveys one's recognition of that which is incumbent on one in the name of the *bienséances*.

With the La Rochefoucauld quotation we are back with the problematic relationship of *jugement* to *esprit*. *Esprit* in seventeenth-century writing has an extremely ambivalent status. Sometimes, as the normal word for the 'mind', it carried strong positive connotations, reflecting a valorization of certain forms of intellectual activity; at other times, when it bears more the meaning of 'wit', it becomes a rather suspicious quality, too little respectful of the established order of language and things, too much the activity, not of an ideal representative individual like the *honnête homme*, but of a concrete singular individual. But it is better to discuss this question later in this book, where what is at stake in the confrontation between *goût* and *esprit* will be slightly more evident.[15]

It is time to sum up the general features of these definitions of 'taste'. The impression they leave is one of nebulosity. No two authorities agree on the precise qualities that go to make up 'taste': *esprit, raison, sentiment, jugement* are variously combined. 'Saint-Evremond' denies that taste can be acquired. Méré avers the contrary. The reader might be puzzled by this. But I think the overall effect is not exactly to create puzzlement. It is akin to that produced by the saturation of abstract nouns in the Bouhours and Méré quotations: it suggests the complexity and richness of 'taste', its capacity to generate and at the same time to exceed discourse. Its very existence authorizes infinite speech about it. To this extent it resembles its near neighbour, the *je ne sais quoi*, 'qui ne subsiste que parcc qu'on ne peut dire ce que c'est'.[16]

The contradictory variety of the definitions, their consciously approximative nature send the reader back to his or her experience (the appearance of the word *sentiment* in two of the quotations is significant). The implication is that even if neither you nor anyone else can say what 'taste' is, you feel it: 'on le sent mieux que l'on ne le peut exprimer', writes Méré (*OC* II, 128). The appeal to spontaneous lived experience is eminently ideological inasmuch as it reproduces the effectivity of the social agencies by which that experience has been produced.

Another common feature of the definitions is the indeterminacy of the abstract terms they deploy. I have argued that this leaves a crucial lacuna in taste-language, which is remedied in the specific discourses in which that language operates. The distinction was earlier drawn between definitions of *goût* in terms of its position within a psychical economy and those which make it over to a certain kind of subject. In practice the first type drifts into the second because the indefiniteness of its terms cannot support a normative discourse of '(good) taste'. This requires the support of a subject defined by the *distinctive* possession of the quality of 'taste', able therefore to control discourse about it, to manipulate it with authority. 'Taste' is an exclusive quality, whether you think of it as conferred by birth ('Saint-Evremond') or as the result of prolonged and careful meditation on *agrémens* and *bienséance* – which can only be the fruit of a certain social experience (Méré). Its subject, however rare, is not an isolated individual: the harmony of his *esprit* with reason must be recognized by other ears than his own (Scudéry). He determines what reason shall count as right, or at any rate recognizes the rightness of the reason dispensed by particular social institutions and formations. 'Taste' has been removed from the sphere of a discourse of human faculties in general, and becomes the instrument of an exclusive authority.

The second meaning given by the dictionaries is listed by A as 'sensibilité'. But its use is purely negative, 'pour marquer qu'un homme n'aime point quelque chose' as F puts it. A gives the examples 'Il n'a pas de goust pour les vers, pour la musique.' They also appear in F, along with 'Il n'a pas de goust pour le mariage, pour la guerre.' F2 adds a sentence from *La Princesse de Clèves*: 'François Ier n'avoit ni le même *goût*, ni la même tendresse pour Henri II son fils.'

So far it looks as if these utterances are neutral statements of an attitude. Some of them are, but not all. Take this other sentence from A: 'Il n'a nul goust pour les choses du ciel.' It is hard to see how this could be anything other than a severe condemnation. Moreover F1 (but, curiously, not F2) glosses 'il n'a point de *goust* pour les Vers, pour la Musique' as 'il n'en est point touché, *ou il ne s'y connoist point*' (my italics). Insensitivity to poetry or music is thus depicted, and condemned, as the fruit of ignorance. But X's disinclination to get married or join the army is not necessarily a sign of his ignorance of hymeneal or martial joys. Not all insensibility is an effect of ignorance. Is it culpable only when it is? Not entirely. Not all ignorances, after all, are necessarily culpable. Earlier in the seventeenth century a nobleman might have prided himself on his ignorance of poetry: Guez de Balzac's story of the Maréchal de Biron is well known: having succeeded in translating, for the king's benefit, a Greek inscription which had defeated some *maîtres des requêtes* who were standing by, he promptly made himself scarce, 'honteux d'en auoir plus sceu que les Maistres des Requestes de ce temps-là'.[17] Conversely, as far as 'les choses du ciel' are concerned, no one could claim to have more than a faint idea of them: yet all alike are supposed to revere them. What condemns the lack of a certain taste is thus not so much its being due to ignorance but the consensual importance attached to its object. Semantics alone will not do justice to the *force* of utterances of the type 'il n'a pas de goût pour ...' They may, although they need not, serve to position their subject within an ideological economy of desire.

The same is potentially true of the third sense (*sentiment, plaisir*). At first sight, and in certain cases, this use appears straightforward, in a sentence for example like 'ses amis le voyaient avec assiduité, & avec *goût*' (F2). But there are territorial disputes between this sense and sense (1) (*discernement*). Thus, under sense (1), F2 lists the sentence 'les manieres de cet homme-là sont au *goût* de tout le monde'. But the almost identical sentence 'cest ouvrage est au goust de tout le monde' is placed by A under sense (3). This may be because F2 is simply copying F1, which does not separately recognize this sense. But this explanation would not cover the illustrative sentences which F2 comes up with off its own bat. Compare the following examples:

1. Les adversitez épurent nos desirs, & nous font perdre le *goût* du monde (Bossuet).
2. Une vuë interieure de Dieu lui ôtoit tout le *goût* des plaisirs du siecle (Flećhier).
3. Un esprit sain, puise à la Cour le *goût* de la solitude, & de la retraite (La Bruyère).

The first of these is listed by F2 under sense (3), the other two under sense (1). All three would, it seems to me, make perfect sense under (3). Nor can I explain why the Bossuet and Fléchier quotations should be placed under different headings when they are making the same point within the same context of spirituality. But, leaving this question aside, let us try to make sense of the quotations from Fléchier and La Bruyère on the assumption that they are using *goût* in the sense of a capacity to respond in general. This is plausible. The disillusioned courtier learns to enjoy getting away from the court. The devout person's sense of God is so strong that worldly pleasures no longer make an impact.

But if this capacity to respond is all that is meant by *goût* (*discernement*), then we come back to the problem of the origins of normativity in the discourse of taste. It cannot be guaranteed by the fact that a discernment or selection has taken place. That simply means that a particular subject has rated one thing above another, or, as in the Fléchier quotation, has ceased to rate a whole category of objects. There is no logical implication that this choice is right or wrong. What validates a particular act of discernment can only be the valuation placed on the object by discourse.

This point might be illustrated by departing temporarily from the text of the dictionary for a brief examination of a couple of other passages from an author already quoted, Bossuet. According to Bossuet, the Christian is fortified by adversity: 'Là on expie ses péchés; là on épure ses intentions; là on transporte ses désirs de la terre au ciel; là on perd tout le goût du monde.'[18] For this final utterance to have its requisite force (for it not to appear as the record of a disaster), the order of religious discourse has to be secured in various ways, some on the level of rhetorical technique, like the fourfold anaphoric repetition of 'là', but including, crucially, the sustained antithesis between the world and heaven, which carries its own implicit hierarchy of values.

Again, in the *Oraison funèbre d'Henriette d'Angleterre*, when Bossuet talks of the princess's reading of works of history, we are told that 'là notre admirable princesse étudiait les devoirs de ceux dont la vie compose l'histoire; elle y perdait insensiblement le goût des romans et de leurs fades héros' (*Oraisons funèbres*, p. 167). The latter statement derives its force simply from the antithesis it helps to establish between two kinds of reading, one directed towards pleasure, the other towards moral instruction, between insipid fiction and substantial reality. And what secures this antithesis in an order of value is the princess's own relation to history as the scene of her own existence. It is an ideology of rank and its attendant philosophy of history that determines this loss of taste as a positive gain. The loss of other tastes can be anything but positive: in the oration for Anne de Gonzague, Bossuet, describing her tribulations, cries out 'Encore s'il eût plu à Dieu de lui conserver ce goût sensible de la piéte qu'il avait renouvelé dans son cœur au commencement de sa pénitence!' (p. 284). As it happens, this loss of her taste for piety is part of God's plan for Anne de Gonzague, but in itself and in the short term it is experienced as pure suffering.

What these examples show is that *goût* in the sense of *sentiment*, *plaisir* can be used to make statements of considerable discursive force: but that, at the same time, the word *goût*, so used, has no intrinsic normative content, as it does in the *discernement* sense, where the use of the word, and even more the expression *bon goût*, implies in itself an order of values with which particular preferences or inclinations can be brought into relation. In these sentences from Bossuet, as in the parallel examples from F2, we see that *goût* functions to produce value-judgments only by association with a scheme of values conveyed by other elements of the utterance. To conflate, as F2 does, these two different uses, by assimilating sentences of the 'perdre le goût de quelque chose' type to the *discernement* type is at first sight confusing. And one could indeed attribute it to lexicographical incompetence. But perhaps it rather reflects a sense of a certain solidarity between 'taste' (*discernement*) as a value and the religious and ethical values alluded to in those sentences from Fléchier and La Bruyère;

as if any taste that upheld the values of religion or philosophical wisdom were *ipso facto* an exercise of the faculty of good taste. But this tends to hollow out the pretensions of *goût* (*discernement*) to a certain cognitive objectivity. To the extent that these preferences are discernments, as F2 suggests we should regard them, discernment is revealed as merely registering values already in place.

Another sentence listed by F2 under sense (1) certainly uses the language of *discernement*, but harnesses 'taste' to a particular object as senses (2) and (3) do: 'Il n'est rien de plus rare que ce discernement exquis, & ce goût rafiné de l'Ame pour sa veritable nourriture.' This is credited to the 'AB. DE S.R.', who does not feature in the list of abbreviations, but who can be identified as the abbé de Saint-Réal. The type of preference here alluded to, for one kind of food over another, is regarded as a discernment of objective qualities. The reference to the proper food of the soul suggests a religious context, although it is true that, as we have seen, Bouhours defines taste as 'un sentiment naturel de l'ame' without any obvious religious implications. The Saint-Réal quotation may be set against one from Nicole, also cited by F2: 'Nous n'avons point de goût spirituel, pour discerner sûrement les bons alimens d'avec les mauvais.'[19] Whereas Saint-Réal says that spiritual taste is rare, Nicole simply denies its existence. But the quotations have this in common, that they transpose not only the activity of tasting from the literal to the figurative sphere but its object as well: figurative 'taste' has figurative 'food' to operate on. This is not the case with any of the other quotations, except for one from La Bruyère which sustains the metaphor by attaching taste-words to the object of taste: 'Les mauvais auteurs gâtent le goût du public, l'accoutumant à des choses fades, & insipides.'[20] But these words denote hedonic shortcomings, which is not what Saint-Réal and Nicole are concerned with. To eat the wrong sort of food is, for them, to imperil one's survival. Of course you can argue that a diet of pap is bad for the spiritual health of the community, but this is, I think, a nineteenth-century kind of argument which it is risky to read back into a seventeenth-century text. What La Bruyère probably means is that a public accustomed to platitude will fail to identify real merit when it comes along.

There are grounds, I think, for suggesting a distinction between religious-moral and *mondain* discourses of taste, with regard, firstly, to their handling of the metaphor, and, secondly, to their ideological function. Two quotations in a dictionary may seem to provide rather a slender basis for talking about a religious-moral *discourse* of taste. It is true that, as Renée Kohn points out, following Cayrou, the word *goût* can have particular resonances in religious discourse, where it can denote, in Cayrou's words, 'la félicité de l'âme savourant un bien ardemment désiré'.[21] But it is not this sense of *goût* that is in question here. And how religious are these two utterances, anyway? While the Nicole quotation is fairly obviously concerned with religion, the assumption may seem premature in the case of Saint-Réal. Does concern with 'the proper food of the soul' necessarily exclude *mondain* preoccupations? The point is, however, that the utterance simply doesn't *look* as if it comes from a *mondain* position: it would be recognized as probably belonging to a religious and moral discourse. And in point of fact it does. It comes from Saint-Réal's treatise *De l'usage de l'histoire*, where he argues that familiar history is full of incidents that could provide a starting-point for moral reflexion but that these are overlooked by the majority of readers because 'il n'est rien de plus que ce discernement *de l'esprit pour ce qui est d'usage & pour ce qui n'en est pas*; ce goût rafiné de l'Ame pour sa véritable nourriture'.[22] The concern with moral enlightenment thus sets the utterance in a different frame of reference from that of Méré's, say, concerned with *agréments* and *bienséance*. The metaphor of taste, moreover, fits easily into religious patterns of thought: physical taste preserves life, spiritual 'taste' preserves spiritual 'life', the latter one of the best-established of Christian metaphors. Du Tremblay's discussion of taste, as we have seen, likewise combines religious preoccupations with the sustained application of the taste-metaphor.[23] Even though Nicole denies that we have a spiritual sense of taste, he implicitly agrees with Du Tremblay as to the function such a taste would perform − distinguishing between true and false spiritual nourishment. The structure of what it thus seems reasonable to call a potential religious discourse of taste is differentiated from that of the *mondain* discourse by a figural lacuna in the latter. Here, the activity of taste seems to lack a corresponding 'nourishment' as its object, despite the occasional reference to the object of 'taste' as a food or the figurative application of taste-words to the object, as in the La Bruyère example.[24] But this is not a structural feature of the *mondain* discourse. By comparison with the religious variety, it is superficially incoherent, unmotivated. What coherence it does have is not on the level of the figure: it comes from the figure's articulations with other elements of discourse (*honnêteté*, for one). Its underlying motivation is no doubt only partially conscious: it is, as I shall argue, to produce ideological differentiations.

Not that 'taste' is not credited with an object: namely, as Méré says in the passage here quoted, the judgment of *agréments* and *bienséance.* But is the subject's relation to them as transparent as the human being's dependence on food? The answer is that it is made to be. The discourse of 'taste' serves to constitute its cultural object as natural, presenting it with, in Althusser's phrase, all the 'false obviousness of the given',[25] i.e., the produced.

It has been argued above that tastes are largely determined as good by their implicit attribution to a valued subject. An example of this can be found in another of the sentences which F2 gives in order to illustrate the meaning *discernement* (it is quoted by R): 'Le *goût* de Paris s'est trouvé conforme au *goût* d'Athenes.' (It comes from Racine's preface to his *Iphigénie.*) Out of context, the meaning of *goût* in this sentence can only be "what Paris or Athens likes". It corresponds to sense (3) of *goût*: *sentiment, plaisir.* It is placed under sense (1) because of the implicit valorization of Athenian taste as *ipso facto* good. If one were to replace 'Athens' by 'province', one would be left with a statement that within the frame of reference of the cultural discourse would seem frankly incredible; certainly there would be no implication that the taste in question was good; or that any form of valid discernment was in question. What appears to have happened here, then, is that the semantic content of the word *goût* has been (mis-)interpreted in terms of the value attached by a potent cultural discourse to the subject of the taste in question: if Athens liked something it must be good. The assumption could be formulated in more subtle terms, those explicitly posited by Racine: that reason and good sense are the same in every age; the fact that our response should coincide with the ancients' is a powerful indication that both are grounded in some essential human nature. But the point remains that for this purpose only privileged categories of subject are allowed to count as human. You could not, within Racine's terms of reference here, urge the continuing appeal of Charlemagne stories among the people to vindicate either their good taste or the instrinsic worth of the subject-matter; and yet the same logic would apply.[26]

This points to a basic ambivalence in the notion of taste. It is both a mental faculty and an unoffical institution. Its value is assured in the first instance by the operation of a psychological mechanism − *esprit, jugement, raison, sentiment* in some kind of combination. But tastes are also validated in practice by their attribution to a subject (for instance, the people of Athens) which is assumed to possess these qualities, or because the value of their object is taken for granted, consensually or within a certain sectional discourse. However, the good tastes so constituted are at the same time valorized by their implicit association with the sovereign values of *raison, esprit,* and so forth. These can be silently marshalled against any taste that does not conform to the institution. It is difficult to see how in the cultural context of late seventeenth-century France one could vindicate the poetry of the Pléiade or the *libertins* in the name of good taste. To illustrate sense (4), which we shall come to shortly, A gives the sentence 'Les pointes & les jeux de mots dans des pieces d'eloquence sont d'un meschant goust.' But this is more than an example: it is a pronounce-ment to be taken literally. What it condemns is of course the style of writing of the early part of the century with its abundance of con-ceits and wordplay: a condemnation that doubtless stretches back in time to take in Ronsard as well.[27] To substitute 'excellent' for 'meschant' here would make perfect sense, but in the given cultural context it would render the utterance literally unspeakable.

So much for the first three senses of *goût* and the sentences that seem to hover uncertainly between them. The fourth sense is separately recognized only in A, although its range is partly covered in F2's treat-ment of sense (5). Sense (4) ('Maniere dont une chose est faite, caractere particulier de quelque ouvrage', A) is concerned with evalua-tion: 'Cet ouvrage est du bon goust. Ce meuble est de bon goust, de mauvais goust. Cet homme-là travaille dans un fort mauvais goust.' There follows the condemnation of conceits and wordplay. Sense (5) ('Caractere d'un Autheur, d'un Peintre, d'un Sculpteur, ou mesme, Caractere general d'un siecle', A) serves to assign a work to its origin: 'Ces vers-là sont bien dans le goust de Ronsard. ce tableau est dans le goust de Michel Ange, de Raphaël. Je reconnois le goust du Titien. cette piece est bien du goust de l'onziéme siecle.'

F is vaguer. F1 says that *goût* is used 'des bastimens, des statuës, des tableaux'; F2 adds 'et de tout ce qui est bien inventé, & bien travaillé'. This roughly corresponds to A's version of sense (5). Within F2 it is content that determines the attribution of utterances to one or other heading. Thus 'Mr Blondel a fait un Traitté du bon *goust* dans son livre d'Architecture', listed by F1 under the *discernement* sense, is shifted by F2 into the company of other sentences referring to the visual arts, irrespective of whether *goût* means the same thing in all of them. It thus endorses the recognition of the visual arts as an isolable sphere of practice. With A the case is slightly different. The reference to furniture under sense (4) shows that furniture comes within the scope of the evaluative discourse of taste. But sense (5) refers specifically to the individual styles of poets, painters and sculptors. Although no separate mention is made of architects, it is clear that A is recognizing the 'fine' arts as distinct from the 'decorative' arts. It is thus ratifying a trend which dates from the Italian Renaissance but which was only recently beginning to establish itself in France as a natural assumption about culture.

The use of *goût* to mean a recognizable style attached to an individual producer or a historical period reduces the scope of taste as pure evaluation. This will become clear if we examine the presuppositions of the various sentences quoted by A. It is true that if, from a seventeenth-century critical point of view, you recognize a poem as being 'dans le goust de Ronsard' you will probably proceed to criticize it severely. All the same to recognize a style as specifically Ronsardian requires a subtlety and literary culture in excess of that required simply to pronounce it bad in view of the unquestioned canons of the time. Similarly, to recognize a piece of work (of what kind is not clear) as belonging to the eleventh century is to go further than dismissing it as barbarous. The sentence 'il a écrit dans le goust de son siecle', also quoted by A, may be accompanied by an evaluation of the quality of that particular taste; it does not preclude an appeal to a sempiternal order of values. Nevertheless it succeeds in relating the productions of individual authors to a definite historical context.

This use of *goût* in the sense of the style of an age thus imports a historicizing dimension which limits the freedom of pure evaluation. It alludes to the antiquarianism, marginal in its age, of a Ménage in the realm of language, or of a Gaignières in that of the material relics of the past (manuscripts, portraits, maps, and so forth).[28]

The other use, where *goût* refers to the individual style of an artist, bears witness to a rather different set of practices. Like the *discernement* sense, it privileges the individual's subjectivity ('*je reconnois* le goust du Titien', my italics). But what is at stake is not a bipolar logic of evaluation (good/bad) but a potentially open-ended set of references to origin (Titian, Michelangelo, Raphael etc.). It is true that a true/false logic is superimposed on this series: I might 'recognize' a Tintoretto as a Titian. None the less, the scope of evaluation is again curtailed − there is no necessary implication that Titian is better than Michelangelo or vice versa; they are just identifiably different. This is not the case with those utterances where 'le goût d'Athenes', for instance, stands for 'good taste'.

At least, not at first sight. In fact, although the sentences that illustrate these uses of *goût* do not contain explicit evaluations, they do connect with discourses and practices of evaluation. In order to show this another sortie outside the confines of the dictionary entries is required. F gives the sentence 'Les uns ont le goust des tableaux de Poussin, les autres de Rubens.' (This confirms my point that F tends to categorize utterances by their field of reference rather than by their meaning; for this one could plausibly have been listed under sense (3) (*sentiment, plaisir*), since it means simply that some people *like* Poussin rather than Rubens, and conversely.) These preferences are cited with an appearance of neutrality. Yet the choice of these painters is not indifferent: it alludes to an important contemporary controversy. Poussin here stands as the representative of the official doctrine of the Académie royale de peinture et de sculpture under Le Brun, that drawing takes precedence over colour. Rubens (and the Venetians) as 'colourists' were relegated to a secondary position.[29] This official dogmatism was initially reflected in market trends. Until the mid-1660s, the King, the big collectors, and the leading citizens of Paris were all eager to acquire Poussins. But a few years earlier, the first signs of a turnaround had become evident. Gradually, Rubenses became desirable commodities, and prices for Poussins fell.[30] The stylistic preferences conveyed by this use of *goût* thus inevitably position the subject *vis-à-vis* a market structure, even if they do not lead to any economic action on his or her part. There was furthermore an ideological dimension latent in the preference for colour over drawing and vice versa: Blunt points out that whereas the appeal of drawing was held to be principally to the learned, that of colour was accessible to all (*Art and Architecture in France*, p.361). How 'democratic' this colourist position is may be questionable: it might merely connote an alignment with *les honnêtes gens* (the general ruling-class public) against *les savants*, a familiar opposition that we shall encounter again.

Clearly, the new form of taste-recognition was supported by a particular set of cultural and economic relations focused on the practice of 'collecting'. This activity must be placed in context. In the early years of the seventeenth century it acquired the ideological function of celebrating monarchical power. The royal collection was systematically expanded by Richelieu for this purpose. In 1630 the royal collection had contained some 200 pictures (Holst, *Creators, Collectors and Connoisseurs*, p.157); 500 were added through Richelieu's gift to Louis XIII of the Palais Cardinal, containing paintings by Raphael, Titian, Leonardo, Giovanni Bellini, Poussin, Claude, and Philippe de Champaigne, not to mention a wealth of statues, portrait busts and bronzes. The Cardinal's agents in Germany and Italy were instructed to look out for any opportunity to snap up a masterpiece. Richelieu was clearly a very knowledgeable art lover, but, as Taylor puts it, 'his acquisitions were programmatic and in conformity with his theory of government'.[31] Mazarin was even more enthusiastic for art. Colbert inventoried the collection he left at his death to earmark items for the king, although the bulk of it went to Mazarin's heirs. The continuing expansion of the royal collection both under and after Colbert matched the deliberate attempt by the Crown to monopolize artistic patronage and production. One of the more shameless manifestations of this was Louis XIV's tendency to relieve his financiers and courtiers of their art treasures for derisory prices (Holst, *Creators, Collectors and Connoisseurs*, p.157). The recognition of individual artists, and of the value of art, was thus at the same time a recognition of the prestige of monarchy.

The existence and growing importance of a market in works of art significantly modified the economics of culture. Aristocratic culture had always presupposed wealth because of the role within it of conspicuous consumption: largesse to dependants, food and drink, palatial residences, fine clothes. The rich and vulgar could and did seek to ape their betters in this respect. As far as clothes were concerned there was, however, a rigidly encoded sartorial hierarchy, clothes, for obvious reasons, serving as prime signifiers of one's social position. For this reason they represented, as Ariès has noted, a considerable outlay.[32] Of course the taboo could be broken, giving rise to Montchrétien's complaint that a shopman and a nobleman were nowadays indistinguishable, and his claim that 'ceste conformité d'ornement introduit la corruption de nostre ancienne discipline.'[33] But though corrosive of social and ideological order, such transgressions are up to a point semiotically conservative, in that they reinforce the equation between fine clothes and social status. This semiotic ideology of clothes is of course founded on presence, on the (literal) contiguity of subject and signifier. (Thus La Bruyère's rejection of vestimentary symbolism is also a refusal of presence: 'Envoyez-moi cet habit et ces bijoux de Philémon; je vous quitte de la personne', 'Du mérite personnel', 24.) For this reason clothing, as Stanton amply demonstrates, continues to play an important albeit modified role within the culture of *honnêteté* – also founded on the presence of subjects to one another: another example of the affiliations between *honnêteté* and traditional aristocratic culture.[34]

Disproportion between the owner and his or her possessions was perceived in other domains besides clothing, as Jean Alter shows. The opulence of a town house might be seen as unsuitable to a bourgeois owner. None the less, the coding between this kind of possession and the social position of its owner was less rigid than in the case of clothing. What was really scandalous, according to Alter, was less the perceived contradiction between low social position and luxurious lifestyle than the supposedly squalid origins of the wealth that made the lifestyle possible.[35]

Moreover, as signifiers, these other categories of possession do not presuppose the presence of the subject: in extreme cases they cancel the subject; 'tous demandent à voir la maison, et personne à voir Monsieur', says La Bruyère of one bourgeois palace ('De la mode', 2). Paintings of course are of this type. To this extent they belong to a different ideological semiotic from *honnêteté*: they signify wealth in the abstract, not justified and occluded by the social position of its owner.

But this is not all. The art object differs from the traditional material supports of aristocratic culture in that while fulfilling a use-value (giving pleasure, conveying a favourable impression of its owner), it retains its exchange-value. The art object fulfils not only the ends of aristocratic conspicuous consumption but those of bourgeois investment. It is instructive to note Mme de Sévigné's reaction to her son-in-law's art collecting: 'La rage de M. de Grignan pour emprunter, et pour des tableaux et des meubles, est une chose qui serait entièrement incroyable si on ne la voyait. Comment cela se peut-il accorder avec la naissance, sa gloire, et l'amitié qu'il vous doit?'[36] Her friend Coulanges, however, writing to Mme de Grignan (and not, as Holst says (*Creators, Collectors and Connoisseurs*, p. 158), to Mme de Sévigné herself) defends the pictures as investments: 'C'est de l'or en barre que les tableaux, vous les vendrez toujours au double quand il vous plaira' (Mme de Sévigné, *Correspondance*, vol. II, p. 47). In other words, consciously or not, Grignan is behaving with perfect bourgeois rationality, borrowing in order to invest with the possibility of returns far higher than the original loan. Does Mme de Sévigné perceive this, rightly or wrongly, as the motive of his conduct and despise it as vulgar; or does she think that painting and furniture are not what a nobleman should spend his money on? Certainly she is horrified by his apparent lack of concern for his wife and family's financial security. In any case, the episode testifies to the penetration of the commodity in the form of the art object into ruling-class culture, bringing with it the characteristically bourgeois practice of investment. What is more, this process is sanctioned by the privileged category of *goût*: for a discerning palate is an obvious necessity if one is to detect the distinctive flavour of an individual master's work. It is not, however, as has been argued, quite the same type of taste as was celebrated by Bouhours, Méré and the rest in their definitions of *bon goût*. The aesthetic values perceived in this kind of taste-reaction are inextricably entangled with commercial ones, and the identification of a picture's producer does not necessarily fall into the oppositional pattern (good/bad) of the logic of good taste. Artistic taste, like good taste in general, can serve to valorize its subject, but in a different way from taste displayed in clothes or conversation, because it does not presuppose the subject's presence. It therefore liberates him or her from the control of *honnête* culture, based on intersubjective exchange and on the construction of a total personality. The owner of a gallery full of Titians, Tintorettos, and Poussins may be a total failure in conversation, a disaster as to his personal appearance and manner, and totally ignorant of the *bienséances* and *agréments* of social life. He may not even possess taste himself but may have paid someone to do his collecting for him: no matter, he has taste in the essential sense; for, as Marx observes, the owner of money can buy clever people for himself, 'and is not he who has power over clever people cleverer than them?'[37] In other words artistic taste does not presuppose the process of socialization and acculturation by which, as we shall see, good taste in general is formed. The higher the standing of the visual arts, the greater the cultural importance of money as such, the more dispersed the cultural hegemony of *les honnêtes gens*. It is significant in this connexion that La Bruyère denies the name of good taste to the enthusiasm of the hobbyist, including the collector: 'La curiosité n'est pas un goût pour ce qui est bon ou ce qui est beau, mais pour ce qui est rare, unique, pour ce qu'on a et ce que les autres n'ont point' ('De la mode', 2; the passage will be analysed in detail in chapter 6). The collection of art objects, as a culturally valorized pursuit, reveals the economic underpinnings of the dominant culture which taste in general had somehow spiritualized away.

The point of the foregoing is not of course to suggest that aristocrats could not be art patrons, which would be a ridiculous idea. It is rather that art collecting offered the rich non-aristocrat or would-be aristocrat a socially acceptable way of spending money that was less subject than other forms of consumption to the influence of aristocratic ideology. Patronage trends in the mid-seventeenth century bear this out. Blunt notes that in the late sixteenth and early seventeenth centuries the great noble families were prominent as patrons of art and architecture. By the mid-seventeenth century, however, the situation had changed: Mansart, Le Vau, Poussin and Vouet had hardly any patrons among the *noblesse d'épée*. Their commissions came from the great officers of the Crown, the *parlementaires*, and the financiers – except for Poussin whose patrons were usually of solid if not particularly distinguished professional stock.[38] Objectively, then, as well as ideologically, the affiliations of art collection were with a different world from that of aristocratic culture.

One final sentence from F merits attention: 'Le bon goût consiste à se former une idée des choses la plus parfaite qu'on peut & à la suivre.' This amounts to a definition of good taste: why is it not listed with the other definitions under sense (1)? Its terms do not confine its reference to the visual arts. *Idée* can mean a mental image of a physical object, but it can equally denote a more abstract conception, as shown by the couplet from Boileau quoted by F2 under *Idée*: 'Selon que notre idée est plus ou moins obscure, / L'expression la suit, ou moins nette, ou plus pure.'[39] However, R associates *goût* and *idée* in the context of painting when it defines *goût* (as a 'terme de peinture') as 'idée qui suit l'inclination que les peintres ont pour certaines choses, maniere'. This is, in effect, a more complex definition of *goût* as equivalent to 'style'. What the sentence from F does, then, is to import a normative element into the use of *goût* to mean 'style'. This kind of *bon goût* entails intellectual activity on the part of the subject. What differentiates this from the activity of judgment described under sense (1), however, is that it is oriented to the production of values (perfection) rather than to their recognition in objects of consumption. To place this definition of *bon goût* under sense (5) rather than sense (1) is to ratify the separation between producers and consumers of culture. They are united around the common value of *bon goût*, but their relation to it is not the same. The subject of productive good taste is involved in a practice, forming ideas and producing works in accordance with them. According to Méré, this is true of consumptional good taste as well: it is a knowledge to be acquired by means of careful reflection. The other writers, however, describe 'good taste' in terms of an economy of the faculties: not a general human economy, though, since taste appears to be the privilege of a few. For those writers, consumptional good taste is the fruit of an essential superiority, not the accidental superiority that comes from mastering a technique. Although good taste may be found among both producers and consumers, it is most perfectly realized in the latter, and serves to ratify their superior position.

What I want to argue, then, is that the dictionary treatment of *goût* in the contexts of the visual arts and of material objects points to a complex relationship between this kind of taste and good taste in general. Firstly, the hiving-off of these contexts within the dictionary entry reflects an emergent division between visual and material culture on the one hand and the larger sphere of judgment and behaviour where good taste as a general value is held to prevail. Again, the various sub-senses of *goût* defined under senses (4) and (5) allude to modes of identifying and placing cultural objects that cut across the simple evaluation of them as good or bad. In short, the use of *goût* in these contexts posits a subject that is by no means identical with the subject of taste in sense (1). It is, no doubt, possible to have a beautiful house, beautiful furniture, beautiful pictures, beautiful clothes, and a beautiful personality: to be the ultimate 'person of taste'. Yet the recognition and valorization of taste in material objects, rather than, or even together with, taste in conversation, reading, and general social behaviour weakens the autonomy of the *honnête homme*. This is not the autonomy of some ideal figure, the embodiment of abstract moral and 'aesthetic' excellence: the *honnête homme* is a signifier of seigneurial-absolutist social relations. But, as a would-be man of taste (in the fullest possible sense), he is subjected to the constitutive power not only of social position but of wealth as well. The strictly economic thus absorbs some of the terrain of the ideological. The increasing dependence (economic, social, and cultural) of the seventeenth-century nobility on the monarchy was in part a dependence on money as an autonomous force: since dependence on the Crown meant dependence on the financiers on whom the Crown itself depended, people whose wealth, essentially usurious in origin, was by no means the 'natural' accompaniment of a social position, as aristocratic wealth has always been regarded, by itself at least. The association of 'taste' with luxurious material objects (investments) testifies obliquely to this increased importance of finance capital, and to the concomitant percolation of capitalist attitudes among members of the dominant class (from which many of the succeeding century's industrial entrepreneurs, as Goubert has noted, were to spring; *L'Ancien Régime*, I, p. 234). In other words, lexicography here shows the traces of significant social and cultural trends. But before these attained their full significance, a rather different social development became evident: the nobility's incorporation of 'culture' in the narrow sense into its way of life, as a supplement or even an alternative to the traditional military and/or political career, and the concomitant growth of the ideal of the *honnête homme*. The notion of taste, in the sense of a faculty for the discernment of good from bad in various spheres of social practice, soon entered into close relationships with the discourse of *honnêteté*, and it is with these relationships that the next two chapters are principally concerned.

3

MÉRÉ: TASTE AND THE IDEOLOGY OF *HONNÊTETÉ*

Méré's discourse of value is far more systematic and coherent than that of any other writer here studied. A comprehensive analysis of his statements dealing with taste would ramify to a quite unmanageable extent. I shall therefore leave aside the question of the place of taste within a discourse of the mental faculties and concentrate instead on the way in which the discourse of taste in Méré places its subjects within the social formation. This involves examining the relationship of 'taste' with other concepts, such as *honnêteté* and *bienséance*, which have clear social implications.

In the *Conversations* the production of taste in the young appears as crucial to their socialization. Taste is not, in general, an inborn capacity. The Maréchal observes that young people may have prudence enough to distinguish between good and harmful objects, but 'ce qu'on appelle ... avoir le goust bon, il ne faut pas l'attendre des jeunes gens, à moins qu'ils n'y soient extremément nez, ou que l'on n'ait eu grand soin de les y élever'.[1] Méré agrees. Children are impressed by 'le spectacle et la decoration', which is undesirable, 'acause qu'ils ont tous cela de commun avecque le peuple, et mesme ceux qui sont nez Princes' (*OC* I, 56). To produce taste in children of the dominant class is to reproduce on the ideological level their difference from the subordinate classes.

Méré himself notes the origin of the metaphor of taste in eating and drinking (*OC* II, 128), and there is indeed a close parallel between the formation of taste and the cultivation of table manners. As Jean-Claude Bonnet has shown in a study of works on *civilité*, children of the early modern period (children, that is, of the dominant or at least the educated classes) were taught to eschew the eating habits (based on a quite different relation to production) of the 'oaf' or 'country bumpkin', and thus to recognize themselves as a different kind of human being.[2] I have already mentioned the parallel established by Norbert Elias between the 'civilizing' of eating and that of speech, the latter domain clearly falling under the sway of 'taste'.[3]

Méré himself stresses the importance of eating habits: 'il n'y a rien qui siéie plus mal et qui donne plus mauvais air que d'avoir de mauvais gousts'. The unfortunate example of this is a certain M. Guogué: 'il devroit se deffaire de ses mauvais gousts pour la sausse douce, et pour lait [*sic*] avec du beurre, de sa vanité de bourgeois et de ses excuses' (*RHL* 31, p. 495). The wretched Guogué's alimentary proclivities and his 'vanité de bourgeois' are elsewhere tied together as objects of ridicule, which suggests that for Méré his 'bad taste' is linked with his class-position (*RHL* 32, p. 452).

Moving back to the more general figurative sense of taste, we observe that its rarity ('peu de gens ont le goust bon', *OC* II, 39) is made an index of its worth: 'je ne voy rien de si rare, ni qu'on doive tant rechercher, que d'avoir du goust, et de l'avoir fin' (*OC* II, 91). To equate value and rarity is habitual with Méré: *honnêteté* is hard to find (*L* II, 522), as is 'un sens net' (*RHL* 29, p. 95). In general 'le petit nombre ... est le meilleur' (*OC* I, 6). The equation is ideologically potentiated by the equation of the ignorant multitude with the *peuple*. As John Lough shows in some detail, the sense of this word is ambiguous. At times it carries positive overtones, as when it denotes the theatrical public, or its enlightened middle-class elements; at others, it means simply 'the rabble'.[4] In Méré, its connotations are invariably negative, but its reference is not confined to the popular masses: it can take in the middle classes as well. Indeed, its ideological force in Méré arises largely from its obliteration of the distinction between the two groups.

Cicero's oratory, we are told, delighted the people but was ridiculed by 'les plus éclairez' (*L* II, 373). 'La haute intelligence trouve le bonheur en des choses que les gens du commun ne goustent pas, comme elle en méprise d'autres que le peuple admire' (*OC* II, 62). 'Sentences' are proscribed from conversation: 'le peuple et les gens du commun en sont charmez; mais les honnestes gens ne les peuvent souffrir' (*OC* II, 120). 'Pomposity' of speech is to be distinguished from the 'nobility' it takes itself for, because ·'les grands Princes, qui regardent la fortune au dessous d'eux, n'en parlent que negligemment, au lieu que le Peuple l'admire' (*OC* III, 116). In the following and final example, the antitheses of value are notably overdetermined:

Que peut-on s'imaginer de plus mauvais goût, que la fausse Eloquence, pour les personnes qui s'y connoissent, ni de plus désagreable que les faux agrémens? Aussi je ne vois rien, dont je sois plus choqué, ni qui trompe si aisement les gens du commun, que certaines vertus contrefaites, que l'ignorance introduit dans le monde.   (*OC* III, 99–100)

The oppositions present or latent in the text are set out in the following table; elements explicitly mentioned are underlined:

Taste	Good	Bad
Eloquence	True	False
Agréments	True	False
Knowledge	Present	Absent ('trompe', 'ignorance')
Virtue	True	False
Subjects	'je'; 'les personnes qui s'y connoissent'	'les gens du commun'

Reading the columns vertically generates a powerful ideological signified. The speaker is constituted as a privileged subject, aligned with others in a positive relation to taste, knowledge, and other values, in contradistinction to 'les gens du commun'. The latter term is admittedly vague. It could just mean ordinary people of whatever social class. None the less, the foregoing examples show it as virtually interchangeable with 'peuple'. The discourse of 'taste' in constituted by its juxtaposition and fusion of axiological terms (terms of value) and social categories. It is difficult, but not impossible, to distinguish the two strands, and the use of terms like 'peuple' or 'gens du commun' as metonymies for negative value is no reason for denying them their social reference.

It is now time to look at the relations between 'taste' and the other values that constitute the elite as defined by Méré. Of these, the chief are *honnêteté* and *bienséance*. 'Bad taste' is declared to be counter-indicative of *honnêteté* (*L* I, 57); conversely, for a man to be considered as perfectly *honnête* 'il faudroit, que toutes les personnes de bon goût ne pussent le voir, ni même en oüir parler, sans lui vouloir du bien, ni sans désirer son amitié' (*OC* III, 78). *Honnêteté* is also defined as excelling 'en tout ce qui regarde les agrémens et les bienséances de la vie' (*OC* III, 70). Since 'le bon goût ne vient que d'une connoissance exquise & juste à juger du bien & du mal pour toute sorte de bien-seance & d'agrément' (*L* I, 218), it is clear that taste is the knowledge, or more strictly the effect of the knowledge, presupposed by *honnêteté*. The connexion of taste with *bienséance* is borne out repeatedly. 'Un grand goust de la bienséance' (*OC* II, 126) is one of the qualities required for success in conversation. Good taste does not depend on the kind of knowledge denoted by *savoir*: witness those people 'qui sçavent tout, et qu'on ne sçauroit pourtant mettre dans le sentiment de ce qui sied bien' (*OC* II, 128). Méré distinguishes two types of 'justesse': the second is concerned with matters of *bienséance*, and it is a function of *goût* and *sentiment* (*OC* I, 14).[5] Again, 'la bienséance est si delicate, qu'elle ne souffre rien de mauvais goût' (*OC* III, 126). From this it appears that the subject of taste may be identified with the subject of *honnêteté* and of *bienséance*.

Domna C. Stanton sees *honnêteté*, and by implication taste, as a valorization of the superior individual.[6] Yet the individualism of the discourse of taste is never pure: it is always conditioned by an appeal to collective modes of perception. An example of this can be found in what is apparently a vigorous assertion of the individual's supreme jurisdiction, a letter from Méré to the critic Costar which casts doubt on the very utility of critics. Méré argues that one has to judge writers by one's 'sentiment particulier' rather than deferring to even the best critics: otherwise there would be an infinite regress of authority (Scaliger says Virgil is good: but how do we know Scaliger is any good?) (*L* I, 133). The best way to arrive at a sound judgment is through unprejudiced attention to one's own reactions in reading: 'Quand Virgile me vient à la main je ne m'attens non plus de voir rien de rare que si j'allois lire un Autheur qui me seroit inconnu; ainsi les choses qui se présentent devant mes yeux produisent naturellement leurs effets en moy, & c'est le moyen ce me semble de juger sincerement' (*L* I, 134–5). Among the effects thus naturally produced in Méré is the conviction that Virgil was ignorant of the *bienséances* that govern 'le Commerce du monde', and, furthermore, that the *Aeneid* is boring (*L* I, 135–6). The problem, for a judgmental discourse like Méré's, is of course to determine the worth of these 'spontaneous' reactions: as a character in Marivaux remarks, 'Quand on a le goût faux, c'est une triste qualité que d'être sincère.'[7] The discourse implies, evidently, that the subject of taste should possess what Virgil lacks, a knowledge of 'le Commerce du monde' and the *bienséances* that regulate it, and this accords with what we have already seen. But the evidence that the *Aeneid* is boring is of a rather different nature: 'je connois des gens de bon goût qui ne la sçauroient lire un quart d'heure durant, sans quitter le livre avec de grands signes de si [*sic*] estre ennuyez' (*L* I, 136). The individual's discernment is thus eked out by the appeal to 'persons of taste' whom he knows; and he and they are located within a network of intersubjective relations. These relations are cemented in another way by taste-discourse, when Méré compliments his correspondents on their taste, or cites their testimony to his own.[8] Taste circulates among subjects as a unifying value, capable of excluding those outside its discursive circle.

By invoking, however, the authority of 'persons of taste', Méré paradoxically destabilizes his position as much as he secures it.

We have, after all, only his word for their good taste, and for that matter only his interpretation of their reactions (the supposed signs of boredom in the case of the *Aeneid*). His appeal to their authority is merely a displacement of his own. Taste is constituted in discourse, and cannot stand outside it to validate itself. Méré's unperceived dilemma thus curiously inverts the one in which he has landed Costar. The latter was supposedly saying 'Virgil is worth reading because Scaliger says so', an inference that committed him either to an infinite regress of authorities or to an ultimate assertion of his own authority. In Méré's case, we have an infinite repetition of the same authority – his own – reflected in any number of other 'persons of taste', who are, however, constituted as such only by his own recognition. In other words, there is a self-assertion in the discourse of taste, but it is conveyed through an identification, albeit imaginary, with a collective subject – even in Méré, whose remarks quoted in the *Propos* verge at times on the megalomaniac.[9]

The appeal to the authority of 'persons of taste' is not by any means a casual argumentative ploy. It appears repeatedly in Méré's writings. Elsewhere in the same letter to Costar he says that 'la meilleure preuve qu'une chose doit plaire c'est quand elle plaît en effet, & principalement aux personnes de bon goût' (*L* I, 141). To appeal to the reader or spectator's pleasure as the criterion of value is of course typical of classical French writing about literature, but it will be noted that Méré here refines on the celebrated Molière formula that 'la grande règle de toutes les règles est de plaire' by conferring special importance on the pleasure of people of taste.[10] We shall see below how Boileau's appeal to audience-response differs ideologically from Méré's.[11]

Identifying these 'people of taste' is a pre-condition of the subject's access to value, which is naturally through their intermediary.[12] Eloquence is acquired 'avec les personnes de bon goût' and by reading 'les Auteurs les plus épurez' (*OC* III, 106). 'Vous ne sauriez trop étudier, trop mediter, trop consulter les personnes de bon goût', says Méré elsewhere (*L* II, 429–30). Likewise for *honnêteté*: 'C'est le plus seur pour se rendre honneste homme, que d'avoir recours aux honnestes gens' (*OC* I, 44). To urge deference to the already established authority of 'persons of taste' confirms existing cultural hierarchies in monopolistic possession of cultural values; it presupposes, moreover, a subject who enjoys the *entrée* to the particular social world these people frequent. As we shall see, this is by no means the case for all and sundry. Given, furthermore, that cultural values are anti-popular, one who is recognized as embodying them is thereby identified as belonging, if only 'spiritually', to the dominant class.

'People of taste' are cited in support of certain general social values, sobriety of language for instance, since 'les beautez d'éclat en fait de paroles ... déplaisent d'abord aux personnes de bon goût' (*L* I, 3). There is a certain 'air noble, que les personnes de bon goût aiment bien mieux, que tant de rolles que le monde joüe' (*OC* III, 145) and a 'veritable grandeur qui plaist aux personnes de bon goust' (*OC* II, 22). But perhaps more interesting is the way in which they are invoked to validate particular tastes. A friend of Méré's sees the woman he loves in her *cabinet*: 'elle tenoit un livre d'Astrée entre ses mains, & sur ses genoux le Jerusalem du Tasse, car elle ... faisoit cas de ces deux livres comme une personne de bon-goût' (*L* I, 52–3). Her taste confirms her worth as an erotic object. Méré deems a correspondent's enthusiasm for Homer a proof of his excellent taste (*L* I, 94), and jocularly cites Plutarch to the effect that any man of good taste would rather spend the night reading the *Iliad* than in bed with Helen (*L* I, 98). But these individual tastes, so far from being arbitrary, are ideologically motivated: 'Homère connoissoit si bien la bienséance! En plusieurs choses, ce qu'il dit est de si bon air!' (*RHL* 29, p. 96). A taste for Virgil, on Méré's showing, would jeopardize its subject's claim to knowledge of the *bienséances*, and therefore his or her pretensions to *honnêteté* and 'taste'.

If 'taste' is, as has been argued, discursively connected with *honnêteté*, then 'les personnes de bon goût' cannot be considered independently of 'les honnêtes gens'. Moreover, the link between taste and *honnêteté* is of its nature not only discursive: taste is a concrete social practice pertaining to a group that identifies itself as *les honnêtes gens*. In what follows, I shall examine how the discourse of *honnêteté* constructs itself by reference to real social categories, albeit in an oblique or distorted form. The following quotation from Raymond Williams will serve to indicate both the aims and the boundaries of this project:

The point is not to question the intelligence or the cultivation of such self-defining groups. It is rather to relate them, in their specific forms, to those wider conditions which the concepts of an 'aristocracy' or a 'minority' both imply and obscure. This means asking questions about the social formation of such groups, within a deliberate context of a much wider history, involving very general relationships of social class and education.[13]

Honnêteté operates in the first instance to preserve social stratification by requiring the subject to act out his or her place within the hierarchy through conformity to the appropriate ideological codes. In any situation, 'le party le plus honneste est celuy qui paroist le plus conforme à l'estat de vie où l'on se trouve' (*OC* II, 66). To act in this way is to give the best possible proof of one's *esprit*; intellectual values are recruited as supports for ideological performances. Taste co-operates with *honnêteté* here, for it is the yardstick of *bienséance* and *agrément* (*L* I, 218), and these are 'les preuves certaines, que les choses que l'on dit, et celles que l'on fait, sont de la sorte qu'il faut qu'elles soient: Cela dépend assez de se conformer à la condition où l'on se trouve, comme au personnage que l'on joüe' (*OC* III, 126).

This prescription imposes a double-bind on members of the subordinate classes who might aspire to *honnêteté*. For if they do not signify their awareness of their inferiority, they offend against *honnêteté* and *bienséance*; yet *honnêteté*, as will presently appear, excludes whatever is associated with membership of an inferior social group. This calls into question the claim, made by Auerbach for instance, that *honnêteté* was not a class ideal, because 'not contingent on birth or on the manner of living of any particular caste'.[14] The word 'caste' gives the game away here, presupposing as it does that social divisions in the *ancien régime* were based entirely on birth. Magendie shows how noble birth, desiderated by Castiglione in his ideal courtier, gradually ceased to feature in definitions of the *honnête homme*;[15] but this does not lift *honnêteté* out of the sphere of ideology. I have argue above (pp. 24–38) that the dominant group in the society of the *ancien régime* was not a caste founded on birth but a class formed by a certain relation to production. If this relation is inscribed within the discourse of *honnêteté*, then *honnêteté* can hardly be considered as independent of class. None the less, the great majority of members of this class had been placed there by birth and it had a distinctive lifestyle to which, as we have seen, new members tended to conform. The lifestyle and its concomitant values did much to shape the discourse of *honnêteté*. Only a narrow view of class ideology can lead us to see the *honnête homme* as a classless type. J.-P. Dens correctly observes that 'une haute naissance, ou à défaut, de la fortune, sont des conditions indispensables pour etre honnête' (*L'Honnête Homme*, p. 14), but he does not show how these pre-requisites actually condition the discourse of *honnêteté*, endowing it with a specific ideological effectivity.

Honnêtes gens have taste; they know the *bienséances*. But it is not always easy to live up to these, as when you are depressed and find yourself surrounded by bores. Sit up straight, however, says Méré, and think of the heroes of antiquity and the knights-errant of romance. Their inspiring examples may be supplemented from nearer home:

Un pere, un oncle, un aïeul tout percé de coups, qui n'entend jamais parler d'une action lâche, ou peu digne d'un brave homme, sans rugir comme un vieux lion, il imprime dans une ame encore jeune et tendre, des sentimens d'honneur, que le temps ne sauroit effacer. (*OC* III, 98)

Domna C. Stanton rightly emphasizes the agonistic element in *honnête* culture (*The Aristocrat as Art*, pp. 63–6), but here we have something more than that: the shaping of social behaviour by the values and practices of the military aristocracy, the extension of authorities from the battlefield to the salon. The continuity between the two areas is founded on birth and breeding: the subject addressed by Méré can draw on these sources of inspiration because he comes from a military family (as well as being conversant with the lives of the heroes of antiquity). *Honnête* culture is thus brought within the scope of nobiliary patriarchy. With people who have not been bred to the aristocratic way of life, 'pour la Cour et pour la Guerre', 'on sent dans leur mine et dans leurs actions, que cette nourriture leur manque, et cela leur sied toûjours mal' (*OC* III, 99). This perception is closely related to the taste-judgment, a *sentiment* whose object is *bienséance*.

It was earlier seen that the *honnête homme* is someone whom any person of taste would like to know. But the judgment of taste in his favour is anchored in the image of a specific political structure. To be counted as perfectly *honnête*:

Il faudroit qu'un homme, sans être Prince ni Ministre d'Etat, ni General d'Armée, eût un merite si noble et si rare, qu'un Roi, qui seroit encore plus intelligent, que celui dont la grande sagesse attira de si loin la Princesse du Midi, et qu'une Reine qui surpasseroit en délicatesse la charmante Cleopatre, le pussent préferer à tous ceux qui les approchent, sans que les plus envieux y dussent rien trouver à redire: il faudroit, que toutes les personnes de bon goût ne pussent le voir, ni même en oüir parler, sans lui vouloir du bien, ni sans désirer son amitié. (*OC* III, 78)

The order of values recognized by taste is thus embodied in the ideal figures of monarchical authority and located at the court. So although, as Magendie showed, the ideal of *honnêteté* was developed away from the court (*La Politesse mondaine*, pp. 120–4), it exhibits in this passage a fundamental affinity with court values − not, then, with a 'pure' feudal-aristocratic ideology, but with a feudal-absolutist one.

Not only is the *honnête homme* recognized as such by the powers-that-be, he is himself a bearer of power; trying to put one over on him is a mug's game, 'car bien loin que l'on puisse traiter les honnêtes gens de haut-en bas, ils sont nez pour prendre le dessus d'une maniere agréable qui les fait aimer' (*OC* III, 145–6). The *honnête homme* is a born aristocrat in the figurative sense at least; he is the embodiment of princely values: 'je ne voudrois ... pas que dans les actions d'un honnête-homme on pût rien découvrir qui ne fût digne d'un Prince' (*OC* III, 144). The difference between him and a real prince is more accidental than essential: 'un honneste homme doit vivre à peu pres comme un grand Prince qui se rencontre en un päis étranger sans sujets et sans suite, et que la fortune reduit à se conduire comme un honneste particulier' (*OC* II, 21). *Honnête* speech, typified by that of Socrates and Alcibiades in Plato, is not identical to the princely speech exemplified by Francis I and Charles V, Caesar and Pompey, or Caesar and Cleopatra (as imagined by Méré). None the less, they are both authoritative types, defined by a shared opposition to the plebeian. 'Les termes pompeux' and 'les phrases figurées' form a language that may dazzle the ignorant, but that is 'aussi peu du monde, que celui du Peuple ... jamais les grands Princes, ni les honnêtes-gens ne l'ont parlé' (*OC* III, 116).

The *honnête homme* thus participates ideologically in a monarchical-nobiliary order; his destiny is realized at the court. Now it might be objected that this order is a purely ideal one, featuring kings wiser than Solomon, queens more charming than Cleopatra. As both Lathuillère and Stanton have pointed out, Méré is severely critical of the court at times.[16] Courtiers are unable or unwilling to improve themselves (*OC* II, 123). They are oblivious of their families and their place of origin (*L* II, 525). (Méré puts his finger here on a crucial shift in the position of the French aristocracy, more and more cut off from its territorial roots, increasingly dependent on the central government apparatus.) But the passage quoted by both Lathuillère and Stanton to illustrate Méré's self-distancing from the court is the following:

Ce n'est pas qu'on n'y puisse apprendre à bien vivre et à bien parler. Mais pour ne s'y pas tromper, il est bon de se souvenir que cette Cour qu'on prend pour modelle, est une affluence de toute sorte de gens; que les uns n'y font que passer, que les autres n'en sont que depuis peu, et que la pluspart quoy qu'ils y soient nez ne sont pas à imiter. (*OC* II, 111)

Two points emerge. Firstly, the court is a socially composite institution, a mixture of regulars and birds of passage. That someone is at the court does not necessarily make him or her an adequate representative of it. Méré implies that one should take seniority and position at court into account when deciding whether to follow a person's example. Secondly, values and institutions do not systematically correspond, in that a lifetime at court does not guarantee one's *honnêteté* or the quality of one's speech.

But Méré appeals beyond the court to the paramount authority of the 'grand Monde', with which the court should not be confused:

Cette Cour, quoy que la plus belle, et peut-estre la plus grande de la terre, a pourtant ses defauts et ses bornes. Mais le grand Monde qui s'estend par tout est plus accomply; de sorte que pour ce qui regarde ces façons de vivre et de proceder qu'on aime, il faut considerer la Cour et le grand Monde separément, et ne pas ignorer que la Cour, ou par coustume, ou par caprice, approuve quelquefois des choses, que le grand Monde ne souffriroit pas.

(*OC* II, 111)

This 'grand Monde' is partly but not entirely an ideal construct: the term denotes high society outside the court rather than inside it. The 'grand Monde' may be more exigent, and more authoritative, than the court, it may correct the errors of the latter, but the two are none the less ideologically akin:

Qui veut bien juger [des choses] du grand Monde, et mesme de celles de la Cour; il est necessaire de penetrer ce qu'en pourroient dire les plus honnestes gens de toutes les Cours, s'ils estoient assemblez, pour en connoistre la juste valeur. (*OC* II, 111)

The 'grand Monde' ideally fulfils the role of a kind of super-court, correcting whatever is merely local or temporary in the court of France. Authority does not rest with a single court, but it does reside in courts in general. Although Méré distinguishes here between the 'grand Monde' and the court, he usually in fact associates them. In the following example, they are united in the guardianship of monarchical and nobiliary values; note also how the monarchy is represented as a support of aristocratic ideology: 'on l'est toûjours plus [i.e. plus cavalier] à la Cour d'un Prince, que dans une République. Il me semble aussi que les mœurs des villes, et leurs façons de faire ne sont pas nobles; vous sçavez que le grand monde ne les peut souffrir' (*OC* I, 87). A single manner, the only agreeable kind, is common to both, sharply and significantly distinguished from the manner that goes with a profession (*OC* III, 142). Women of the court and the 'grand Monde' think that a certain carelessness of speech and dress is rather *distingué*: their benighted city counterparts fail to realize this (*L* I, 156–7).

So when Méré criticizes the court so as to limit its cultural authority, he devolves plenary cultural authority upon a formation, the 'grand

Monde,' that is not only an ideal but a real social force, and that is generally so aligned with the court as to confirm the status of *honnêteté* as essentially a court, therefore a nobiliary, value. Similarly, the assimilation of the *honnête homme* to the prince (whether or not in reduced circumstances) does not efface the terms' social reference by turning them purely into metaphors for an ideal. On the contrary. In behaving as he thinks a prince would, or should, behave, the *honnête homme* recognizes simultaneously that he is subject to certain values and that they are characteristically realized by a prince fulfilling his ideological role; his own realization is therefore seen as dependent on the monarchical order, however unworthily it may be represented by a particular monarch. Where power resides with princes, to celebrate conduct as princely is to validate princely power.

The discourse of *honnêteté*, then, postulates a subject participating in a nobiliary scheme of values under the aegis of a monarchical order. Given the discursive connexion between the two elements, this obviously applies to 'taste' as well. But the subject of 'taste' is also socially positioned by the opposition established between taste and other knowledges with their socially positioned subjects. It is systematically distinguished from the kinds of knowledge that proceed by rules. Thus, in the letter to Costar cited above Méré observes that 'ceux qui s'attachent fort aux regles n'ont que bien peu de goût' (*L* I, 138). Taste determines the scope of the rules: 'il ne faut suivre ny regle ny methode qu'autant que le bon goût les approuve' (*L* I, 217). This looks like a piece of advice to a budding writer, and so it is, as the letter it comes from makes clear; but it also secures an ideological relation of authority. Two categories of person are implicated in the subordination of rules to taste: the scholars who codify the rules and the writers who apply them (someone like Vaugelas would fulfil both roles). The correspondent ('Monsieur de ***') is called upon to signify, by his independence *vis-à-vis* the rules (by his taste, in other words), that he is different from the professional scholar or author who would, it is supposed, regard himself as bound by them: to uphold the dignity of his rank and the self-sufficiency of the culture to which, as a presumed *honnête homme*, he belongs. The professional could apply this truth about taste to himself by not sticking too closely to the rules of his trade, and in so doing he would be acknowledging the right of *honnête* culture to set standards binding on him as well.[17]

Méré acknowledges the importance of study as a supplement to the cultivation of one's taste in society. One learns to speak well 'avec les personnes de bon goût', but also by reading 'les Auteurs les plus épurez' (*OC* III, 106). Reading and writing can confer 'une justesse, une pureté de langage, une netteté d'expression, et sur tout une marche asseurée qu'on n'apprend point dans le commerce du monde', and they develop the art of expression, important 'parce qu'elle vient principalement du bon goust' (not, then, from a taught rhetorical technique) 'et qu'elle en donne à ceux qui s'y plaisent' (*OC* II, 94). One may, thus, *state* the importance, even the indispensability, of study; but not *signify* it in one's behaviour: 'vous devez vous en servir avec tant d'adresse qu'on ne s'en puisse apercevoir'. If one studies at all, it is in order to 's'expliquer de l'air qui sied le mieux' (and which therefore gratifies taste) 'parmi les gens de la Cour fine & galante' (*L* II, 636). Language must signify, so as to celebrate, the culture of that world: 'le stile ne sauroit assez sentir la Cour et le monde, ni trop peu l'art et l'étude' (*OC* III, 129). Authors go wrong because most of them 'tiennent plus de l'étude, que la bienseance ne voudroit' (*OC* III, 116). The suggestion that they have some kind of proprietorial authority over discourse raises Méré's hackles: when a correspondent remarks that someone 'écrit fort bien pour un cavalier', he retorts that it would make more sense to say that 'un Autheur écrit fort bien pour un homme d'étude. Car pour se prendre de bonne grace à parler, il faut estre du monde & fort honneste-homme' (*L* II, 428). He is rather pleased with a put-down he once administered to an author who stepped out of line:

Je disois à quelqu'un fort sçavant, qu'il parloit en autheur; 'Et quoy, me répondit cét homme, ne le suis-je pas?' 'Vous ne l'estes que trop, repris-je en riant, et vous feriez beaucoup mieux de parler en galant homme; car quelque sçavant qu'on puisse estre, il ne faut rien dire qui ne soit entendu de ceux qui ont de l'esprit, et qui sçavent le monde.' (*OC* II, 119)

The author has had the temerity to suggest that there are more things in heaven and earth than are dreamt of in *honnête* philosophy; he has signified his own difference from *les gens du monde* as if it were not a mark of inferiority; and he has got his come-uppance. As Méré remarks, 'c'est la conformité qui fait qu'on se plaist ensemble': this is a reason for, on occasion, holding back the knowledge one possesses: 'l'air noble et naturel est le principal agrément de l'Eloquence, et parmy les personnes du monde, ce qui tient de l'estude est presque toûjours mal receu' (*OC* II, 106). Note the equation here between the noble and the natural. It recurs in the statement that 'je voudrois qu'on fût honnête-homme, sans témoigner d'en avoir jamais eu la pensée. Que cela sied bien, quand il semble que ce soit un present du Ciel!' (*OC* III, 143); 'Quand on admire une chose, on aime bien mieux qu'elle vienne de la Fortune que de la Science, ou du talent d'un particulier. Car ce qui vient de la Fortune est comme une faveur du Ciel' (*OC* II, 109). Bernadette B. de Mendoza argues that Méré departs from his contemporaries' insistence that people's qualities are inborn (and thus from what she rightly identifies as an aristocratic position) by his habitual stress on the acquirability of qualities like taste and *honnêteté* through individual effort and a process of assimilation in the society of other people.[18] But by requiring such values to conceal the conditions of their own production, to pass themselves off as innate, it is clear that Méré is simply displacing the aristocratic position without in any way challenging it.

It is fair to say that Méré's attitudes to individual authors are generally ideologically motivated. Homer, as we saw, is outstanding because of his knowledge of the *bienséances*, Virgil culpable for transgressing them. The *bienséances* are not so much artistic conventions here as representational proprieties. For all his craftsmanship, or perhaps because of it, Horace frequently displays a 'mauvais air'. Cicero and Boileau are attacked for 'pedantry', in Cicero's case an effect of his lack of the right social experience: 'Cicéron ne pouvoit pas estre agréable: il n'avoit vû ny femmes, ny débauchés, ny gens de plaisir, ny des joueurs' (*RHL* 32, p. 434). Even philosophers are judged by *mondain* standards: Descartes is a 'maistre de roquets' (*RHL* 31, p. 492), and 'il n'y a point de philosophie qui donne si mauvais air que celle d'Aristote' (*RHL* 32, p. 453). Socrates and Plato, however, are beyond criticism.[19]

The anecdote is sometimes recounted of the gallery attendant who tells a disgruntled visitor: 'It is not the *pictures* that are on trial.' Boileau, as will be seen, would have agreed. Méré, it is clear, would not. And the dents he inflicts on the prestige of great authors cannot but be detrimental to the standing of those whose stock-in-trade they are: the scholars. Their lack of taste is axiomatic: 'ces gens si Doctes ... d'ordinaire ont ... peu de goût' (*L* I, 138). Instead of teaching *honnêteté*, schoolmasters deal in 'fausses subtilitez [qui] ne peuvent plaire aux gens de bon goût' (*L* II, 365). Nor can academic and *honnête* culture be united, except by the *honnête homme* who unobtrusively assimilates what humanism has to offer:

quand on dit de quelqu'un de cét ordre [i.e., an academic, but in particular a follower of Aristotle] qu'il est sçavant en honneste homme, on se trompe pour l'ordinaire, et ... c'est je ne sçai quoi de faux et de poli tout ensemble, qui dégoûte encore davantage.   (*OC* I, 30)

What is at stake in this quarrel with the scholars is represented by Méré as control of the central ideological agency, if one may speak of the monarch in so disrespectfully abstract a fashion. When kings try to raise the cultural level of their courts, they always look to mathematicians, historians, linguists, philosophers, instead of 'quelqu'un qui connust en tout le bien et le mal' or 'les plus honnestes gens' (*OC* II, 74). The anti-'pédant' discourse seems to have an anti-governmental edge. Ch.-H. Boudhors suggests that 'le plus pédant homme qui soit en France' is a royal minister or official: certainly Méré observes that 'quand un pédant gouverne, les pédans sont en vogue' (*RHL* 31, pp. 493–4; see p. 493, n. 9). Government officials (*maîtres des requêtes* and *intendants*) are, by *mondain* standards, even worse than pedants (*RHL* 32, p. 68). Anti-pedantry here conveys the traditional aristocratic hostility to the officials of middle-class or *robe* origin by whom France was actually governed.

Language is, of course, a privileged site of this ideological confrontation. A passage already quoted more than once illustrates how the confrontation takes place through a significant series of oppositions in which value and social categories are inextricable. As we saw, the grand style of 'termes pompeux' and 'phrases figurées' is not noble, although it dazzles the ignorant, because princes, being above fortune, speak of it carelessly, whereas 'le Peuple l'admire' (*OC* III, 116). Obviously, then, 'le Peuple' are one with 'les ignorans et les duppes', social and intellectual levels coinciding. When 'le Peuple' see some one strutting around in 'faux or' and 'fausse broderie', they take him for a *grand seigneur*, just as 'les gens du commun, bien qu'ils soient de la Cour, soient persuadez que la plus grande beauté de l'Eloquence consiste en ces fausses parures, que les personnes de bon goût ne peuvent souffrir' (*OC* III, 117). These 'fausses parures' are obviously the rhetorical ornaments that were earlier objected to. 'Good taste' by implication induces the subject to adopt the same attitude to language as princes display.

But are social and axiological categories really so closely fused? What about these 'gens du commun … de la Cour'? Méré might be referring here to noblemen who are 'mentally negligible', as Jeeves says of Bertie. He might be, although the point would still remain that through their stupidity they are failing to live out their ideological role as noblemen and adopting a 'popular' attitude to language. In fact, though, he is not referring to them. His example of this kind of linguistic misconception is an Academician. Now some Academicians were certainly noble; but this one evidently isn't, and not just because he has the popular taste for brilliance, admiring a seductive but fallacious comparison in Seneca. He objects to the (figurative and jocular) use of the words *maillot* and *démailloter* as 'low'. What he doesn't realize is that 'les Princes savent ce que c'est que *maillot* et *démailloter*, et les plus éclairez, si cela venoit à propos, ne feroient pas difficulté de le dire' (*OC* III, 117). In other words, he doesn't know from experience (unlike Méré) how princes talk; he is not of a rank to mix with them. Their practice is constituted as the yardstick of linguistic register.

The values, 'taste' among them, invoked in this passage from Méré, thus serve to fuse social and linguistic authority. The superficial brilliance that 'taste' rejects and ignorance admires comes from an attitude of inferiority to Fortune that is imputed to 'le Peuple'. 'Taste' endorses a certain plainness and simplicity of speech, the linguistic reflection of an attitude of superiority to the world said to result directly from the social position of the prince. It invites its subjects to see themselves as different from the common herd, to identify with princely values, to regard the prince's attitude to the world as setting linguistic standards valid for them, and his practice as authoritative. The last injunction naturally presupposes some degree of literal proximity to the prince – the position of a courtier, a member of a princely household, or a man of rank.

I should add once again that the social references of a passage such as this are not simply the figurative husk from which a 'spiritual' kernel of values is to be extracted. The values are anchored in real social practices and social relations, as processed, evidently, by a certain discourse. Thus, a statement such as 'les ... Princes ... regardent la fortune au dessous d'eux ... au lieu que le Peuple l'admire' (*OC* III, 116) is nothing if not discursive. It does not, on its own terms, invite empirical confirmation or falsification. But it fits ideologically, it feels right from Méré's point of view, and it is supposed to feel right to the reader. It presents him or her with an image of the world that, through the operation of very basic ideological mechanisms in a whole process of socialization, he or she has been schooled to recognize as real, and that can therefore produce real effects: in this case, as I have argued, solidarity with the monarchical order (if not with its administrative aspects) and self-distantiation from 'le Peuple'.

But the ideological effects of this passage are more complex. The kind of figurative language it condemns is unknown in the practice of princes and *honnêtes gens*. It is all too common among public speakers, however, and the popular admiration it arouses is the source of 'ce ramage d'Avocats et de faiseurs de Panegyriques' (*OC* III, 116–17). Although this is followed by a contemptuous reference to the style of preachers, the major target of Méré's attack is the legal profession. He defines it as essentially plebeian, drawing on an anecdote of Cicero's (*De oratore*, I. 18) about a Greek philosopher who tells a Roman orator that 'les gens du Palais ne se connoissent à rien, et que les plus éloquens parloient comme des Manœuvres' (*OC* III, 110). Lawyers are frequently declared to be socio-culturally inferior: 'l'air qui sent le Palais', along with 'le mauvais goût' and a host of other characteristics, is declared to be incompatible with *honnêteté* (*L* I, 57). When an *avocat* goes into society, if he wishes to appear an *honnête homme*, 'il doit laisser dans son cabinet toutes les choses qui ont l'odeur ou le goût du Palais' (*OC* III, 143). The sensory metaphors are significant, imputing objective social significance to these things, but also presupposing a collective taste on the part of *mondain* society, sensitive to what is different from, therefore inferior to, itself. This kind of taste quite obviously postulates a subject in a privileged social position. Defining *honnête* culture by the exclusion of characteristically legal elements is to align it with the court aristocracy in its century-long battle against the *robe* for cultural hegemony. The group that for so long had enjoyed a monopoly of (high) culture, and whose association with humanism had been particularly fruitful, is now called upon to renounce its identity on pain of exclusion from culture.

Although it is significant that Méré should single out the legal profession here, he does so merely as an example; to display in society one's attachment to any profession is frowned upon: 'dans la vie ordinaire tout ce qui tient du métier, déplaît' (*OC* III, 142). As Dens points out (*L'Honnête Homme*, p. 14), what is condemned is not the exercise of a profession as such but the appearance of it. There are no exceptions to the ban, not even the classic, and ideologically constitutive, aristocratic profession of arms: 'la guerre ... est le plus beau mêtier du monde, ... mais à le bien prendre, un honneste homme n'a point de mestier' (*OC* I, 11). This is a logically but also an ideologically valid application of the principle that excludes a professional manner from society: to allow swashbuckling in the drawing-room would be tantamount to accepting the identification of the aristocracy with the single role of war-making, and thus jeopardizing its claim to a distinctive and privileged cultural role. Apart from this instance, the ban functions as a valorization of independence from personal labour. It privileges the situation of the landowner, but also that of the *rentier* or the holder of a lucrative sinecure. It thus helps to further the ongoing assimilation of those two categories into the dominant class under the sign of *honnêteté*.

This does not mean that an *honnête homme* should refrain from talking about 'la plus-part des Arts', provided he does so 'en homme du monde, plûtôt qu'en artisan' (*OC* III, 142). The sayings of Socrates are noble, even though he spent much of his time talking to craftsmen about their craft. Nobility of style is not a function of subject-matter but of the manner in which it is treated (*L* I, 219). In other words, a discourse is 'nobilized' by its capacity to signify the social and ideological differentiations that may exist between the *honnête* speaking subject and the object of discourse.

'Taste', to sum up, defines itself by contrast with 'popular' modes of judging, speaking, and behaving, and associates itself with monarchical practices and values. It thus tends to privilege, in the first instance, the position of the court nobility, who are nearest to the ruler, not only literally, but in their supposed essential nature: for both monarch and nobleman participate in the prestige of the innate, to which *honnêteté* pays tribute by passing itself off as a gift from above. 'Taste' reinforces aristocratic claims to cultural hegemony in another way, by identifying as 'popular' all that is anchored in a non-aristocratic way of life. It is not found in the universities (which never appealed much to the aristocracy)[20] or in the humanistic culture of the *gens de robe*. It precludes overt involvement with a specific occupation, and thus both normalizes and valorizes the position of living on unearned income. All this does not formally exclude the *roturier*, but it makes his admission to *honnêteté* and 'taste' contingent on his acceptance of the validity and self-sufficiency of aristocratic standards. 'Taste', then, as defined within this discourse, reinforces the seigneurial grip on the French social formation, not least because it tacitly sanctions another support of the system − the drive towards seigneurialization of the wealthier members of the middle class, and the officials in particular.

But class relations are not the only sort that enter into the discourse of 'taste'. It also bears on relations between the sexes. The cultural importance of women in seventeenth-century France is well known. The image of women improved considerably, as Ian Maclean has shown, during the first half of the century.[21] But, as he makes clear, the 'feminist' discourse of the period was full of tensions and contradictions. Women could be heroic: but the *femme forte* was celebrated (largely by male celibates like Père Le Moyne) as an *exceptional* figure; and with the end of the Fronde, as Maclean puts it, 'the rule of common sense' returned (*Woman Triumphant*, p. 265). Women were put back in their place and men reoccupied the driving seat.

To what extent did the discourse of *honnêteté* contribute to the improvement in the image, and maybe the actual condition, of women? There is no space here to sift this matter in full, although it should be recorded to Méré's credit that in the name of *honnêteté* he criticizes the view, attributed to Tasso, that any woman will yield to protracted pestering (*OC* III, 101). But it is possible to tease out some of the ideological implications of statements by Méré about 'taste' in which women feature either as subjects or as objects.

Certainly, women are not to be excluded from culture. If one speaks of the natural world, 'il faut que ce qu'on en dit se r'apporte à l'usage des Cours, & que mesme les Dames le puissent gouter' (*L* I, 316). And it is important to 'former le sens et le discours aux jeunes Princes, et mesme aux jeunes Princesses' (*OC* I, 111). But, more than this, women are acknowledged as in some respects enjoying a special cultural status. For instance, they seem to be particularly gifted with good taste. The correspondents whose good taste Méré recognizes are women more often than not.[22] He repudiates the view that women are less intelligent: they have a 'délicatesse d'esprit qui n'est pas si commune aux hommes' (*OC* I, 17–18), and they do what they do more gracefully than men, 'soit que l'avantage de plaire leur soit plus naturel, ou que sentant que c'est-là leur fort, elles s'en fassent dés leur enfance comme un métier' (*OC* I, 18). The hesitation between natural and cultural explanations is significant, as is the elision of the question: please whom?

For Méré the ideological value of woman (as a discursive entity) is that she is the supreme incarnation of the natural. How can Mme de Lesdiguières's letters be so good when she has had so little formal education? He wonders whether 'par un instinct de justesse & de proportion que la nature a mis en nous, un esprit qui se sent dans un beau corps, et qui se communique par un esprit comme la vostre, s'accoûtume insensiblement à ne rien dire qui n'ait du rapport à tant de grace & de beauté' (*L* I, 100–1). The linking of her intellectual gifts with her physical qualities underscores their natural (therefore in this case mysterious) origin. She embodies 'les graces ... si libertines qu'elles renvoient bien loin l'Art & l'Etude' (*L* I, 100). Steele said of someone that 'to love her is a liberal education': to love Mme de Lesdiguières is to recognize the superfluity of all educational institutions, unable to equal the achievements of nature. Méré elsewhere proclaims *galanterie* in women incompatible with 'pedantry' (*RHL* 30, p. 89).

Women, moreover, have a special role in the cultivation of *honnêteté*. It cannot be learned exclusively in male society: 'le commerce des femmes est encore plus à rechercher' (*OC* III, 74). But the reason given is revealing: 'Les hommes sont ordinairement ensemble tout d'une piece, sans maniere et sans façon, et si les uns veulent plaire aux autres, ce n'est gueres que par quelque vertu solide, ou par quelque service effectif' (*OC* III, 74–5). Men may be essentially coarser, but they are more firmly anchored in the real world in which things get done, in relation to which women are marginal. This very marginality, however, defines them as quintessential to *honnête* society, which represents itself as marginal to the world of politics, administration, power. *Honnêteté* is the creation of 'certain Faineans sans mêtier, mais [non] sans merite ... qui ne s'empressent pas pour gouverner, et pour tenir la premiere place auprés des Rois' (*OC* III, 70). If *honnête* culture is, as Stanton implies, a continuous and apparently gratuitous semiosis, it is women who most fully incarnate it, with their 'maniere délicate et mysterieuse' and their 'façons', which not every man can respond to (*OC* III, 75).[23] But this pre-eminence of women as such gives *honnête* relationships a virtual erotic character. Men are transformed by the desire to win the good graces of woman – 'c'est de l'amour, que naissent la plûpart des vrais agrémens' – and by the same token 'jamais une Dame ne sera parfaitement aimable, qu'elle n'ait eu dessein de gagner un honnête-homme' (*OC* III, 75). In other words, the values that typically reside in women are fully actualized only in relations between the sexes, which also bring out men's potentiality for *honnêteté*.

The use of taste-language is particularly interesting in this context. Writing to a 'Madame la Maréchale de ***', no doubt Mme de Clérambault, Méré acknowledges that a man who could love her as she wishes to be loved would be happy, but protests all the same: 'Mais, Madame, qu'il est mal aisé de s'en tenir là quand on a le goust de ce qui doit plaire' (*L* I, 348).[24] The man's taste, presenting itself as normative ('ce qui *doit* plaire') is invoked to counter the restrictions Mme de Clérambault would impose on her lover: her pleasure (in both senses: will and gratification) is displaced by the affirmation of the male subject's taste.

Women as objects provide the basis for Méré's discussion of *beauté* and *agrément*. The comparison of literary to feminine beauty is a commonplace of the period.[25] Usually, it is a rhetorical figure and nothing more: it *conveys* a truth about poetry, but simply *presupposes* a truth about women. It doesn't really refer to them. But when Méré distinguishes *beauté* and *agrément* by differentiating types of women he is actually saying something about male–female relations as well as abstract values: indeed, to speak of 'abstract values' in this connexion is falsely to abstract them from the relations in which they are essentially embodied (as I have argued in connexion with *honnêteté*, princes, and the 'people').

Beauté and *agrément* are not the same. The former is objective, as Boudhors says, not a matter of taste (p. 72, n. 2 in Méré, *OC* I, 161). The latter, however, along with *bienséance*, is one of the two constitutive objects of the taste-judgment (*L* I, 218). *Beauté*, as taste bears witness, is less powerful than *agrément*: 'Quoy qu'une chose soit belle et reguliere, à moins qu'on ne puisse dire qu'elle est agreable, ceux qui ont le goust fin la laissent volontiers apres l'avoir loüée' (*OC* II, 36). In other words, 'on loue les plus belles femmes, mais on aime les plus jolies' (*OC* I, 72); the context shows that to be 'jolie' is an effect of *agrément* rather than *beauté*. This is, in effect, a lesson to women:

Les Dames qui songent plus à devenir belles qu'agreables, sont mal conseillées: quand cela leur arrive, c'est le plus mauvais moyen du monde pour se faire aimer long-temps. Car dés qu'on possede une belle chose, il arrive pour l'ordinaire qu'on ne l'estime plus tant ... Mais il n'en va pas ainsi d'une chose agreable; En effet lors qu'on aime une femme parce qu'elle est belle, cet amour passe quelquefois bien viste: mais quand ce sont de vrais et de profonds Agrémens qui font naistre l'affection, on n'en revient pas de la sorte; et d'ordinaire plus on a de faveur plus on est charmé.   (*OC* II, 37–8)

Women are enjoined to work towards being *agréable*, in order to stimulate the taste, and thereby conserve the affections, of men. The discourse of taste and *agrément* functions ideologically inasmuch as it calls on women to recognize themselves ('une Dame se doit savoir meilleur gré qu'on la trouve agreable que belle', *L* II, 528) in a way that will affect their behaviour. The appeal is, of course, to women's perception of their own real interests. The 'agreeable' woman is safe from being discarded by a sated lover; she enjoys the security of constant affection, beneficial both to her ego and to her reputation (perhaps Mme de Clèves should have taken Méré's correspondence course).

To this extent, the discourse of *agrément* emancipates women from subjection to the automatic rhythms within which male desire is/was lived: craving, gratification, satiation. In another way, it of course presupposes those rhythms as natural, and that women's fulfilment lies in being the object of a long-standing affection which they are able to gratify. It offers women at best the chance to profit from a certain play in the workings of ideology, both attenuating and confirming their subjection.

The discourses of taste and *honnêteté* promote an image of the

Méré

sexes as different but complementary, each partner recognizing the other as an exceptional creature and finding in the other's recognition his or her own fulfilment. This particular intersubjective relation is only one instance of a situation characteristic of the discourse of 'taste', whereby the recognition of the other person's taste invites a reciprocal acknowledgement of one's own; but it is an extremely powerful one, in view of the general prestige accorded by the culture to love. This itself is an inheritance from traditional aristocratic culture, which *honnêteté* both continues and sublimates. It may be said, then, that the incorporation of gender difference in the form of complementarity into the discourse of taste/*honnêteté* intensifies its characteristic ideological effects.

Foucault argues that discourse transmits power but also undermines and exposes it.[26] Can taste-discourse be said to subvert the order it tends to reinforce? If taste is the judge of *bienséances* it can sort out 'true' ones from 'false' ones. Conversely, 'la fausse bienséance nous oste le goût de la veritable' (*OC* III, 95). 'Fausse bienséance' is the pressure exerted by irrational or even wicked customs, such as (Méré's example) suttee in India. Blind adherence to the customs of one's country is a mark of '[les] gens du commun' (*OC* III, 95), which must be the best of all possible reasons for cultivating a wider outlook. None the less, Méré's attitude is basically one of conformity to the established order, even though one's taste may find things to disapprove of within it:

Comme les institutions de ceux qui nous ont précedez, nous reglent malgré nous, il faut observer ce qu'on approuve dans les Cours et dans les Päis, où nous avons à passer nôtre vie, et ne pas offenser la reverence publique; mais pour ne pas être d'un méchant goût, on se doit bien garder d'aimer dans son cœur des choses, que la raison ne permet, que parce que le monde s'y est accoûtumé. (*OC* III, 94)

'Taste' here estranges its subjects intellectually from the established order. But it coexists with a perception of that order as authoritative because traditional. By dissipating the illusion that the prevailing customs are rational in themselves, 'taste' foregrounds the adventitious rationality they derive from long continuance – for reason, albeit grudgingly, actually 'permits' them on this account. 'Taste' and a sense of tradition, then, combined as they are in this specific discursive framework, produce an ideological compromise whereby the individual's sense of what is reasonable in itself is caught up within an awareness of the larger requirements of the social order. Pascal's *raison des effets* leaves the subject in a rather similar position. The knowledge that one's respect for dukes is not essentially founded on their personal qualities raises one's compliance with etiquette from the level of unthinking reflex to that of willed gesture: one *accepts responsibility* for the maintenance of the social order.[27] So in the army one salutes the uniform and not the man; but this is not because the army broadmindedly accepts that not all its officers are all they should be: it is an essential preservative of discipline against the corrosive effect of individual criticism. Although in certain cases, then, 'taste' may appear to subvert the existing structures of power and authority, it would be truer to say that it resettles their mental foundations on a surer basis than the claim to rationality. Its critical perceptions do not eventuate in action.

Except in one case that again limits their scope. Princes, says Méré, are to blame when they allow bad customs to flourish, and a subject concerned with his master's *honnêteté* and glory will urge him to extirpate them (*OC* III, 96). So the point where critical taste is allowed to take on a pragmatic function is where it contributes to the ideological reproduction of the monarchical order.

There is, however, another way in which taste and *honnêteté* can be looked upon as subversive. They can sometimes call hierarchies of rank into question. *Honnêteté* can actually put one at a disadvantage with certain *grands seigneurs* by challenging their propensity to self-assertion: 'ils savent qu'ils ne sauroient se mettre au dessus d'un honnête homme, par un avantage bien réel, et que le seul merite fait les veritables distinctions' (*OC* III, 160). *Honnêteté* and 'taste' tend to diminish the significance of rank in interpersonal relations:

> Les Dames du premier rang et les plus grandes Princesses quand elles sont de bon goût, ne se plaisent qu'avec les honnêtes gens, et quelques-unes des plus considerables m'ont appris qu'elles n'ont de l'esprit, qu'en leur compagnie, et qu'elles les trouvent d'autant plus agréables, qu'ils sont plus hardis.
> (*OC* III, 160)

As in the definition of the *honnête homme* discussed above (*OC* III, 78), the recognition of value is entrusted to 'taste' and power in conjunction. 'Aesthetic' values and social relations turn out to be inextricably interwined. *Honnêteté* grows in the shadow of social hierarchies, even though its own scale of values is not that of the peerage-book. If at the individual level rank does not necessarily conform to merit, rank and merit coalesce at the level of the dominant class as a whole. Outside that class's influence, there is no apparent social basis for the existence of *honnêteté*, merit, 'taste'.

'Taste' is only released from its dependence on the nobiliary order where interpersonal relations lose their cultural importance, as in the city theatres, where a public exercising an impersonal form of cultural authority could take shape in relative independence from the court. In general, the relative decline of personal cultural influence and the concomitant growth of an impersonal public is the effect of the commercialization of culture. I shall be returning to this topic in chapter 7, on Boileau; suffice it to say for the moment that this development will radically modify the whole discourse of taste, annulling the ideological effect that, I have argued, it carries out in Méré: the orientation of culture, in its broadest sense, to the ideological reproduction of the alliance between a socially dominant nobility and a politically dominant monarchy that characterizes the feudal-absolutist regime.

When E.B.O. Borgerhoff (*The Freedom of French Classicism*, pp. 83–4) expresses his dislike of Méré as an individual, it is hard not to agree. He does not seem to have been a very nice man. Saint-Evremond one somehow thinks of as rather nicer. All the same, the next chapter, which deals with him, will evoke a strong sense of *déjà vu*. The same positions, the same gestures, are there as in Méré, although there are emphases specific to each. We are dealing, in short, not with a series of more or less intelligent, more or less articulate, more or less admirable individuals reacting to the world, but with a discourse.

4

SAINT-EVREMOND: TASTE AND CULTURAL HEGEMONY

The word *goût* appears in the last sentence of what may well be the last letter Saint-Evremond ever wrote.[1] During his last days, according to his doctor, he retained 'un vif ressouvenir des choses qui pouvoient flatter le goust et me disoit la dessus tous les jours quelque chose de nouveau'.[2] Taste was a lifelong interest with him: 'Le Comte d'Olonne, le Marquis de Boisdauphin et lui, furent nommés les Côteaux, pour avoir voulu rafiner sur le goût, et sur la délicatesse de la table' (*OP* I, xliii). The point is not simply that Saint-Evremond liked both eating and reading. It is rather that the category of 'taste' binds together a whole range of cultural practices in such a way as to assure the cultural dominance of a distinctive kind of subject. A valuable practice is one that provides opportunities for this kind of subject to exercise his or her taste and thus endorses his or her distinctiveness. Saint-Evremond develops a certain concept of taste, which is given a concrete content by a certain representation of contemporary culture, and of past cultures, and by an appeal to various kinds of authority.

The first of these is the appeal to 'persons of taste' to validate a specific opinion or attitude. Saint-Evremond asserts that 'les Machines … ne plairont guere au Théatre à des personnes de bon goût' (*OP* III, 161–2). Euripides's handling of the character of Achilles will be condemned by 'tous les gens de bon goût' (*OP* III, 334). Petronius is 'loüé par tous les gens de bon goût' (*OP* III, 376). 'Mr. Guillaut', the representative of common sense in Saint-Evremond's comedy *Les Opéra*, dismisses Italian music as the art 'sur quatre Notes, d'ennuyer quatre heures les personnes de bon-goût'.[3] The same gesture is made in reference to food and drink: Saint-Evremond informs Olonne that wines from Champagne are the fashion, whereas 'ceux de Bourgoigne ont perdu tout leur credit avec les gens de bon goût, et à peine conservent ils un reste de vieille reputation chés les marchands' (*L* I, 256).

'People of taste' are constituted as the target of cultural discourses and practices: if only Italian singers would sing properly, Saint-Evremond tells them, 'Les méchans Connoisseurs vous admireroient moins, / Mais aux Gens de bon goût vous plairiez davantage' (*L* II, 189). The oxymoronic formula 'méchans Connoisseurs' is significant: good taste is contrasted with its opposite not as knowledge to ignorance but as 'true' to 'false' knowledge. But the only grounds offered here for distinguishing between the two are the specific attitudes endorsed by the author, which the reader may or may not share. Saint-Evremond says that the use of stage-machinery is in bad taste, which is exactly what La Bruyère says of Saint-Evremond's opinion ('Des ouvrages de l'esprit', 47). So far, the appeal to 'people of taste' seems to be purely arbitrary.

This way of supporting an opinion invites the reader to submit to an authority vested in third parties. The connexion between speaker – interlocutor relationships and their common recognition of a third-party authority is already apparent in Saint-Evremond's criticism of Euripides mentioned above. The dramatist should not have shown Achilles so unmoved by Iphigeneia's plight:

On m'avoüera que l'humanité demandoit de la pitié; que la nature, que la bienseance même exigeoient de la tendresse, et tous les gens de bon goût blameront le Poëte d'avoir trop consideré le caractere, lors qu'il falloit avoir de grands égards pour la passion.   (*OP* III, 334)

The interlocutor ('on': the pronoun partakes of both second and third persons) is called upon to adopt the speaker's attitude, which is reinforced by the appeal to third parties ('persons of taste'), as well as to abstract values (*humanité, nature, bienséance*). This double discursive structure is frequently present even in the apparently straightforward situation of a compliment to the interlocutor on his or her good taste. This frequently unites interlocutor and speaker in a common attitude to other categories of people. Talking to scholars, Saint-Evremond tells his friend Hervart, 'me laisse à desirer votre bon goût' (*L* I, 190). The duchesse Mazarin is told 'vous devez conte ... aux Délicats de vôtre bon-goût' (*L* II, 85). Here 'taste' binds together a circle of associates; in the previous example it served to exclude. The circle of taste is perfectly closed when the good taste of each participant is represented as not only the image but the effect of the other's. Saint-Evremond is gratified by Olonne's praise of his taste, and adds 'Vous avez intérest qu'il soit bon, juste et délicat; car l'idée du vôtre, que je conserve toûjours, régle le mien' (*L* I, 355).

'People of taste' tend not to go for the obvious reaction. Saint-Evremond refuses to thank the comte de Lionne for the help he has given: 'connoissant la délicatesse de votre goût, je crois vous plaire mieux par une ingratitude recherchée que par une reconnoissance trop commune' (*L* I, 125). But this is a natural corollary of the fact that such people are rare. Indeed, the quality of a taste is almost proportional to its rarity. Good taste is rare in England, but those who have it 'l'ont aussi délicat que gens du monde' (*OP* III, 158). Likewise, 'il n'y a point de païs où la raison soit plus rare qu'elle est en France; quand elle s'y trouve, il n'y en a pas de plus pure dans l'Univers' (*OP* III, 125). There are in France 'des Esprits bien sains, qui jamais ne se dégoûtent de ce qui doit plaire, et jamais ne se plaisent à ce qui doit donner du dégoût: mais la multitude, ou ignorante ou préoccupée, étouffe le petit nombre des connoisseurs' (*OP* III, 125).

'Taste' draws some people in, it excludes others; it is rare; it confers authority. The abbé de Chaulieu, whose own taste is praised by Saint-Evremond (again differentially: it is better than Voiture's or Sarrasin's, *L* II, 316), returns the compliment by referring to him as

> ... cet homme si fameux
> De qui le goût seul décide
> Du bon et du merveilleux.   (*L* II, 310)

The link between 'taste' and authority is embodied in Petronius. In Nero's court 'une chose passoit pour grossiere quand elle n'avoit pas son approbation ... Tout se rapportoit à la delicatesse d'un goust si exquis' (*OP* I, 176). Against the 'faux jugement' of his own age, Petronius upheld the reputation of Cicero, Virgil and Horace, in whose time great writers were so abundant that 'il estoit juste de se soûmettre à leurs sentimens, et on ne pouvoit recevoir avec trop de docilité leurs decisions' (*OP* III, 376).

These utterances should be taken in conjunction with more general attributions of social and cultural authority. 'Depuis vôtre départ', Saint-Evremond writes to the marquis de Miremont, 'la conversation languit, la dispute est morte, les rangs sont confondus: il n'y a plus de distinction dans la qualité, ni dans le mérite' (*L* II, 169). The juxtaposition of social and cultural authority is significant. Both Louis XIV and William III are praised for their taste (*L* II, 97, 170). Augustus shared, and one may suppose fostered, 'le goût exquis de son siécle' (*OP* II, 344). The equation of social, political and cultural values is generalized in the statement that 'le bon goût se rencontre ordinairement dans les écrits des personnes considerables' (*OP* IV, 110). The sentence begins, 'Un choix delicat me reduit à peu de livres'; the critic's perceptions serve to make the order of literary value correspond with the social order.

But there are problems with cultural authority: it can enforce bad taste as well. The authors Nervèze, Coëffeteau, Cohon, and Balzac were all responsible for the spread of different forms of 'bad taste' (*OP* III, 377–8).[4] Saint-Evremond goes back on his praise of Augustus (*OP* II, 345), and opines that Maecenas exercised a harmful influence on 'taste' (*OP* IV, 111). Tyrannical friends want us to 'faire violence à nôtre Naturel, asservir nôtre Jugement, renoncer a nôtre Goût' (*OP* III, 287). There are valid, then, and invalid authorities; the point is knowing how to distinguish between them.

The major *de facto* source of cultural authority is the court; Mairet's *Sophonisbe* is historically inauthentic, but was extremely successful 'pour avoir rencontré le goust des Dames, et le vray esprit des gens de la Cour' (*OP* II, 90). Not that the taste that prevails at court can be identified automatically with good taste, although one might be tempted to think so:

Je ne m'estonne point que le bon goût ne se trouve pas en des lieux où regne la barbarie, et qu'il n'y ait pas de discernement, où les Lettres, les Arts, et les disciplines sont perduës ... mais ce qui est estonnant, c'est de voir dans la Cour la plus polie, le bon et le mauvais goût, le vray et le faux esprit, tour à tour à la mode comme les habits.   (*OP* III, 121).

The reason assigned to this is that good judges, like good authors, are rare, and thus, 'chacun cherchant à donner de la reputation à ce qui lui plaît, il arrive que la multitude fait valoir ce qui a du rapport à son mauvais goût' (*OP* III, 124). In other words, good taste is not to be expected in the body of courtiers as a whole. Those of Saint-Evremond's youth had 'peu de delicatesse' (*OP* III, 122). But taste is, nevertheless, a court value. Saint-Evremond mentions one Henry Jermyn 'qui renonçant à la Cour, en avoit porté la civilité et le bon gout à la campagne' (*L* I, 309).

For Saint-Evremond, the acquisition of taste is dependent on personal relations with those who already possess it. Furthermore, taste is not merely subject to the bipolar logic of 'good' and 'bad', but is capable of the more subtle quality of *délicatesse*. These two themes coincide in the statement that taste must have a foundation in one's nature, but that 'l'experience et le commerce des gens délicats achevent de nous y former' (*OC* III, 128). Again, in his third-person self-portrait Saint-Evremond says that 'il cherche les plus délicats pour donner de la délicatesse à son goût' (*OC* IV, 308). What distinguishes 'les Délicats' is that 'l'Esprit a plus de part [à leur] goût qu'à celuy des autres' (*OP* IV, 18). Now *délicatesse* is identified as a court value. For all his faults, Seneca does display an impressive fund of knowledge, but this is largely because he lived in a 'Cour delicate' (*OP* I, 159). However, he was deservedly ridiculed by the 'petits-maîtres delicats' who surrounded Nero (*OP* I, 155). Petronius was a 'Courtisan delicat' (*OP* I, 169), and the supreme representative of a certain culture: 'Cette Cour là estoit comme une escole de voluptez recherchées, où tout se rapportoit à la delicatesse d'un goust si exquis' (*OP* I, 176). The taste of such people confers on them a hegemonic status: 'Sans les Délicats, la galanterie seroit inconnue, la musique rude, les repas mal-propres et grossiers' (*OP* IV, 18). This particular juxtaposition of practices warns us not to understand 'culture' here in the narrow and self-validating sense it sometimes bears.[5] Moreover, a moment's reflection will make it clear that the role of these 'Delicats' in each of these activities is quite different. They are active participants in *galanterie*, they may dabble in music but are not professional musicians, and they certainly don't cook their own meals. But their shifts of subject-position are simply taken for granted by Saint-Evremond, as perfectly natural. They are clearly identical to the 'Honnêtes-gens de la Cour' to whose authority Mr. Guillaut advises 'les Savans en quelque matiere que ce puisse estre' to defer, seeing that 'le Bon-goût se forme avec eux' (*Les Opéra*, p. 64). The composer Cambert is cited as an artist who suffered from this lack of direction.

Honnêteté, says Saint-Evremond, is an outgrowth of reason (*OP* III, 13–14), and it is universal:

J'avois cru autrefois qu'il n'y avoit d'honnêtes gens qu'en nostre Cour ... Mais à la fin j'ay connu par experience qu'il y en avoit par tout ... A la verité le fond d'une qualite essentielle est par tout le méme.   (*OP* IV, 127–8)

Well, universal in a sense. The notion that *honnêtes gens* were rare outside France was originally founded on climatic considerations, 'la mollesse des pais chauds, et une espece de barbarie des païs froids' (*OP* IV, 127). What he has abandoned, then, is the belief in climatic determinism. But even when he thought the French climate special, he still believed that its effects were felt only 'en nostre Cour'. The abandonment of climatic determinism leaves social determinism intact. Although Holland has some admirable features (see the 'Lettre écrite de La Haye', *OP* II, 24–33), it contains 'moins d'honnestes gens ... que d'habiles' (*OP* II, 27); and it happens to be a country without a court (*OP* II, 24; *L* I, 157). The *honnête homme* is consti-tuted, in a more general sense, as the subject of pleasures and benefits produced by somebody else. In his 'Jugement sur les sciences où peut s'appliquer un honneste homme', Saint-Evremond acknowledges that mathematics is a very worthwhile pursuit – for somebody else: it produces 'commoditez' and 'embellissemens' that enrich our lives, but for '[les] personnes de bon sens' it is enough to be able to benefit from these, without worrying about how they are produced: 'nous avons plus d'interest à joüir du monde qu'à le connoître' (*OP* II, 12). It is the same with poetry:

Il faut qu'il y ait d'excellens poëtes pour nostre plaisir, comme de grands mathematiciens pour nostre utilité: mais il suffit pour nous de nous bien connoitre à leurs ouvrages, et nous n'avons que faire de rêver souvent comme les uns, ni d'épuiser nos esprits à mediter, comme les autres.

(*OP* IV, 113–14)

The 'we' of this discourse is identified with the *honnête homme* from whom the poet is differentiated: sometimes the latter deals in 'le langage des Dieux', sometimes in that of '[les] fous', seldom in that of an *honnête homme* (*OP* IV, 112).

The fact is that the values of *honnêteté* and *délicatesse* cannot be understood apart from the differentiations they produce. That which separates cultural consumers from producers has already appeared clearly enough. But there are other distinctions, no less ideologically potent. The chief of these are between the 'person of taste' and the scholar, or the professional in general; between the courtier and the *robin*; and between the discourse of *délicatesse* and *honnêteté* and that of Christian morality.

The entry under *Savants* in Flaubert's *Dictionnaire des idées reçues* begins 'Les blaguer'. Like many another seventeenth-century writer, Saint-Evremond would seem to have memorized this lesson in advance. For some reason or other, a *savant* with taste seems to be a contradiction in terms. Learning and taste are distributed among different categories of people: 'vous devez conte … aux Savans de vôtre lecture', writes Saint-Evremond to Mme Mazarin, 'aux Délicats de vôtre bon-goût' (*L* II, 85). He says of himself that 'il ne s'attache point aux sentimens des sçavans pour acquerir la science, mais aux plus sensez pour fortifier sa raison; tantot il cherche les plus délicats pour donner de la délicatesse à son goût' (*OP* IV, 308). Learning and taste have a natural antipathy, overcome only in an exceptional case like Hervart's: 'Quand je parle à des gens polis, je trouve à redire vos connoissances; l'entretien des Savans me laisse à desirer votre bon goût' (*L* I, 190). Their difference from 'people of taste' is a sign of *les savants*' inferiority; learned culture is at best a *pis aller*:

Quand je suis privé du commerce des gens du monde, j'ay recours à celuy des sçavans, et si j'en rencontre qui sçachent les belles lettres, je ne crois pas perdre beaucoup de passer de la delicatesse de nostre tems à celle des autres siecles. Mais rarement on trouve des personnes de bon goût, ce qui fait que la connoissance des belles lettres devient en plusieurs sçavans une erudition fort ennuyeuse. (*OP* IV, 129)

There corresponds to this scheme of values a general prejudice in favour of collective rather than individual activity. Reading is a substitute for 'la conversation des honnêtes gens' and '[le] commerce des plaisirs' (*OP* II, 6). Study and meditation spoil a person for the company of *les honnêtes gens* (*OP* II, 134).

This repudiation of the cultural authority of scholars is supported by a twofold attitude to what appears as the typical object of scholarly knowledge, namely the textual corpus of antiquity. The scholar is not allowed to bathe in the reflected glory of 'his' texts, partly because that glory is questionable, partly because they are not his. To begin with, the standards of the ancients are quite different from those of today, sometimes for better, sometimes for worse. Thus it seems a pity that a fine play like Corneille's *Attila*, which would have been admired in antiquity, should fail to please its modern audience (*L* I, 137, 143). But an authentic *Oedipus* would nowadays appear 'barbare, ... funeste, ... opposé aux vrais sentimens qu'on doit avoir' (*OP* IV, 182). Moreover, whereas 'la verité n'estoit pas du goût des premiers siecles' (*OP* III, 356), 'le genie de nôtre siecle est tout opposé à cet esprit de fables et de faux mysteres' (*OP* III, 357). Religion, politics, morals and manners have all changed so as to render the ancient artistic models unserviceable: 'il nous faut comme un nouvel art pour bien entrer dans le goût et dans le genie du siecle où nous sommes' (*OP* III, 348). The scholar cannot, therefore, lay claim to cultural authority as the guardian of the values embodied in ancient texts, for most of them are no longer valid. In any case, of those that are, he cannot claim to be the guardian. Saint-Evremond observes that critics can explain the works of a grammarian, whose mentality is akin to their own, 'mais ils ne prendront jamais [l'esprit] d'un honnéte homme des anciens, car le leur y est tout à fait contraire' (*OP* IV, 130). Reading, in fact, is an extension in time and space of ordinary social intercourse: 'J'aime à connoitre dans les Epistres de Ciceron et son caractere et celuy des gens de qualité qui luy écrivent' (*OP* IV, 110). In other words, the scholar unused to frequenting the company of contemporary *gens de qualité* is debarred from appreciating the substantial qualities of their ancient predecessors. Power and culture are close kin to each other: power over culture is inherited by the powerful from their predecessors: by an *homme de qualité* like

Saint-Evremond, not by the culture-labourers who are that and nothing else.

It is true, however, that scholars are not the only sort of people whose grasp of antiquity is defective. Few people have what Saint-Evremond calls 'le bon goust de l'Antiquité' (*OP* II, 90), an appreciation of the distinctive character of different nations, historical periods and individuals (*OP* II, 88–9). Corneille would appear to be the sole exception and he has 'le malheur de ne plaire pas à nostre siecle' (*OP* II, 90). This virtue pertains not only to the author but to the spectator as well: ideally, 'il éloigne son esprit de tout ce qu'il voit en usage, tâche à se defaire du goust de son temps, renonce à son propre naturel, s'il est opposé à celuy des personnes qu'on represente'. And this is a rational response, since 'la raison ... est de tous les temps' (*OP* II, 89). There is a contradiction here between this and the evolutionary view of reason as peculiarly embodied in contemporary taste, while that of antiquity fed on fables and mystifications. Be that as it may, this kind of taste seems to be a personal attribute, not grounded in any privileged social experience, nor yet conferred by any special training. Usually, however, good taste is more precisely located by Saint-Evremond.

In the examples quoted above, the word *savants* has the sense of 'scholars', but it can also bear the more general sense of culture-professionals of whatever kind. This appears from Mr. Guillaut's already-quoted injunction to 'les Savans en quelque matiere que ce puisse estre' to submit to the authority of 'les Honnêtes-gens de la Cour', those guardians of good taste. They are empowered to determine how other people shall apply their skill and knowledge. Collective activity is valued precisely as the sphere in which this hegemony is exercised: 'La Science peut s'aquerir avec les Savans de Profession; le bon usage de la Science ne s'aquiert que dans le Monde' (*Les Opéra*, p. 64). Individual activity is suspect because it withdraws its practitioners from this hegemonic space, whether their role in it is dominant or subordinate. The abstract values invoked by Saint-Evremond are tied to acts of recognizing one's difference from or similarity to others, one's place in a hierarchy of sociocultural relations. In the examples quoted above (pp. 111–12), it is not learning as such that has been found wanting so much as the actual company of its votaries. The professional is told to learn his trade among his kind, but to learn how to apply it in the society of a different class of person. This latter, the courtier *honnête homme*, likewise recognizes himself by his boredom when with *savants*, his euphoria with those of his own kind. The cultural values invoked in this discourse help to segregate producers from consumers, and to subject the former to the latter.

The second distinction, between courtier and *robin*, emerges most clearly in the 'Observations sur Salluste et Tacite' and the essay 'Sur les historiens françois'. Compared to the ancient Romans, the Frenchmen of Saint-Evremond's day are lamentably specialized (*OP* III, 75). It is rare to combine the understanding of men with that of *les affaires* (*OP* II, 65). By *les affaires*, Saint-Evremond means politics, national and international, administration and diplomacy. Knowledge of these falls to people 'élevez dans les compagnies', by which he means the sovereign courts and in particular the *parlements*, in other words, to the *gens de robe*. But, however competent in their own sphere, such people make a poor show at court, 'grossiers au choix des gens, sans aucun goust du merite, ridicules dans leurs dépenses et dans leurs plaisirs' (*OP* II, 66). In other words, they are the opposite of *les délicats*. Courtiers, however, possess a keen insight into what Jeeves has taught us to call the psychology of the individual; but for lack of a more general understanding of *les affaires*, they become superfluous and even ridiculous (there are similarities here with La Rochefoucauld's description of old age in the essay 'De la retraite'). This is where the *robins* tend to score, since their experience of practical matters puts them in demand (*OP* II, 67–8).

So far, the honours appear to be even between *robins* and courtiers, their characteristic shortcomings cancelling each other out. But not quite. Young *gens de robe* have a 'faux air de Cour qui ... les rend ridicules aux Courtisans' (*OP* II, 68); all *gens de robe* are laughable 'aussi-tost qu'ils veulent sortir de leur profession' (*OP* III, 75). These external pressures on them to keep to their place are more obvious, to themselves and to others, than the inhibitions that deter *gens de qualité* from compromising themselves by learning about the laws of France (*OP* III, 71). The ideal type combines both sets of qualities, but not by an abstract process of fusion: on to his basic 'delicatesse de Cour', he grafts 'la connoissance des affaires, et l'experience de la guerre' (*OP* II, 69). He is a courtier-soldier, therefore typically an aristocrat, who has diversified his hegemonic status by incorporating the characteristic skills of an inferior social group. The distinction between courtier and *robin* is thus weighted in favour of the former.

The third distinction is between the discourse of *délicatesse* and *honnêteté* and that of (Christian) morality. Saint-Evremond stages a dispute on self-interest between two people, one 'vertueux', the other 'corrompu'. These are obviously ethical labels, the second having

114

something of a religious flavour. But by his obsession with amassing wealth and his self-proclaimed contempt for honour (*OP* III, 5), the 'corrompu' is socially marked as low-born. The dispute is arbitrated by an 'honneste et habile Courtisan' (*OP* III, 13). It is important to note that Saint-Evremond is not appealing to some natural mean between virtue and self-interest. It is the courtier who 'fait le temperament' (*L* I, 150). Both participants are in error. But the 'vertueux' at least is raised to the dignity of an interlocutor, whereas the courtier never deigns to address the 'corrompu'. Of the two errors, that of the 'vertueux' is preferable: the avarice and ingratitude boasted of by the 'corrompu' are 'de tres-vilaines qualités' (*OP* III, 16), and 'on se passe plus aisément du bien que ne produit pas une vertu inutile, qu'on ne souffre les effets d'une si dangereuse corruption' (*OP* III, 20). None the less, the 'vertueux' has mistaken his discursive situation: 'Il me semble qui vous debuttez mal avec des Courtisans, de leur prêcher sans cesse la moderation de leurs desirs, eux qui font de l'ambition leur plus grand merite.' While one remains at court, it would be 'mal honneste' to renounce ambition. Courtiers simply do not come under the jurisdiction of the categorical morality preached by the 'vertueux'; they have a code of their own. The stake in this ideological struggle is the control of discourse: 'Trouvez bon que les delicats nomment plaisir, ce que les gens rudes et grossiers ont nommé vice.' But there is a teleological aspect to the question, too: 'la politesse, la galanterie, la science des voluptez, font une partie du merite *presentement*' (*OP* III, 14, my italics). According to the courtier, the original function of reason was to establish 'des loix qui puissent empescher les outrages et les violences' (*OP* III, 14), to put an end to the anarchy in which early mankind lived (see *OP* III, 353). It therefore needed to be rigid and austere. But, this initial task achieved, 'elle s'est adoucie pour introduire l'honnesteté dans le commerce des hommes; elle est devenuë delicate et curieuse dans la recherche des plaisirs, pour rendre la vie aussi agreable qu'elle estoit des-ja seure et honneste' (ibid.). What reason does, then, as time progresses, is not just to enhance the general level of civilization, but to generate further distinctions between human beings according to their level of cultural life. Its action was originally directed towards mankind in general; now it applies only to the elite capable of *honnêteté* and *délicatesse*. Since the latter value appears to be an advance on the former, perhaps one should consider *les délicats* as an elite within an elite. But, as we have seen, these qualities are largely constituted by social position. The moralism of the 'vertueux' is not just outdated, it is essentially appropriated to keeping the subordinate classes in order, and consequently not binding on the courtier.

The chief point of dissension between the courtier and the 'vertueux' is over the nature of pleasure, which the moralistic discourse tends to identify as equivalent to vice. Being concerned with pleasure, taste thus fetches up on the non-moral side of the fence. It is implicated, for instance, in the anti-moral revaluation of Petronius, Seneca and Plutarch. The *arbiter elegantiae* of the proverbially monstrous Nero is 'un des plus honnestes hommes du monde' (*OP* I, 164); his satire has no moral intention: 'c'est plustost un Courtisan delicat qui trouve le ridicule, qu'un Philosophe utile au public qui s'attache à blasmer la corruption' (*OP* I, 169). Seneca and Plutarch, however, are both 'grands Prescheurs de sagesse et de vertu' (*OP* I, 159). Seneca's taste as such is not mentioned, but his style is vigorously criticized, and Saint-Evremond, rightly or wrongly, sees it as the target of Petronius's satire on contemporary style, which is criticism enough (*OP* I, 155–8). Plutarch is far more favourably treated, but even his taste was not 'tout à fait exquis': 'aux choses purement de l'esprit, il n'a rien d'ingenieux ni de delicat' (*OP* I, 161).

But not only is 'taste' subversive of moralistic culture; it even tends to displace morality as an autonomous force. 'Les vrais honnétes gens' have no need of moral instruction: 'ils connoissent le bien par la seule justesse de leur goût et s'y portent de leur propre mouvement' (*L* I, 253). Again, 'il n'y a personne de bon goût qui aime le vice, quand le vice n'est pas agréable' (*L* I, 269). This latter remark comes from a letter to the Duke of Buckingham, who had recently undergone a celebrated conversion, on which Saint-Evremond, if I interpret him correctly, is ironically congratulating him: continence is easy in a northern country, where the 'man of taste' will find nothing to tempt him; but if a real temptation comes along Buckingham will doubtless show the authenticity of his change of heart. Despite the deference, tinged in any case with irony, to the notion of genuine moral virtue, the point remains that the effects attributed to the latter can very often be produced by 'taste' as well. But there is a paradox here: if 'taste' takes over the work of morality proper, it is in a sense confirming morality, so long as its determinations and those of morality coincide. 'Taste' thus both distances its votaries from the official ideological agencies and re-enacts their practical subjection to official ideology; the following passage brings this out particularly clearly:

Que les personnes grossieres et sensuelles se plaignent de nôtre Religion, pour la contrainte qu'elle leur donne; les gens delicats ont à se löuer de ce qu'elle leur épargne les dégouts et les repentirs. Plus entenduë que la philosophie voluptueuse dans la science des plaisirs, plus sage que la philosophie austere dans la science des mœurs, elle épure nostre goût pour la delicatesse et nos sentimens pour l'innocence.   (*OP* IV, 163–4)

The contradictions in the relationship between 'taste' and official religious morality are mirrored in Saint-Evremond's position *vis-à-vis* official culture. In the *Comédie des académistes* and the 'Dissertation sur le mot de Vaste' Saint-Evremond attacks the *Académie française*, the official repository of linguistic values. The choice of the word *vaste* is far from arbitrary, for it serves to evaluate political and military schemes and strategies. Saint-Evremond contends that it is intrinsically pejorative, whereas the *Académie* allows it a positive sense. But there is a very clear implication that a lot of nobodies like the Academicians have no standing in a discussion of lofty political and military matters: they think that to speak of Richelieu's 'esprit vaste' is to pay him a compliment, but if they had had the honour of Turenne's acquaintance 'ils auroient bien veu que l'esprit vaste du Cardinal de Richelieu n'avoit aucune recommandation aupres de luy' (*OP* III, 414). At the beginning of the 'Dissertation' Saint-Evremond contends that the Golden Age of Latin literature was the late Republic rather than the reign of Augustus (*OP* III, 376), which is obviously a side-swipe at the official ideology of the 'siècle de Louis XIV'. All 'people of taste' would praise Petronius for attacking the corruption of contemporary style, and the discriminating individual has a perfect right to follow his example and take issue with the orthodoxies of his time (*OP* III, 377–9). Very good. But the fact is that the cultural orthodoxies of the reign of Louis XIV were propagated just as much through the court as through institutions like the *Académie*. Yet Saint-Evremond's ideal, the 'man of taste', the *délicat*, is a courtier, and as such subject to similar pressures. Besides, although Seneca, the model of a corrupt style according to Saint-Evremond, was Nero's tutor, Petronius, on Saint-Evremond's own showing, was no voice crying in the wilderness, but the leader of a clique of courtiers on the very best of terms with the emperor (see *OP* I, 155–6).

'Saint-Evremond', it has been written, 'does not attempt to isolate taste as a quality, to give a meticulous definition of it, or to expatiate upon the impossibility of defining it.'[6] This is true. It is unnecessary to define what imposes itself in experience, impossible to isolate taste as a mode of perception and evaluation from the experience within which it is characteristically exercised, without which it is unthinkable. But this experience should not be abstracted from its social and material conditions. Taste-discourse is essentially differentiating, oppositional. It excludes or subordinates – the scholar, the culture-professional, the *robin*. It positions its subject at the centre of a social existence; others produce that he may consume, that he shall not lack for operas or ortolans. But he does not control only the cultural present. He is also master of the past, for only an *honnête homme* like himself can properly frequent the *honnêtes gens* of antiquity, only a man of rank can savour the 'good taste' of 'les écrits des personnes considerables'. In so far as history, a privileged zone of discourse, largely consists of military events, it is accessible only to the aristocrat with his military background and experience, even though he may lack the scholar's insight into political and religious systems. But the man of taste can largely dispense with scholarly mediation in his reading; the company of scholars only reminds him of their difference from himself, their lack of taste. On the contrary, dining or conversing with a circle of *délicats* gives him the heartening sensation of being among his social and cultural equals.

Saint-Evremond, of course, nowhere makes noble birth a precondition of access to culture and 'taste'. But he defines cultural values in terms that, partly by excluding other social categories, postulate a nobleman as their natural subject. Anyone else subscribing to them is thereby accepting his or her position as a subordinate within a nobiliary scheme of things. Saint-Evremond's discourse of taste seeks to appropriate culture as a field of nobiliary ideological dominance.

But in so doing it exposes its own contradictions, and along with them the contradictions in the position of the nobility of Saint-Evremond's time. The fact is that 'culture' in the narrow sense, which in this context means primarily literary culture, is for Saint-Evremond of secondary importance. It is a supplement to or substitute for less ethereal forms of pleasure: reading is what one falls back on when at a loss for company. The natural locus of the total culture of *goût* and *délicatesse*, values that serve to unify an elite, is the court. Not everyone there has taste, not even at the court of France. Yet taste is unlikely to flourish anywhere else. Since the transformation of the nobility from a mainly military caste that began in the early seventeenth century, the court is the natural place for them to exercise and extend their new role of cultural dominance. But it is also subject, as they are subject, to the royal authority, whose taste, as manifested in institutions like the *Académie française*, is unreliable, corrupted by bourgeois influence. French culture is menaced with the same fate as that of Rome, which throve under the late Republic – with its proliferation of great men, men of action who were intellectuals, intellectuals who were men of action — and decayed under the emperors. Saint-Evremond's individual fate is curiously symptomatic of the general process. Banished from France for his criticism of government policy over the Treaty of the Pyrenees, he spent the rest of his life in England, a Petronius without a Nero. The institution in which the ideal of aristocratic culture ought most naturally to be realized was not in aristocratic control, and this basic political fact called into question the validity of the whole ideal.

5

LA ROCHEFOUCAULD: TASTES
AND THEIR VICISSITUDES

The epigraph of the *Maximes* appears to entrust the work with the task of unmasking 'virtue' to reveal vice. The principal interest of reading La Rochefoucauld comes, however, less from this than from the repeated calling into question of the terms 'virtue' and 'vice'. Time and again, some professed moral virtue is broken down into its non-moral constituents. Parallel to this is the marginalization of the rational element in human behaviour. Among the concepts that carry out these operations, *amour-propre* (inevitably), *fortune, humeur, intérêt* feature prominently: so too does *goût*. But its meanings are complex, even contradictory; and there is a further problem. If *goût* is, as we shall see, capricious and irrational, and if it is, as it appears to be, part of the human make-up as such, then how can it also designate a faculty of judgment or discernment?[1]

According to La Rochefoucauld, 'il est malaisé de rendre raison des goûts en général'.[2] The formation of tastes is no more intelligible than the world-process as a whole: 'Il y a une révolution générale qui change le goût des esprits, aussi bien que les fortunes du monde' (MS 48). The basic conservatism of this position should be noted: it fosters a belief in timeless values, and perpetual deviations from them, which are then placed to the account of 'human nature'. Particular tastes, however, like the one discussed in the essay 'Des coquettes et des vieillards' may be to some extent intelligible. In any case, it is possible to observe the interaction of *goût* with other factors internal or external to the subject.

Plato appears to have thought that the womb was, rather than a part of the female anatomy, an animal existing inside the woman (*Timaeus*, 91). *Amour-propre* in La Rochefoucauld seems to have the same sort of status; as Odette de Mourgues has noted, the most remarkable stylistic feature of MS 1 is 'the obsessive repetition of the pronoun *il*'.[3] The human being is the subject of *amour-propre* in more than one sense; La Rochefoucauld knows that man, as Malcolm Bowie puts it in an essay on Lacan, 'bears otherness within him'.[4]

This otherness is itself a subject, with tastes of its own. These surface at the level of consciousness in various forms, which conventional psychology assumes to be primary. Not so: 'les passions ne sont que les divers goûts de l'amour-propre' (MP 28). As such, they are inaccessible to introspection; for, just as the conscious personality stands over against the opacity of its unconscious *amour-propre*, *amour-propre* itself is endowed with an unconscious double: 'il est souvent invisible à lui-meme', and one of the symptoms of this is that 'il pense avoir perdu tous les goûts qu'il a rassasiés' (MS 1, p. 134). Starobinski is perfectly right to talk of the *mise en abyme* effect of La Rochefoucauld's picture of the self.[5]

But not only the passions are tastes on the part of *amour-propre*. The virtues are as well, at least to judge by maxim 46: 'L'attachement ou l'indifférence que les philosophes avaient pour la vie n'était qu'un goût de leur amour-propre, dont on ne doit non plus disputer que du goût de la langue ou du choix des couleurs.' This is a very marked example of the anti-normativity of La Rochefoucauld's discourse of taste. Denied their foundation in a universal order, moral values are likewise denied any rational justification, and are ascribed to a purely subjective basis. But does not this position lead to moral nihilism and anarchism? The question leaps to the lips of every respectable person. La Rochefoucauld's implicit answer will be discussed in due course. In the meantime, one should note the immediate ideological function of this use of *goût*: to demolish the moral authority of the ancient philosophers, the Stoics particularly, and their modern epigoni, and beyond them a whole scheme of categorical morality.

As well as the tastes of which the subject is *amour-propre*, and which present themselves to consciousness as passions or moral attitudes, there are the tastes of which we ourselves are the subject. But not the source: 'La persévérance n'est digne ni de blâme ni de louange, parce qu'elle n'est que la durée des goûts et des sentiments, *qu'on ne s'ôte et qu'on ne se donne point*' (177; my emphasis). This externality of 'our' tastes to ourselves is doubtless another effect of the presence of otherness within us; and it counts as a reason for withdrawing them from the jurisdiction of morality.

Even those tastes which are not explicitly attributed to *amour-propre* do not escape its influence. This is partly because they are subject to the passions, which are, as we have seen, the tastes of *amour-propre*. In particular, La Rochefoucauld asserts that 'l'orgueil ... est presque toujours le maître de nos goûts' (R 17, p. 223). This of course raises the problem of the status of La Rochefoucauld's moral terminology, which Jonathan Culler has perceptively discussed.[6]

It might seem that to ascribe our tastes to 'pride' is to bring them within a moral, even theological, frame of reference, such as that of the 'Discours' of La Chapelle-Bessé which served as an introduction to the first edition of the *Maximes*. In it, La Chapelle-Bessé also associates taste and pride in a quotation, or rather misquotation, from Brébeuf:

> Si le jour de la foi n'éclaire la raison,
> Notre goût dépravé tourne tout en poison;
> Toujours de notre orgueil la subtile imposture
> Au bien qu'il semble aimer fait changer de nature.
>
> (reprinted in Truchet's edn, p. 276)

Such similarities favour the recuperation of La Rochefoucauld's discourse by traditional Christian, and in particular Augustinian, morality. They are, however, superficial. La Rochefoucauld makes the link between tastes and pride in the essay 'De l'inconstance', where human feelings, particularly love, are represented as subject to inevitable natural processes of change, and the scope of moral judgment severely attenuated. To put the matter more precisely, if somewhat paradoxically, La Rochefoucauld's use of moral language is evaluative but not normative: it does not, or does not necessarily, connote obligation. To speak of our tastes as dominated by pride is not, for La Rochefoucauld, to suggest automatically that we should eschew them, although for a religious writer it would be. But it does serve to demolish an idealistic view of love (and to discuss love as a taste is in itself to devalue it) as selfless, generous, concerned primarily with the other person.

But *amour-propre* is not bound up with taste only through the medium of the passions. La Rochefoucauld asserts that 'notre amour-propre souffre plus impatiemment la condamnation de nos goûts que de nos opinions' (13). Given that we should like to believe that we have some rational foundation for our opinions, this maxim implies that our ultimate identification is not with the rational part of our personality. The same point is made in the essay 'Du faux': 'On craint encore plus de se montrer faux par le goût que par l'esprit' (p. 208). This brings a normative element, hitherto absent, into relation with taste. But why should people feel more implicated by their tastes than by their opinions? Tastes, it would seem, are powerful indicators of the state of our personality as a whole: 'Quand notre mérite baisse, notre goût baisse aussi' (379). Moreover, they can be read, as we shall see in connexion with 'Du faux', as signs of how correctly we conceive and live our relationships with other people. But this should not be taken as a natural scheme of things. To 'recognize' the truth of La Rochefoucauld's observations here is to place oneself, like him, within an ideological formation where opinions are superficial because they have no practical consequences, where the emphasis is laid instead on appearance and personal style. This is, of course, the position of the dominant class of late seventeenth-century France: dominant, but not responsible, not, in the true sense of the word, a governing class.

La Rochefoucauld's psychology is based on two possibly incompatible images of the human psyche. It sometimes appears as a quasi-theatrical empty space. Here rival forces interact (as in 376, 228, 281), or alternatively a single force develops and transforms itself under the influence of external stimuli but according to the laws of its own internal dynamic, as in maxims 10 or 11. At other times, however, it appears as a nucleus of determinate qualities which obstinately assert themselves, again under the influence of external circumstances. In other words determination by the basic and fundamentally unchangeable nature of the individual coexists with determination by the laws of a general human economy of the passions. The latter form of determination appears in the statement that 'l'orgueil ... est presque toujours le maître de nos goûts', cited above; the former in 252: 'Il est aussi ordinaire de voir changer les goûts qu'il est extraordinaire de voir changer les inclinations.' This is glossed by the *Grands Ecrivains français* edition as meaning that 'les inclinations, invariables en elles-mêmes, ne varient que dans leurs objets', an interpretation quoted and endorsed in the Truchet edition (p. 65, n. 1). Inclinations, as Truchet notes in the same place, are associated with varieties of temperament in MS 1 (p. 135). In 252, then, tastes are represented as superficial, attached to the flux of phenomena which are processed by the subject according to the laws of his or her individual nature.

But these individual laws are modified or suspended by general human ones, and taste shows the effect of this. In 'De l'amour et de la vie' La Rochefoucauld traces a double process of change, in the object ('les mêmes biens ne conservent pas leur même prix') and in the subject ('et ils ne touchent pas toujours également notre goût') (p. 200). It is life itself that devalues life. Changes in taste are the effect of the consumption-process of which taste is the vehicle. We ingest the objects we taste so that they become part of ourselves and thus no longer objects of desire, no longer capable of appealing to our taste. Devaluation has a twofold significance in La Rochefoucauld. It is an effect brought about by the rhetorical strategies of the *Maximes*, when a virtue is reduced to a vice, or to a passion. *Goût* plays its part within this strategy, because to define something as a taste, on the part of the subject or of *amour-propre*, can be, as we have seen, to devalue it. But devaluation is also a referent of the *Maximes* and the *Réflexions diverses*, the devaluation of life brought about by time and the internal entropic tendencies of the emotions: and taste is implicated in this process as well. It is affected by age, and by the state of the body: 'La jeunesse change ses goûts par l'ardeur du sang, et la vieillesse conserve les siens par l'accoutumance' (109). The point of this is to demolish consistency as a value by representing it as the mere product of an absence, the absence of vigour. Taste is the plaything first of physiological, then of psychological forces. But their operations are contradictory: 109 appears to clash with the essay 'De la retraite', where La Rochefoucauld associates ageing with *changes* of taste. But the tastes acquired by old people are not, it would seem, on a level with those they keep from sheer force of habit: the latter are the effect of a blind determinism, but the former obey a kind of natural rationality (the expression 'raisons naturelles' is used (p. 223)). And yet the rationality is not so much in the subject as in the process: it is not so much that decisions are taken as that stimuli are responded to. Old people withdraw from the company of others and abandon former activities, and they are doubtless right to do so, but the credit should not go to their reason but to 'l'orgueil, qui est inséparable de l'amour-propre, [et qui] leur tient alors lieu de raison' (p. 224). This of course subverts the traditional pejorative connotations of *amour-propre* and *orgueil* since they are shown as producing desirable effects, but at the same time it does not give much comfort to moral rationalism. Old people are bound to be unhappy if they remain in society, and the only sensible course of action is to leave it. 'Leur goût, détrompé des désirs inutiles, se tourne alors vers des objets muets et insensibles; les bâtiments, l'agriculture, l'économie, l'étude' (p. 225). There is a value-judgment implicit in 'détrompé': this change of attitude is in accordance with the reality of their situation, therefore a good thing. But the linguistic form in which this point is made is striking: it is not so much the people who are the subject of this change of attitude as their taste; as if this were a process of which they themselves are the site but not the subject. Again, then, *goût* seems to be party to the decentering of the subject.

In 'De la retraite', La Rochefoucauld is trying to give the psychological, and even physiological, rationale for a widespread pattern of behaviour. He attempts something similar in 'Des coquettes et des vieillards'. But the difficulty of accounting for tastes in general is, he says, accentuated in the case of coquettes, although it is possible to generalize about their 'envie de plaire' and their vanity (p. 215).

Here the general emphasis on the arbitrariness and capriciousness of taste is reinforced by a traditional reflex association of women with the irrational. The essay as a whole curiously juxtaposes a discursive strand of rationalism with another of stereotyped bewilderment: mystification in both its senses. This is especially evident in the following passage:

> Mais le plus incompréhensible de tous leurs goûts est, à mon sens, celui qu'elles ont pour les vieillards qui ont été galants. Ce goût paraît trop bizarre, et il y en a trop d'exemples, pour ne chercher pas la cause d'un sentiment tout à la fois si commun et si contraire à l'opinion que l'on a des femmes.
>
> (p. 215)

It looks at first sight as if the subsequent investigation is to clarify the mystery and expose the shortcomings of the Doxa. None the less, despite the attempt to give a rational account of the phenomenon, the language of categorical evaluation persists in a phrase like 'ce goût dépravé des coquettes pour les vieilles gens' (p. 216). The tone of the passage presents another contradiction, between sober realism and whimsicality: the former dominates in the references to the old man, but the coquette is spoken of as capable of raising the dead; she attaches the old man to her triumphal chariot; he is as necessary a part of her train as the dwarves in *Amadis de Gaule*. But behind this ironic exploitation of romance motifs, there are definite ideological certitudes: women are governed by the twin drives of vanity and concern for their reputation; the homage of the old man gratifies the former without imperilling the latter.

The distribution of roles between the participants reveals another set of contrasts, founded on the basic asymmetry that only the woman is explicitly named as the subject of a taste: the essay deals with 'le goût qu'elles ont pour les vieillards' (p. 215), 'ce goût dépravé des coquettes pour les vieilles gens' (p. 216). Her role in the first instance is to appear: 'elles paraissent bonnes et solides en conservant un ami sans conséquence'; his is to act, broadcasting her praises, suppressing rumours about her (if they are true, he won't believe them), generally acting in her interest. At the same time, he is the subject of thought-processes: 'il juge ... il craint ... il se trouve ... heureux ... il se persuade ... il croit ...' (pp. 216–17). She, however, is the subject of discourse; for though he speaks to other people in her behalf, he is never shown as addressing her, whereas 'elle lui fait remarquer ..., elle le prie ..., elle lui avoue ...' (p. 217). It is obvious that these roles are far from arbitrary; they are a function both of the partners' social position (as an old man he enjoys respectability and perhaps a measure of 'crédit' to use in her behalf; as a woman she must take thought for her reputation and keep her husband's suspicions from being aroused) and of the essential nature that goes with it (women are vain, old men blind to their real situation). Indeed, the relationship is so rigidly structured in this way that if one thinks of taste as something personal, capricious, arbitrary, it becomes difficult to use the word in this connexion; this taste is subjective, but in the sense that it appears as a necessary effect of one's constitution as a subject by ideology and 'nature' (that is, ideology). I shall discuss the relation between taste and subject-position below. In the incisiveness of its analysis, 'Des coquettes et des vieillards' is very fine; the whimsicality that blunts it is, however, no accidental defect. The essay confirms Odette de Mourgues's observation that

> wherever the apparent reactions of human beings are different from his own, La Rochefoucauld can comment only at a rather shallow level ... The most glaring proof of this lack of imagination and curiosity is to be found in the maxims on women. As far as women are concerned, there is no discovery, no probing beyond the traditional motivation given for their attitudes.
>
> (pp. 42–3)

There is a contradiction between the analytic intention and the attitude of bewilderment and revulsion: how is it possible to call so strongly motivated a taste 'bizarre' and 'dépravé'? The investigation of a phenomenon 'si contraire à l'opinion que l'on a des femmes' presupposes and reinforces that very opinion.

Taste, however, refuses to be unequivocally identified as determined by self-interest; it has a life of its own: 'On renonce plus aisément à son intérêt qu'à son goût' (390). Its implication in our self-destructive urges associates it, once again, with *amour-propre*, of which La Rochefoucauld writes, 'on le voit quelquefois travailler avec le dernier empressement, et avec des travaux incroyables, à obtenir des choses qui ne lui sont point avantageuses, et qui même lui sont nuisibles, mais qu'il poursuit parce qu'il les veut' (MS 1, p. 135). Like 13, where taste is said to take priority over opinions, 390 stresses the relative unimportance of consciousness and rationality in shaping our lives. The same point is made in 467: 'La vanité nous fait faire plus de choses contre notre goût que la raison.' If virtue occasionally involves subduing our inclinations by reason, and if virtuousness is proportionate to the difficulty of acting virtuously,[7] then taste stands convicted of being an enemy to virtue and reason. That vanity should occasionally override it, and thus do the work of reason, is perfectly normal from a La Rochefoucauldian perspective: the human personality has the capacity to sort itself out but not through the consistent intervention of a regulating agency. 'Ce qui nous empêche souvent de nous abandonner à un seul vice est que nous avons plusieurs', as 195 puts it.

So slight a role do rationality and objective knowledge play in our lives that to represent *goût* as their antithesis is not to condemn it: 'La félicité est dans le goût et non pas dans les choses; et c'est par avoir ce qu'on aime qu'on est heureux, et non par avoir ce que les autres trouvent aimable' (48). No more than taste can happiness be evaluated in accord with a norm.

And yet other texts by La Rochefoucauld show *goût* actually assuming a normative function. How is this possible? The most straightforward explanation is that La Rochefoucauld is using *goût* in the examples just studied in a different sense from that in which it performs a normative function. He himself observes in 'Des goûts' that 'ce terme de *goût* a diverses significations, et il est aisé de s'y méprendre', and he distinguishes between 'le goût qui nous porte vers les choses' and 'le gout qui nous en fait connaître et discerner les qualités' (pp. 201–2). If we adopt this distinction between 'appetitive' and 'cognitive' senses of *goût*, then the examples already looked at could be said to come under the former, which would leave the latter intact to assume its normative role. But this would be premature. In the first place, I shall argue that the distinction, as La Rochefoucauld gives it, is in practice hard to maintain and moreover incompatible with his own use of *goût*. Secondly, even if we accept the possibility of an objective cognitive 'taste', the conditions for its actualization still need to be specified, especially given La Rochefoucauld's own depiction of the personality as largely dominated by irrational forces. He does in fact partly specify them when he says that cognitive 'taste' functions 'en s'attachant aux règles' (p. 202), although the statement must be admitted to be vague.

The notion of taste seems to take on more positive overtones when it is connected with intersubjectivity. The essay 'De la conversation' lays down a series of rules for conversational behaviour. Rather than interrupting or contradicting other people, 'on doit ... entrer dans leur esprit et dans leur goût'. Living with other people suspends certain objective values: 'il faut leur laisser la liberté de se faire entendre, *et même de dire des choses inutiles*' (p. 191; my italics). Although such values are not phased out altogether ('on doit ... louer ce qu'ils disent *autant qu'il mérite d'être loué*', p. 191; my italics), it looks as if other people's taste as such deserves a respect that, considered in the abstract as the taste of an individual, one would not, given the vagaries of taste in general, accord to it. It is possible, further, that 'entering into' other people's taste is seen as a way of escaping from the distorting influences that presumably affect one's own. On the other hand, there is no point in entering into just anybody's taste; La Rochefoucauld's concern is with the 'commerce particulier que les honnêtes gens doivent avoir ensemble' (p. 185).

Intersubjective values are also seen as transcending those pertaining to the individual subject in 81, one of the most complex of the *Maximes*. It begins in typical reductive fashion: 'Nous ne pouvons rien aimer que par rapport à nous, et nous ne faisons que suivre notre goût et notre plaisir quand nous préférons nos amis à nous-mêmes.' The fact that pure altruism is an impossibility does not, however, remove all value from friendship: 'c'est néanmoins par cette préférence seule que l'amitié peut être vraie et parfaite'. A taste that promotes reciprocity is thus capable of attaining the rank of an objective value, despite the impossibility of parting company with one's roots in subjectivity. It marks an escape from the self-destructive, irrational and capricious nature of taste in general. The relationship between the coquette and the old man emerges, in this light, as based on a false intersubjectivity, whereby the coquette, the subject of the taste, exploits the object of it (these are La Rochefoucauld's terms of evaluation, not mine).

The value of a taste thus appears to be related to the extent to which it furthers the collective experience of a group of like-minded people; this is consistent with Starobinski's explication of the 'substitution' of moralities in La Rochefoucauld whereby codes oriented towards the individual, whether that of orthodox morality, or the heroic 'éthique de la force', are superseded by a morality that keeps an elite group of kindred spirits in being.[8] The relationship of taste to the activities of such a group is brought out in the essay 'De la différence des esprits': 'Un bel esprit ... entre dans le goût des autres, et retranche de ses pensées ce qui est inutile ou ce qui peut déplaire' (p. 218). The old firm of *Utile* and *Dulce*, or its French subsidiary *Plaire* and *Instruire* is back in action in the last part of the sentence; what is significant, however, is that not only pleasure but utility is judged by the taste of the interlocutor rather than according to an external objective criterion. If internalizing the taste of others is part of being a *bel esprit*, by the same token, the fact that a *bel esprit* internalizes it reflects favourably on the taste and its subjects. The constitution of values is reciprocal.

It could be argued that this passage helps to throw light on 258: 'Le bon goût vient plus du jugement que de l'esprit.' I mentioned above, in connexion with the entry on *goût* in F2, where this maxim is quoted, that it appears to contradict the statement that 'le jugement n'est que la grandeur de la lumière de l'esprit' (97). As Odette de Mourgues points out, however, *esprit* is being used in different ways in these two passages: in 97, it stands for 'the sum total of our intellectual make-up'; elsewhere (340, 451, 456) it denotes 'a particular gift of mental agility, wit' (*Two French Moralists*, p. 32). In 258 the latter meaning makes far better sense. The function of *jugement*, considered as a synonym for '(la grandeur de) la lumière de l'esprit', is defined in some detail in 97: 'cette lumière pénètre le fond des choses; elle y remarque tout ce qu'il faut remarquer et aperçoit celles qui semblent imperceptibles.' It is possible, however, to go beyond this, and to ascribe to *jugement* the function of censoring the suggestions of *esprit*. Some such role seems to be implied by 456: 'On est quelquefois un sot avec de l'esprit, mais on ne l'est jamais avec du jugement.' The division of labour between *esprit* and *jugement* may be seen as paralleled in the bipartite nature of *bel esprit*. On the one hand, *bel esprit* is productive: 'Un bel esprit pense toujours noblement; il produit avec facilité des choses claires, agréables et naturelles; il les fait voir dans leur plus beau jour, et il les pare de tous les ornements qui leur conviennent' (p. 218). On the other, it contains, as we have seen, a self-censoring faculty, a capacity to anticipate other people's probable reactions, their taste. If these two aspects of *bel esprit* may be equated with *esprit*, in its restricted sense, and *jugement*, then there are plausible grounds for equating *bon goût*, considered as *esprit* regulated by *jugement*, with this ability to internalize the taste of others. This can be no more than a suggestion, based as it is on much extrapolation and on parallels for which there is no precise textual support, but it seems to follow the grain of La Rochefoucauld's argumentation.

La Rochefoucauld's most extended discussions of 'taste' in the normative sense occur in the essays 'Des goûts' and 'Du faux', to which the rest of this chapter will be devoted. The former begins 'Il y a des personnes qui ont plus d'esprit que de goût, et d'autres qui ont plus de goût que d'esprit' (p. 201), and this sets the tone for what follows. What La Rochefoucauld is doing in this essay is not just analysing the nature of *goût*, but distinguishing between various categories of *subject* of taste. The third paragraph brings this out particularly: 'Il y a des gens qui ont le goût faux en tout; d'autres ne l'ont faux qu'en de certaines choses ... D'autres ont des goûts particuliers ... Il y en a qui ont le gout incertain' (p. 202). In other words, the essay offers guidance towards the identification of individuals in respect of their taste. If 'taste' is, as we shall see, a matter of judgment, and judgment is a function of *esprit* in its larger sense, then the first sentence of the essay, on persons who have more, or less, of *goût* than of *esprit* must be using the latter term in the restricted sense we have already encountered.

When La Rochefoucauld says that 'il y a plus de variété et de caprice dans le goût que dans l'esprit', he is merely attributing to *goût* characteristics with which we have already met. Then, however, after warning against confusion between the various senses of *goût*, he proceeds to argue for the existence of two sorts of taste: 'le goût qui nous porte vers les choses, et le goût qui nous en fait connaître et discerner les qualités en s'attachant aux règles' (pp. 201–2). These have been distinguished above as 'appetitive' and 'cognitive' uses of *goût*.

Not that the distinction is self-validating. In point of fact, it is significantly imbalanced. 'Appetitive' taste, with its characteristic variety and capriciousness, appears as a completely arbitrary penchant. 'Cognitive' 'taste' is completely normative: it offers authentic knowledge of the object. In the first place, this very clear-cut distinction scarcely does justice to the complexity of some of the uses of *goût* studied above. Take the reference to the change of taste on the part of old people: 'Leur goût, détrompé des désirs inutiles, se tourne alors vers des objets muets et insensibles' (p. 225). This is clearly an inclination for a particular kind of object, and yet, as was noted, the word 'détrompé' lends it a certain cognitive quality. Even if it should be credited to pride, as a substitute for reason (see p. 224), rather than to reason itself, this taste is a rational response to a certain situation. But it does not register intrinsic relationships of value, as if building, agriculture and study were in themselves superior to an active life in society. The contrary rather is implied. The rationality, such as it is, of this taste consists in its conformity to a certain relation of appropriateness linking the subject and the object. Much the same is true of the coquette's liking for old men; presented as bizarre and incomprehensible, it is also revealed as thoroughly congruent with her 'nature' and position. Now in fact in 'Du faux' La Rochefoucauld will make this congruence between subject and object a criterion of the goodness of a 'taste'. But in 'Des goûts' cognitive 'taste' is presented as the apprehension of objective qualities irrespective of their relationship to the subject.

It could be argued that this contradiction is purely apparent. At this point in 'Des goûts', La Rochefoucauld is simply distinguishing between two meanings of the word *goût*; his business is not to describe the workings and certify the authority of this cognitive 'taste'. But the semantic distinction between two meanings of *goût* is here overlaid by another, evaluative, distinction, between good and bad 'taste'. La Rochefoucauld in fact reproduces the instability of the dictionary definitions of *goût* as a *discernement*. The semantic distinction registers the linguistic fact that *goût* is used in two ways, to denote both an inclination towards a particular object and a capacity to make judgments of value. But this capacity may become the object of a judgment of the kind 'X has good/bad "taste"'. La Rochefoucauld collapses these two stages into one: he identifies the faculty of making judgments in general (which does not postulate a qualified or privileged subject) with that of making *correct* judgments (which does). *Within the terms of the definition*, there is no medium term between correct knowledge of the object and mere inclination towards objects. This is not the case in the rest of 'Des goûts' and in 'Du faux'. There La Rochefoucauld frequently uses *goût* to refer to false judgments, as well as valid ones. But what this shows is that the supposedly cognitive variety of *goût* can in fact offer a pseudo-knowledge of the object just as well as authentic knowledge. It thus forfeits the intrinsically normative and self-validating capacity with which La Rochefoucauld's definition endows it. The force of the definition, however, remains: it serves to relegate any 'taste' which is deemed not to correspond to the model of objective knowledge to the status of a mere inclination or appetite.

All this might be true, yet it does not prove that La Rochefoucauld's basic position – that certain 'tastes' are objectively sound – is untenable. Even if 'taste' does not carry its own authenticating criteria around with it, so that one can think one is exercising a correct discernment when this is not in fact the case, it does not follow that no authenticating criteria exist. La Rochefoucauld seeks to provide them partly by attaching the notion of 'good taste' to the possibility of recognizing different qualitative categories of subject. Much of 'Des goûts', as I have said, is taken up with precisely this kind of classification.

But it can be found elsewhere as well. Take 105: 'Celui-là n'est pas raisonnable à qui le hasard fait trouver la raison, mais celui qui la connaît, qui la discerne, et qui la goûte.' As E. D. James points out, we have here 'the objective discernment of what is in accord with the reason' (p. 351). But we have something else too: a distinction between subjects according to the quality of their reason. Although this follows naturally from what appears to be La Rochefoucauld's basic point about rationality, it is not inseparable from it. The maxim might have been differently phrased to read something like 'Pour être raisonnable il ne suffit pas de trouver la raison par hasard: il faut la connaître, la discerner, et la goûter.' I daresay this lacks some of the stylistic snap of La Rochefoucauld's maxim. But stylistic considerations are not the only ones relevant. The antithesis between subjects ('celui-là', 'celui qui …') is present in the earliest extant forms of the maxim, in the Liancourt manuscript (where it was number 63), the Smith-Lesouëf copy of 1663 (number 68), and the Holland edition (number 23). It is not just a way of making the point, it is actually part of the point. The supposedly equivalent form I have proposed alludes to a universal order of reason and to a single representative subject who may coincide with it by accident but should assimilate it consciously and deliberately. La Rochefoucauld postulates two subjects, although their roles may be fulfilled by a single individual, one adventitiously rational, the other fully so, and a third besides these to distinguish between them. In other words, the maxim as it stands possesses a discursive force absent from its suppositious equivalent: it represents knowledge as an intersubjective process.

La Rochefoucauld's formulation of the distinction between two senses of *goût* is thus far from transparent. First of all, it does not seem to cover his own use of the word, the complexity of which belies the trimness of the definitions. Secondly, by the very rigidity of the distinction between correct knowledge of the object and blind inclination towards it, it excludes rational argument about tastes, for reason, by definition, must be on one side of the argument only. It is not that La Rochefoucauld is talking about an ideal of correct judgment to which reality never corresponds, for he specifically goes on to say that some people do possess 'good taste', albeit perhaps only in certain spheres; and in 'Du vrai' he holds out the possibility of knowing the qualities of objects by measuring them against the ideal of the category to which they belong. The idea of 'taste', then, becomes inseparable from that of an authoritative group of people in whom the ideal is more or less realized. The problem then is to identify them, failing which our own social practice is liable to be vitiated by the failure to 'enter into' the 'taste' of the right people.

In the taxonomy, one might almost say the pathology, of tastes that follows the distinction between the two meanings of *goût*, La Rochefoucauld mixes the two senses more or less indiscriminately. 'Il y a des gens qui ont le goût faux en tout; d'autres ne l'ont faux qu'en de certaines choses, et ils l'ont droit et juste dans ce qui est de leur portée': here *goût* is plainly used as a synonym for 'discernment', but the sentence is surrounded by others using *goût* in the sense of 'inclination': 'Il y a des goûts qui nous approchent imperceptiblement de ce qui se montre à nous; d'autres nous entraînent par leur force ou par leur durée', and 'D'autres ont des goûts particuliers, qu'ils connaissent mauvais, et ne laissent pas de les suivre' (p. 202).

Eventually, we come upon a category of people whose 'taste' is definitely good: 'Il y en a qui sont sensibles à ce qui est bon, et choqués de ce qui ne l'est pas; leurs vues sont nettes et justes, et ils trouvent la raison de leur goût dans leur esprit et dans leur discernement' (p. 202). In this case, an affective reaction ('sensibles', 'choqués') precedes, not only in the order of words, but apparently also in the order of things, the formulation of an intellectual reaction. La Rochefoucauld had earlier asserted the separability of taste-as-inclination from 'taste'-as-discernment: one may like plays without having the 'taste' to judge of them correctly, or one may have the 'taste' but not happen to like plays. In practice, however, he seems to accept that inclination and discernment are linked. But although these people's 'taste' is accepted as valid, the word *goût* here refers to the inclination rather than the discernment: the preference is already formed when discernment steps in to provide reasons. Pascal, incidentally, seems to cast doubt on the authenticity of this reasoning process:

M. de Roannez disait: 'Les raisons me viennent après, mais abord la chose m'agrée ou me choque sans en savoir la raison, et cependant cela me choque par cette raison que je ne découvre qu'ensuite.' Mais je crois, non pas que cela choquait par ces raisons qu'on trouve après, mais qu'on ne trouve ces raisons que parce que cela choque. (*Pensées*, 983)

The implication is of course that these reasons are more in the nature of rationalizations.

As I have said, La Rochefoucauld harnesses the abstract value of 'good taste' to a category of concrete subjects. Here he does more: he constitutes a group of subjects in sole ownership of certain intellectual properties. It is not general human intellectual capacities that furnish them with the reasons that justify their 'taste': it is rather that their individual *esprit* and *discernement* are represented as being in harmony with objective values of good and bad ('ce qui est bon', 'ce qui ne l'est pas'). La Rochefoucauld is not saying that any taste that can appeal to reason is good, which would leave room for rational disagreement about tastes. Rather, only those 'tastes' that conform to the standards alluded to in the term 'good' are allowed to claim an intellectual foundation. The assertion of objective standards, because they are deemed recognizable only by certain individuals, serves here to reinforce the distinct and superior nature of a particular category of subjects of 'taste'. What is more, insofar as these values are objective, they provide a quasi-metaphysical foundation for the unity of the members of that category: harmoniously linked to what is objectively good, they are harmoniously linked to one another.

But this is not the only kind of 'good taste':

Il y en a qui, par une sorte d'instinct dont ils ignorent la cause, décident de ce qui se présente à eux, et prennent toujours le bon parti. Ceux-ci font paraître plus de goût que d'esprit, parce que leur amour-propre et leur humeur ne prévalent point sur leurs lumières naturelles; tout agit de concert en eux, tout y est sur un même ton. Cet accord les fait juger sainement des objets, et leur en forme une idée véritable.   (p. 202)

These people are said to display more 'taste' than *esprit* presumably because their 'taste' can dispense with rational backing: it springs naturally from the total consistency of their personality and persona. This quality, like the *esprit* and *discernement* in which another category of subjects find the reason for their 'taste', is, it would seem, a purely personal prerogative. It does not seem possible to acquire it in any way. However, it looks as if La Rochefoucauld associates it with independence from the 'taste' of other people, because he goes on to say that 'il y a peu de gens qui aient le goût fixe et indépendant de celui des autres; ils suivent l'exemple et la coutume, et ils en empruntent presque tout ce qu'ils ont de goût' (p. 202). In 'Du faux' he does lay down principles for acquiring independent 'taste', which, if followed, doubtless help to produce this harmonious personality. But the stress on independence in the formation of one's 'taste' seems to clash with the earlier insistence on the incorporation of other people's 'taste'-reactions into one's own thinking. The contradiction can none the less be reconciled if we suppose, as seemed plausible, that only the 'taste' of people with recognizably good 'taste' should be internalized. This has the effect, like the restricted ownership of true *esprit* and *discernement*, of keeping cultural values circulating within self-consciously elite groups, secure in their distinctive possession of 'taste', *esprit*, and so on.

'Des goûts' concludes with the familiar assertion of the rarity of 'cette sorte de bon goût qui sait donner le prix à chaque chose, qui en connaît toute la valeur, et qui se porte généralement sur tout' (pp. 202–3). But this is not simply taken for granted: La Rochefoucauld ties it in with his general thinking about the human personality. Good taste is so hard to attain because 'nos connaissances sont trop bornées' (compare 106), and because 'cette juste disposition des qualités qui font bien juger ne se maintient d'ordinaire que sur ce qui ne nous regarde pas directement' (p. 203). Good taste suddenly emerges, not as the inalienable possession of a privileged few, but as an unstable arrangement of qualities that fall apart as soon as we become directly involved: 'Quand il s'agit de nous, notre goût n'a plus cette justesse si necessaire, la préocupation la trouble, tout ce qui a du rapport à nous nous parait sous une autre figure' (p. 203). And now there appears to be no exemption either for the discerning few whose 'vues' are 'nettes et justes' or for the lucky minority whose 'lumières naturelles' are not quenched by *amour-propre* and *humeur*;

> Personne ne voit des mêmes yeux ce qui le touche et ce qui ne le touche pas; notre goût est conduit alors par la pente de l'amour-propre et de l'humeur, qui nous fournissent des vues nouvelles, et nous assujettissent à un nombre infini de changements et d'incertitudes; notre goût n'est plus à nous, nous n'en disposons plus, il change sans notre consentement, et les mêmes objets nous paraissent par tant de côtés différents que nous méconnaissons enfin ce que nous avons vu et ce que nous avons senti.   (p. 203)

It is clear that this radical scepticism is hard to reconcile with the confident normative statements of the preceding sections of the essay. The discontinuity is mirrored in a linguistic shift. The authoritative distribution of subjects of taste into a series of separate categories, conveyed by a string of statements using or postulating the third-person pronoun *ils* is dissolved into an all-encompassing discourse of the first-person *nous*, whose universal implications run counter to the segregative and exclusive discourse of the third person. But this shift parallels a modification in the nature of the object. Earlier in the reflection, the object was a solid aggregate of qualities, which a certain kind of 'taste' could 'connaître et discerner'. Now its appearance changes with a bewildering rapidity, and its successive aspects cannot even be held together by the memory. In the last paragraph of 'Des goûts' the hijacking of 'taste' by *amour-propre* recalls some of the most radical insights of MS 1, the screen it erects between the subject and the 'thing-in-itself': 'c'est par lui-même [amour-propre] que ses désirs sont allumés, plutôt que par la beauté et par le mérite de ses objets; ... son goût est le prix qui les relève et le fard qui les embellit' (pp. 134–5). The 'value' of the object is no longer to be read off by 'good taste' (which supposedly 'sait donner le prix à chaque chose', p. 202), it is a mere projection by the 'taste' of *amour-propre*.

It is true that the sceptical and destructive implications of this final paragraph of 'Des goûts' do not completely subvert the notion of objective good taste. We can still judge correctly, it would seem, when not personally involved with things. But, firstly, as 3 suggests, the activity of *amour-propre* is never wholly present to consciousness. Secondly, 'nous ne pouvons rien aimer que par rapport à nous' (81); but 'tout ce qui a du rapport à nous nous paraît sous une autre figure' (p. 203). Consequently, there is no judging correctly of anything we like, because then there is no direct access to the essential object. Of course, 'on peut avoir le goût assez bon pour bien juger de la comédie sans l'aimer' (p. 202). As long as we don't like anything, we can make correct judgments about it. But who wants to? Thirdly, as 'Du faux' will show, the subject is always implicated in his or her tastes, which are therefore always already distorted. It looks as if the normative discourse of 'taste' will not survive the corrosive influence of *amour-propre*.

But there are conditions, not mentioned in 'Des goûts', in which the position of the subject and the nature of the object are so firmly established as to make possible correct 'taste'-judgments. This is the theme of 'Du faux'. This essay falls into the same pattern as 'Des goûts': a pathology of *fausseté* is combined with a series of normative pronouncements. 'Il y en a dont l'esprit est droit, et le goût faux', says La Rochefoucauld (p. 208), ratifying the autonomy of 'taste' from *esprit*, confirming that it is not rationality that makes a 'taste' good, even though certain people can back up their 'good taste' with reasons. Those who have 'l'esprit faux, ... et quelque droiture dans le goût' (p. 208) are presumably akin to those mentioned in 'Des goûts' whose integrated personality enabled them to judge correctly without recourse to a reasoning process.

Fausseté, however, is virtually universal, because 'nos qualités sont incertaines et confuses, et ... nos vues le sont aussi' (p. 208). (Truchet glosses *qualité* as 'disposition, tendance', p. 644.) Both our cognitive and our evaluative faculties are found wanting: 'on ne voit point les choses précisément comme elles sont, on les estime plus ou moins qu'elles ne valent' (p. 208). But it is not simply the object we fail to apprehend but our relationship to it: the sentence continues 'et on ne les fait point rapporter à nous en la manière qui leur convient, et qui convient à notre état et à nos qualités' (p. 208). This is the first attempt made by La Rochefoucauld to define the subject of 'taste' otherwise than by reference to his or her intellectual and affective make-up. The subject is now additionally constituted by a character and a social position. *Amour-propre* is promiscuous, attracted to any apparent good; we pursue objects out of vanity or temperamental inclination, out of custom or convenience, or simply because other people pursue them, 'sans considérer qu'un même sentiment ne doit pas être également embrassé par toute sorte de personnes, et qu'on s'y doit attacher plus ou moins fortement selon qu'il convient plus ou moins à ceux qui le suivent' (p. 208). The bases of this kind of *convenance* have been hinted at already; they will emerge more clearly in a minute. La Rochefoucauld implicitly acknowledges the connexion between 'taste' and *honnêteté*: 'Les honnêtes gens doivent approuver sans prévention ce qui mérite d'être approuvé, suivre ce qui mérite d'être suivi' (p. 208). But the judgment of 'taste' takes place on two levels: 'Il faut savoir discerner ce qui est bon en général, et ce qui nous est propre' (p. 208). In other words, through this act of discernment one recognizes oneself as a subject, as endowed with rights and duties in virtue of one's identity. This identity is partly naturally, partly socially constituted:

Si les hommes ne voulaient exceller que par leurs propres talents et en suivant leurs devoirs, il n'y aurait rien de faux dans leur goût et dans leur conduite; ils se montreraient tels qu'ils sont; ils jugeraient des choses par leurs lumières, et s'y attacheraient par raison; il y aurait de la proportion dans leurs vues et dans leurs sentiments; leur goût serait vrai, il viendrait d'eux et non pas des autres, et ils le suivraient par choix, et non pas par coutume ou par hasard.

(pp. 208–9)

Access to the objective values of reason and 'taste' thus comes via the recognition of oneself as subject to duties and to a code that ties certain objects to certain personal qualities.

The first-stage error of 'taste' is to approve what should not be approved, or vice versa. The second-stage error is to attempt 'se faire valoir par des qualités qui sont bonnes de soi, mais qui ne nous conviennent pas' (p. 209). The consonance between a subject and a quality is not worked out on a purely individual level: it is determined by the ideological code that assigns certain qualities to a particular gender or social position. This is clear from such examples as: 'un magistrat est faux quand il se pique d'être brave, quoi qu'il puisse être hardi dans de certaines recontres'; he may, indeed should, display the courage appropriate to a magistrate, namely firmness when it comes to repressing the turbulent masses, but 'il serait faux et ridicule de se battre en duel' (p. 209), since that kind of courage, which is what *brave* refers to, is proper only to noblemen.

'Taste' here supplements the juridical order, for until the suppression of duelling by Louis XIV, following in the footsteps of Richelieu, the duel had been regarded as a privilege of the *gentilhomme*.[9] Likewise, 'une femme peut aimer les sciences, mais toutes les sciences ne lui conviennent pas toujours, et l'entêtement de certaines sciences ne lui convient jamais, et est toujours faux' (p. 209). Like Clitandre's famous or notorious speech in *Les Femmes savantes* (I, iii, 218–26), although not to the same extent, this utterance seeks to validate itself by loading its terms: of course *entêtement* is undesirable, because it is 'excessive'; it all depends, though, on who places the dividing-line between an acceptable interest and an *entêtement*. And does La Rochefoucauld mean to suggest that 'l'entêtement de certaines sciences' is all right for a certain category of man? The whole utterance generates a beautiful double-bind by its very vagueness: the woman is told 'You may study the sciences, but you may not, because you are a woman, study certain ones.' If the woman responds by asking 'Which ones?', she immediately characterizes her 'taste', and her identity as a woman, as false, because her sense of 'being a woman' should have told her in advance which sciences are unsuitable for her. Better, then, to lay off the sciences altogether, except for those which 'by common consent' are compatible with femininity.

The last substantive paragraph of 'Du faux', followed only by a discussion of the ways in which kings can belie their status, links the values of *raison* and *bon sens* – by which, according to La Rochefoucauld, our 'taste' should be determined – to this double recognition of the value of the object in itself and of our proper relationship to it; in practice, however, few people live up to this standard (p. 209).

We saw in 'Des goûts' that certain 'tastes' had a rational basis, perceptible, however, not to intelligence in general (since one may be intelligent and have bad taste) but to the intelligence of a select few. In the penultimate paragraph of 'Du faux', La Rochefoucauld similarly attaches reason and good sense, by which our 'taste', he says, should be directed, to the double recognition of the value of the object in itself and of our proper relationship to it, as determined by ideology. The few with 'good taste' in its rational variety are thus identified as perfectly conversant with the codes that associate their social position with particular judgments and attributes. As for those with instinctive 'taste', they are even more blessed; nature itself has, it would seem, endowed them with the capacity to perceive immediately and painlessly whatever is appropriate to their individual qualities and social position.

La Rochefoucauld, therefore, has done what he was required to do: namely, provide some kind of criterion for distinguishing correct 'taste' from misjudgment or mere inclination. 'Good taste' is supported by the values of reason, good sense, intelligence, and discernment. But they themselves are abstract categories like 'taste': how are they to be recognized in actual experience? Firstly, through the recognition of authoritative subjects who are presumed to embody them. But on what ground? In the last analysis, their perfect conformity to the codes whose multiple and simultaneous operation serves to produce the subject in a variety of mutually reinforcing forms. The point is not simply the commonsense one that we should foster our real abilities and not waste too much time on activities we have no natural talent for. Individual abilities and propensities (*qualités*) are only part of the question. Such 'qualities' are themselves largely produced by discourse, and are inserted into class-differentiated ideological schemas. Take the case of courage. As 215 shows, this is partly an individual, even a physical quality; it takes different forms in different people, most of which involve some kind of shortcoming. But to call someone *brave* in this context is not akin to saying that he has red hair. It has specific implications: not, for instance, that he would shin up an Alp with perfect sang-froid, an activity that the seventeenth century would have looked on as silly. It implies that he will in certain circumstances behave as a nobleman is called upon to do by the code of his class: if insulted, for instance, he will demand satisfaction. It is for this reason that, as we have seen, a magistrate cannot be *brave*, because then he would be behaving like a nobleman: he would be ridiculous, 'false'. 'Taste' governs the whole of life, and life is the living-out of one's class- and intra-class position, and the position imposed by one's gender, according to the schemas which associate it with particular values and practices. These schemas and the social structure they serve to reproduce and validate are take for granted by La Rochefoucauld, and from his point of view they offer a crucial advantage: they serve as a defence against the ravages of *amour-propre*. If one has well and truly identified oneself as a subject, limited to a certain space of legitimate desire, the risk of wrongly identifying a particular object as good because it appeals to one's *amour-propre* is much diminished. To see oneself as a subject is to see oneself in a certain relationship to other people; and if this is correctly envisaged, one is less likely to be led astray by others' example. On the one hand, one is better prepared to enter into the taste of those people whose reactions are recognizably worth consulting. La Rochefoucauld's discourse of 'taste' reinforces the small circle of choice spirits at the same time as the larger-scale ideological structures of class and gender.

'Il ne se soucie que d'être', says La Rochefoucauld of *amour-propre*; '... dans le meme temps qu'il se ruine en un endroit, il se rétablit en un autre' (MS 1, p. 135). It is curious how, in this respect, *amour-propre* resembles the ideology of a class: in particular, that of La Rochefoucauld's own class, the nobility of the *ancien régime*. Ruined, apparently, by the encroachments of the central power, deprived of their political function, but retaining their socio-economic base in the seigneurial system, they re-established themselves as a hegemonic cultural group, dispensing standards for themselves and other groups – standards which helped to enforce the acceptance of their own authority. Among these, 'taste', as defined by La Rochefoucauld, plays the vital role of inducing the individual to recognize himself or herself as bound, and rightly bound, by the codes that help to preserve each class as a separate identifiable entity with its proper position in the social hierarchy.

6

LA BRUYÈRE: TASTE-DISCOURSE
AND THE ABSENT SUBJECT

The text of *Les Caractères* builds into itself problems of its own reception, which are partly problems of placing it within its culture (or for that matter, ours): 'Si on ne goûte point ces *Caractères*, je m'en étonne; et si on les goûte, je m'en étonne de même' ('Des esprits forts', 50). This coda to the work takes up a theme already set out at the beginning of the text (or before the beginning of the text proper) in the 'Discours sur Théophraste'.[1] The problem there investigated lies both with the kind of text involved and with its potential audience. It would be better to speak of 'audiences', for , La Bruyère notes, there are many different kinds of reader: some read to satisfy their imagination, others to form their judgment; some look for demonstrative reasoning, others for delicate allusions. Then again there is a special problem facing works that take man himself as their object: a problem presented by La Bruyère first and foremost in terms of a contradiction between scholarly and *mondain* cultures. The scholarly vice is complete inattention to the contemporary world, while those who observe that world most closely – 'les femmes, ... les gens de la cour, et tous ceux qui n'ont que beaucoup d'esprit sans érudition' (p. 3) – pay no attention to anything else: they are ignorant of history and cannot even respond to the preaching of the Gospel. In other words, a text addressed to them can only with difficulty mobilize traditional moral concepts and examples.

Again, from a court position, the city is in effect invisible (because beneath notice) and therefore unrepresentable; while the court cannot be represented from outside ('il faut même y avoir vécu pour le connaître'), and must in any case be represented 'avec les ménagements qui lui sont dus' (p. 4), which means that it cannot be accurately portrayed for outsiders. The problem, then, is finding a place from which to speak and a public to address. And this situation is aggravated by problems of moral discourse as such: it is not so much that, as Swift put it, 'Satire is a sort of glass, wherein beholders do generally discover everybody's face but their own'; rather that 'il est naturel aux hommes

141

de ne point convenir de la beauté ou de la délicatesse d'un trait de morale qui les peint, qui les désigne, et où ils se reconnaissent eux-mêmes' (p. 4). Classical literary theory holds that aesthetic gratification reinforces the apprehension of truth; but here the aesthetic response emerges as an alibi for fallen human nature's resistance to the truth.

Secondly, moral discourse falls into a variety of genres, systematic inventories of the vices and virtues on the one hand, and the analysis of the passions, usually explained with reference to bodily processes, on the other (pp. 4–5). La Bruyère identifies Theophrastus with a third option: the moral and physical principles so often expounded by ancients and moderns alike can be taken for granted, and the surest path to the goal of moral writing – which is the reform of morals – is to apply these principles to the contemporary world, so as to exhibit the moral implications of behaviour open to common observation (p. 5).

This kind of moral discourse is not only the most efficacious: it seems (although La Bruyère does not actually make this point) to offer a possibility of reconciling the conflicting cultural demands of scholars and *le monde*; it gratifies the *mondain* appetite for close observation of the contemporary world, but it relates that observation to an inheritance of truth of which scholars are the custodians. Yet the status of La Bruyère's enterprise remains problematic: he is introducing a set of 'Characters' from antiquity that itself introduces a collection of modern 'Caractères'. As defined by La Bruyère, 'characteristic' moral discourse requires immediacy – it deals in 'images ... familières' (p. 5). Yet – as La Bruyère knows very well – Theophrastus's representation of characters is ancient and alien. To ward off the threat of its rejection as unreadable, he has to insist on the relativity and historical variability of *manners*, while insisting on the unchangeability of 'le cœur et ... les passions' (p. 13). There is a double implication here: reading Theophrastus, one can reabsorb this lesson of human moral immutability beneath the appearance of difference; equally, one learns to recognize difference as intrinsic to history, as there at the heart of one's own historical world: 'Nous, qui sommes si modernes, serons anciens dans quelques siècles' (p. 11). In other words, part of the enterprise of *Les Caractères* is the demonstration to the world of France under Louis XIV (which one is tempted to write in a single word, *à la* Queneau) of its own difference; and the questioning of its own identity in such passages (rightly seen as pre-echoing Montesquieu and Voltaire) as 'De la cour', 74, or 'De la ville', 19. Evidently, this relativism has its ideological limitations, though in a sense it would be fair to say that it is less hampered than *enabled* by the assertion of human moral unchangeability, and the related assumption of unchanging religious truths. These mutually reinforcing textual elements cannot, however, always be kept from undermining each other: it is almost impossible, given the presence in the text of defamiliarizing strategies, *not* to read 'Des esprits forts', 29, as a defamiliarizing, relativizing text – which it patently is not meant to be. None the less, it is this simultaneous affirmation of unchanging human nature and changing human manners that gives *Les Caractères* much of its ideological character.

But 'taste' is also one of the objects of the discourse of *Les Caractères*. And just as the text as a whole is negotiating problems of placing itself within its culture, of reconciling its *mondain* and its *savant* affiliations, it also faces the related problem of placing 'taste' somewhere in its world of morals and manners.

La Bruyère's *Caractères* has been called 'la bible de l'honnête homme'.[2] But while a code of *honnêteté* can be reconstructed from it, while it presupposes certain of the values of *honnêteté*, it is in no sense a formal and exhaustive treatise on the subject. The powerful discursive articulation between *goût* and *honnêteté* plays no overt part in La Bruyère's text, although doubtless, if asked, he would have accepted their congruence. Without an explicit commitment to *honnêteté*, there can be no explicit commitment to a discourse of *goût* of the type of Méré's or Saint-Evremond's. *Les Caractères*, and the discourse of *goût* it contains, belong to a different discursive and ideological formation.

This is apparent in two respects. Firstly, in La Bruyère, 'good taste' has a privileged and limited sphere of action: that of the 'arts' and, more specifically, the literary. These certainly come within the scope of Méré's or Saint-Evremond's notion of taste, yet they are not coextensive with it. 'Taste', for these writers, had a whole realm of social intercourse for its domain. It was concerned with the 'art of pleasing' individuals (in practice, members of a certain class) in an infinity of possible ways. In this sense, 'good taste' for La Bruyère is something more limited than it is for Méré or Saint-Evremond.

Yet in another way the role of *goût* in his discourse is more extensive. There is a simple reason for this. Méré's discourse of taste is essentially one of 'good' and 'bad' taste. As I have tried to show, the distinctions he makes between what is good and what is bad inherently involve class criteria. In La Bruyère, the use of *goût* to denote a simple, apparently neutral, preference, occurs far more often and is far more significant than in Méré. Such preferences are linked, indeed, with social categories in such a way as to take on a positive or negative value-charge. But the process is less obtrusive than in Méré. La Bruyère is interested in socially placing and in thereby evaluating specific tastes. But in doing so he is less concerned to construct a notion of 'good taste' by a kind of *via negativa* than to affirm a full range of social, moral, and even religious values within which 'good taste' plays a relatively subordinate role. Its marginality indeed corresponds to the limitation noted above by which 'taste' comes to be associated with a determinate sphere of social practice: the 'arts'.

All this could be put another way. La Bruyère's authorial stance is to a significant extent removed from what he is observing, so that much of what he says appears disinterested. This applies to his use of *goût*: the point is (apparently) to observe, and take pleasure if possible in observing, a wide variety of tastes; whereas a more involved subject such as Méré (self-styled paragon of *honnêteté*) is committed inescapably to evaluating them.[3] There is also the complicating factor of La Bruyère's irony, which often makes it difficult to be sure, at first reading, whether a given taste is to be approved or condemned. What this means is that the function of *goût* in La Bruyère's discourse of values cannot be adequately treated on the basis of texts where *goût* appears in the sense of '(the faculty of) "good taste"'. It is also necessary to examine the more subtle relationships between preferences (*goûts*) of all kinds and the general discourse of values.

It is, first of all, worth looking at the texts concerned with the literal sense of 'taste' as a physical response, especially because *goût* in these utterances can operate according to discursive patterns similar to those exhibited by utterances using *goût* in its figurative sense. 'Des biens de fortune', 25, uses *goût* in the sense of 'palate': in kitchens, 'l'on voit réduit en art et en méthode le secret de flatter votre goût'. Here 'flatter' and the intimacy established by 'votre' themselves flatter the reader: much trouble is taken on his behalf (the creation of a whole culinary science); he is a gourmet capable of relishing his food. *Goût* here is associated with euphoria, a sensation La Bruyère proceeds to deflate by revealing, in rather materialist fashion, the sordid conditions of its production. In 'De la cour', 74, the young courtiers have lost all their pleasure in wine through over-indulgence; they turn to spirits to 'réveiller leur goût déjà éteint'. The reader is invited to prize his or her taste-sensations, the better to appreciate how low these sybarites have sunk. In the portrait of Cliton the epicure ('De l'homme', 122), we read that 'il n'est guère permis d'avoir du goût pour ce qu'il désapprouve'; he is 'l'arbitre des bons morceaux', in virtue of his 'palais sûr'. 'Good taste' is here presented as objectionably authoritative. In 'De la mode', 1, the subjection of *goût*, among other things, to fashion is a proof of man's pettiness. Fashion determines actual taste-sensations as well as taste-discourses: 'La viande noire est hors de mode, et par cette raison insipide.'[4]

In connexion with food and drink, then, the position of 'taste' is equivocal. It is accepted as an established value, but its authority tends to shade into tyranny. This suspicion weakens the connexion between 'taste' and the total social practice of a privileged social group, so evident in Méré and Saint-Evremond; to that extent, it weakens the discourse of taste as a whole by violating its integrity. Coming now to the figurative uses of *goût*, I shall begin with the two most explicitly devoted to the notion of 'good taste'. 'Il y a dans l'art', says La Bruyère in 'Des ouvrages de l'esprit', 10, 'un point de perfection, comme de bonté ou de maturité dans la nature. Celui qui le sent et qui l'aime a le goût parfait; celui qui ne le sent pas, et qui aime en deçà ou au delà, a le goût defecteueux. Il y a donc un bon et un mauvais goût, et l'on dispute des goûts avec fondement.' The analogy between art and nature, a familiar one, is voiced here gratuitously, and somewhat questionably. What constitutes 'art' as such is precisely its difference, as a human transforming process, from nature. It is not clear to what extent values can be simply translated from one level to the other.

The two realms, of course, appear to have in common the fact that both can be 'tasted', one literally, the other figuratively. But the figural displacement is precisely what La Bruyère is seeking to validate here. In other words, his establishment of the notion of 'good taste' depends on the prior assumption that reading, say, is as natural a process as gathering berries was for primitive man; on acceptance, that is, of the presuppositions of the discourse of taste. The resolution of the acknowledged problem of justifying one's taste is thus achieved purely on the figural level.

More than that, it is arguably a pseudo-resolution. La Bruyère does not attempt to locate 'good taste' with respect to some psychical economy of faculties: reason, *sentiment*, *esprit*, and so forth. What determines a taste as good is not where it comes from in the mind, but, apparently, the nature, good or bad, the degree of 'perfection', of its object. This is a problematic attitude. It conflates two positions:

1. Bananas (say) undergo a transformation from green to ripe to squishy.

2. It is better (or more rational, or what have you) to like ripe bananas.

But (2) does not by any means follow from (1). It may be that most people do not like green bananas. But a preference for them cannot be disputed or refuted, as, according to La Bruyère, tastes can be. Of course, one may well experience one's response to bananas on a scale of maturity: I may like green bananas in general, but find this one too green. The point is that one's own response is an adequate and indisputable guide here. Let us apply the analogy, in a plausible form, to poetry. Let us say that poetry can be too 'prosaic' or too 'ornate' (Crabbe on the one hand, Góngora on the other?). Somewhere in between we find 'perfection'. But, leaving aside the question of whether it could be *rational* to sacrifice Crabbe and Góngora, it remains the case that 'perfection' is subjectively determined within certain discourses. A given poem, say, Johnson's elegy on the death of Robert Levet, may be pronounced too 'ornate' (in virtue of its eighteenth-century stylistic traits) by a Wordsworthian, while to a partisan of the Metaphysicals it may appear 'prosaic'. For a third person, it will be 'perfect'. The scale operates in all three cases; it is the placing on it that remains problematic. And it is this placing that, on the basis of his analogy, La Bruyère seeks to establish as objective.

If the determination of 'perfection' is subjective, this doesn't necessarily mean it is arbitrary. The arbitrary can be excluded in two ways: one, by valorizing the taste of certain subjects above that of others; two, by allowing certain other values to determine what shall count as perfection. Frain du Tremblay saw this well. As he says, what constitutes a taste as 'good' is the worth of the person who holds it. And this is in turn determined by other values (for Du Tremblay explicitly religious ones), which are taken for granted.[5] We shall find this latter procedure in La Bruyère; indeed, in this very *remarque*, if interpreted in an alternative fashion. What counts for the moment is his exclusion, from this passage, of the subject of 'taste'. This object-oriented discourse of (rational, disputable) 'taste' bears, in the instability pointed to above, the mark of the absence of the (value-bearing) subject.

In the alternative reading of this passage (which by no means excludes the one just discussed), the analogy between culture and nature concerns not only values but processes. Cultures rise and decline: the products of one stage in the process are valued over those of another, Virgil over both Ennius and Claudian. Should we understand the *point de perfection* in these terms? Admittedly, the problem of identifying the apogee of a given culture is, like the subject, elided from La Bruyère's text. But this is where the second procedure, the constitution of 'taste' by other cultural values, may come into play. A certain historical doxa provides the necessary supplement. The age of Augustus and the *siècle de Louis XIV* salute each other respectfully across the centuries. The works of Virgil, Horace, Ovid and Livy outshine those of earlier or later Latin writers, as those of Louis XIV's time excel those of all earlier French literature – as 'good taste' would tell you.

This pattern of response is not 'in' La Bruyère. It is one, however, that his text might activate. (It is present, for example, in Bouhours: 'good taste' involves a preference for recent French, and for classical, literature above that of Italy and Spain, and for the Latin Golden Age above the Silver.)[6] Moreover, there is an ideological stake in the identification of the *point de perfection*. Ludovician neo-Augustanism acts as a prop of the regime; significantly, the exiled and critical Saint-Evremond saw the late Republic as marking the true apex of Latin literature, and the works of Augustus's reign as already degenerate.[7] La Bruyère does not make his position clear here. None the less, if the *point de perfection* is temporally constituted, as a rigorous reading of the analogy would imply, then this passage points to the ideological discourse of the Ludovician cultural version of history; it unquestionably leaves it in place. It has to be said that La Bruyère's comments on individual writers in 'Des ouvrages de l'esprit', 37–45, and on linguistic and cultural evolution in 'Des ouvrages de l'esprit', 60, and 'De quelques usages', 73, reveal, alongside a certain teleologism, an awareness of the eccentricities of cultural time: on the one hand, 'Ronsard et les auteurs ses contemporains ont plus nui au style qu'ils ne lui ont servi: ils l'ont retardé dans le chemin de la perfection' ('Des ouvrages de l'esprit', 42); on the other, 'Marot, par son tour et par son style, semble avoir écrit depuis Ronsard' (ibid., 41). In 'De quelques usages', 73, he criticizes facile comparisons between pieces of writing from different periods. I am not, then, arguing that he crudely attaches 'good taste' to the Ludovician ideology, merely that he leaves room for this association to be made. What 'Des ouvrages de l'esprit', 10, reveals, on either interpretation or both, is a lacuna in the discourse of good taste, a need for authorization from elsewhere – from the privileged subject or from a specific – generally accepted – view of history.

The second of La Bruyère's texts devoted to 'good taste' in general is 'Des jugements', 56. This, like the fragment just before it or 'Des femmes', 24, shows La Bruyère attempting to tidy up, or to impose a particular pattern on, a complex linguistic or conceptual area. The key terms of the discourse, placed by their shared position on an equal footing, are *esprit* and *bon sens*. The other terms, *talent* and *goût*, are defined in relation to them, in terms either quantitative ('entre esprit et talent il y a la proportion du tout à sa partie') or causal ('entre le bon sens et le bon goût il y a la différence de la cause à son effet').

After the general statements, La Bruyère proceeds to reflect on the apparent paradox that great abilities in one domain confer no all-round advantage in life. He seems unwilling to accord the title of 'homme d'esprit' to the fine musician, for instance, who is a perfect nonentity when not actually performing. This is probably what he has in mind in making *talent* simply a part of *esprit*. No such limitation seems to apply to *bon goût*. It is simply *bon sens* in action, not restricted, on this showing, to any single category of objects. It is thus more comprehensive than *talent*; more unitary, too, than *esprit*. The *bon sens/bon goût* axis is not riven by any of the mysteries, even scandals, that linger round *esprit*: why should a clever man be a fool at cards, and an imbecile so skilful? how can a brilliant writer perform so wretchedly in conversation? 'Taste' is unproblematic: once placed in relation to *bon sens*, there is nothing more to say about it, and the rest of the passage is devoted to *esprit*. The greater discursive security of 'taste' reflects and ratifies that of the consumer (the consumer class). Cultural production is a more enigmatic affair, left to people who may be totally incompetent at life in general. Not that *esprit* is solely concerned with productive cultural activity: the passage also mentions participation (playing cards). None the less, music and writing bulk large in it. Significantly, their practice does not entail the possession of taste — a distinguished writer (evidently Corneille) 'ne juge de la bonté de sa pièce que par l'argent qui lui en revient'. The passage, then, registers the gap between the subject of taste and the producer of cultural objects, and privileges the former, the *honnête homme*, as the more complete individual, above the latter.

I noted that La Bruyère excludes the subject from his discourse of taste in 'Des ouvrages de l'esprit', 10. None the less, he often uses *goût* with a subjective dimension, to denote a personal opinion. This use poses problems. Take 'Des ouvrages de l'esprit', 2: 'Il faut chercher seulement à penser et à parler juste, sans vouloir amener les autres à notre goût et à nos sentiments; c'est une trop grande entreprise.' This asserts both the existence of an objective order and the in-communicability of one's perceptions of it; a state of affairs that renders difficult the rational disputation over tastes that La Bruyère asserted was possible. Sometimes the presence of a subjective element confers value on a taste: thus Ménippe 'croit souvent dire son goût ou expliquer sa pensée, lorsqu'il n'est que l'écho de quelqu'un qu'il vient de quitter' ('Du merite personnel', 40). The point is not whether Ménippe is right or wrong in what he says, but that it is not really he who is speaking. Yet elsewhere the subjective dimension devalues 'taste'. La Bruyère takes over the distinction between *agrément* and *beauté* which is to be found in La Rochefoucauld (maxim 240) and Méré.[8] But whereas Méré had privileged *agrément* precisely because taste is required to perceive it, for La Bruyère this is an index of its un-reality: 'L'agrément est arbitraire: la beauté est quelque chose de plus réel et de plus indépendant du goût et de l'opinion' ('Des femmes', 11).

The subjectivity of *goût*, in this sense of 'opinion', is thus a focus of instability; it confers positive and negative value by turns. The instability is produced by the absence, in La Bruyère's writing on taste, of a coherent discourse of the subject of taste, such as we find in Méré. In saying this, I am neither approving Méré nor blaming La Bruyère; the heterogeneity, the inconsistencies, of *Les Caractères* give it a richness that far exceeds the resources of Méré's monothematicism. Some of the larger implications of this discrepancy are discussed in the conclusion to this chapter.

However, the discursive contexts of other passages bestow a certain concrete content on La Bruyère's discourse of taste, with its hitherto problematic subject. If taste is hard to communicate, we should perhaps expect it to be rare, and it is: 'il y a peu d'hommes dont l'esprit soit accompagné d'un goût sûr et d'une critique judicieuse' ('Des ouvrages de l'esprit', 11). Here is the familiar emphasis on the rarity of taste, accompanied by the suspicion of *esprit* (and of production?) encountered earlier. Moreover, *goût* is further defined in opposition to *vivacité*: the passage begins 'Il y a beaucoup plus de vivacité que de goût parmi les hommes ...'. The most relevant sense of *vivacité* is 'la subtilité & le brillant de l'esprit' (Richelet) or, as the *Dictionnaire de l'Académie* puts it, 'la penetration de l'esprit, la promptitude à concevoir'. In this sense, it can be both opposed to the reliability of *bon sens* and represented, unfavourably, as a national characteristic. Take the following illustrative quotations from dictionaries:

Les Espagnols & les Italiens font paroître beaucoup de *vivacité* d'esprit dans leurs Poësies, mais cette vivacité n'est point à comparer au bon sens des Grecs, ni des Latins.   (Richelet)

Les Africains avoient plus de *vivacité* d'esprit, que de bon sens, & de jugement.
(Furetière, *Dictionnaire universel*, second edn, 1701)

Des qualitez aussi opposées, que la *vivacité* & le bon sens, ne se rencontrent
pas toujours ensemble.   (ibid., attributed to Bouhours)

These utterances hint at the potential ideological significance of La
Bruyère's subordination of *vivacité* to *goût*. He appears to be
repudiating, as Bouhours did more explicitly in *La Manière de bien
penser dans les ouvrages d'esprit*, the literary influences of Spain and
Italy, and indeed the whole tradition of what, for want of a less
unsatisfactory word, one may as well resign oneself to calling the
baroque.

This nationalist-classicist position is reinforced by the warning in
'De la société', 17, against *imagination*, a quality arguably akin to
vivacité: 'elle ne produit souvent que des idées vaines et puériles, qui
ne servent point à perfectionner le goût et à nous rendre meilleurs:
nos pensées doivent être prises dans le bon sens et la droite raison'.
The valorization, endorsed by 'taste', of the commonsensical, of the
obvious certitudes of experience, brings out the conformism of
classical culture; it provides a check on the individual's subjectivity,
as does the harnessing of 'taste' to morality. This latter step distinguishes La Bruyère's discourse of taste from the aristocratic-*honnête*
discourse where *honnête* values tend to subsume those of morality.[9]

La Bruyère speaks in this passage of taste as perfectible; but it is,
by the same token, also corruptible: 'C'est prendre le change, et
cultiver un mauvais goût, que de dire, comme l'on fait, que la machine
n'est qu'un amusement d'enfants, et qui ne convient qu'aux Marion-
nettes' ('Des ouvrages de l'esprit', 47). Not only can the dissemination
of stock attitudes provide a threat to good taste; so may the
mechanisms of literary distribution. La Bruyère observes that a
bookful of platitudes will get past the censor, 'comme ce discours n'est
ni contre la religion ni contre l'Etat, et qu'il ne fera point d'autre
désordre dans le public que de lui gâter le goût et l'accoutumer à des
choses froides et insipides' ('De la chaire', 23). 'Taste' can also be
jeopardized by moral failings, themselves describable as tastes. The
moral objection to sneering at others ('c'est une chose monstrueuse
que le goût et la facilité qui est en nous de railler, d'improuver et de
mépriser les autres', 'De l'homme', 78) is reinforced by a taste-
judgment: 'Il ne faut point mettre un ridicule où il n'y en a point:
c'est se gâter le goût, c'est corrompre son jugement et celui des autres'
('Des ouvrages de l'esprit', 68). Taste, it is however implied, is a
prerequisite for the moralist: for the reflection proceeds, 'mais le

ridicule qui est quelque part, il faut l'y voir, l'en tirer avec grâce, et d'une manière qui plaise et qui instruise'. Association with and opposition to certain values thus help to provide 'taste' with a concrete content. So too do the various forms of conditioning the subject of taste is represented as exposed to. In 'Du cœur', 82, La Bruyère observes that 'l'on dépend des lieux pour l'esprit, l'humeur, la passion, le goût et les sentiments'. This would appear to be a relativist position, but it need not be if we assume that certain environments are privileged to foster 'good taste'. And this appears to be the case. La Bruyère marvels that a particular objectionable form of humour should have achieved such currency 'dans un pays qui est le centre du bon goût et de la politesse' ('De la société', 71). This passage tends to confirm the presence of nationalistic implications in some of the abstract formulations discussed above. However, alongside the national factor, there are social ones: 'Cette manière basse de plaisanter a passé du peuple, à qui elle appartient, jusque dans une grande partie de la jeunesse de la cour, qu'elle a déjà infectée.' Sections of the court are thus *de facto* popular in character (compare the great ones of this world mentioned in 'Des grands', 53: 'tous méprisent le peuple, et ils sont peuple'). None the less, this state of things is presented as the violation of an ideal antithesis; what is second nature to the people is after all an alien infection at the court. It is as if La Bruyère is alluding to Vaugelas's commitment of linguistic authority to 'la plus *saine* partie de la cour' (*Remarques*, Préface, II.3; my emphasis), in respect of whom alone is France the centre of 'good taste'.

Not surprisingly. For the court is after all the cultural centre of France, and affects taste accordingly: 'Les princes, sans autre science ni autre règle, ont un goût de comparaison: ils sont nés et élevés au milieu et comme dans le centre des meilleures choses, à quoi ils rapportent ce qu'ils lisent, ce qu'ils voient et ce qu'ils entendent. Tout ce qui s'éloigne trop de LULLI, de RACINE et de LE BRUN est condamné' ('Des grands', 42). Taste here is determined as good by the apparently taken-for-granted excellence of its objects; the subject of this good taste is constituted entirely by his social and therefore cultural position. Between him and the object there exists a perfect concordance. (However, beneath this felicitous closure of the discourse of taste, there are more subversive, ironic implications; a hint that this very coherence is a kind of blindness and a repressive force.)

A slight shift in position, still within the privileged domain of the court, and 'taste' too is modified. Courtiers are never satisfied, however great a prince's efforts to please them, because 'leur goût, si on les en croit, est encore au delà de toute l'affectation qu'on aurait à les satisfaire, et d'une dépense toute royale que l'on ferait pour y réussir' ('De l'homme', 145). La Bruyère explains this reaction in moralistic-humanist terms: *vanité, mauvaise délicatesse, malignité* are all invoked; human nature is seen as peeping through the habitual complaisance of the courtier. Yet it is easy to suggest a materialist interpretation: the courtiers' taste-discourse is a means of affirming, against all the appearances, their independence from royal control, a last aristocratic self-assertion against the pressures of political, social and economic subordination to the monarchy. It is no accident (as they say) that Saint-Simon should have found Louis XIV deficient in taste.[10]

Suspicious as he is of the courtiers' self-interested taste-discourse, La Bruyère none the less endorses their claims to cultural superiority over the *ville*. Père Séraphin has preached to empty churches in the city, whereas 'les courtisans, à force de goût et de connaître les bienséances, lui ont applaudi' ('De la chaire', 5). But the compliment is not unequivocal. *Goût* is by no means an adequate level of response to religious discourse; it sanctions the deplorable division of the Church into productive and consumptional sectors: 'celui de dire la vérité dans toute son étendue, sans égards, sans déguisement; celui de l'écouter avidement, avec goût, avec admiration, avec éloges, et de n'en faire cependant ni pis ni mieux' ('De la chaire', 12). Take the congregation in 'De la chaire', 11, moved by Théodore's admirable sermon — to the extent of pronouncing it better than its predecessor. This taste-judgment (although the word *goût* is not used here) is a positive stumbling-block.

In these passages, which establish, record, or endorse claims to taste-authority based on the social position of the subject, the authority is questioned even when recognized. The prince's taste is formed by a lifetime's exposure to the best in every sphere; yet it is blinkered, even repressive. The courtiers' pretensions to taste are ungrateful, and arguably self-interested. True, their taste is better than the citizens', but it operates in areas where taste is not enough.

Membership of vaguer collectivities than these can also condition one's taste. Vaguest of all, perhaps, is the time one lives in, with its dominant taste. La Bruyère evinces a certain mistrust of this: 'Celui qui n'a égard en écrivant qu'au goût de son siècle songe plus à sa personne qu'à ses écrits: il faut toujours tendre à la perfection, et alors cette justice qui nous est quelquefois refusée par nos contemporains, la postérité sait nous la rendre' ('Des ouvrages de l'esprit', 67). This position, combining essentialism with a sense of the historical vagaries of taste, marks, as Odette de Mourgues has noted, a departure from the consensus of French classical writers, for whom 'respect for the "goût du siècle" was axiomatic'.[11]

But there is another significant, albeit tacit, dissent here, in the contention that the writings are more important than the individual. The whole discourse of *honnêteté* implies the contrary: its privileging of presence and speech above writing does not need a Derrida to detect it. The recognition of *honnêteté*, it will be remembered, takes place ideally in the gesture by which the perfect monarch beckons the person of his or her choice from among the crowds around the throne. *Honnêteté* is an ideal of communication by speech and action, and those two aspects are so bound up with each other that they cannot be considered in isolation (Méré, *OC* III, pp. 103–4). Writing, on this showing, is a merely partial form of communication. What eloquence means, according to Méré, is first and foremost excellence in conversation (*OC* II, p. 102). The nexus between *honnêteté* and the erotic likewise defines it as a discourse of presence.[12] *Honnêteté*, in short, is a pattern of total behaviour, and its object therefore is the individual *qua* individual rather than the discourses he or she utters. *Honnête* can of course be predicated of the absent – of Julius Caesar, say – but only by imagining him as a presence. Significantly, the offences Méré observes in Caesar are to do with his writing (*OC* III, p. 87), which does not prevent him from being the greatest man in history, along with Socrates (*OC* III, p. 140). In other words, *honnêteté* of necessity privileges the *goût du siècle*, provided the age in question is itself *honnête*. La Bruyère's attitude on the other hand hints at new socio-cultural relations: the comparative impersonality of the capitalist book market, the greater social fragmentation of Enlightenment culture, no longer exclusively focused on one privileged centre. (This attitude reaches its logical conclusion in *Le Neveu de Rameau*, where the person and behaviour of the historical Racine are declared to be of negligible interest.)[13]

Furthermore, by enfranchising the writer from the taste of his century, and committing him to a possibly lonely and unrecognized search for perfection, La Bruyère unobtrusively subverts not only a metaphysics of presence but an ideology of cultural relations according to which the professional is to submit his works for approval to 'les Honnêtes-gens de la Cour', as Saint-Evremond puts it (*Les Opéra*, p. 64). The insistence of writers on taste on the need to form one's taste by cultivating the living exemplars of that quality has the effect of confirming them and their heirs in perpetual possession of cultural authority – and thus of conserving existing hegemonic structures. La Bruyère does not explicitly contest this attitude, and logically it is not incompatible with his own. Indifference to the dominant taste of one's age can coexist with deference to the taste of a privileged few. But about these La Bruyère's silence is virtually total. *Les gens de goût* are not the linchpin of his discourse of taste in the way that they are of Méré's and Saint-Evremond's.

More concrete than the taste of an age is the taste of the public. The notion of the 'public' in seventeenth-century France has been studied by Lough with reference to theatre audiences. These were inherently diverse in social composition, and it was clear that the responses of *les honnêtes gens* could not pretend to exclusive significance: those of the *parterre*, say, counted as well.[14] La Bruyère's use of *public* in 'De la chaire', 23, betokens an awareness of similar pressures operating outside the context of drama. The public is an impersonal formation, called into being by the emergence of impersonal, intrinsically commercial, cultural relations alongside those of the salon or small gathering of *honnêtes gens*: self-constituted repositories of 'good taste' conceiving themselves as an assemblage of *individuals* whose merit guarantees the upholding of standards, indifferent to or contemptuous of any verdict besides their own. Significantly, La Bruyère shows the public as vulnerable to the effects of individuals' cupidity: Dioscore simply writes for money, and in this context it matters little whether the fifty *pistoles* he requires are to come from a grateful aristocratic dedicatee or from a bookseller. Not surprisingly, then, La Bruyère expresses his contempt for the *Mercure galant* by representing it as capitalizing on the stupidity of the public: 'Il y a autant d'invention à s'enricher par un sot livre qu'il y a de sottise à l'acheter: c'est ignorer le goût du peuple que de ne pas hasarder quelquefois de grandes fadaises' ('Des ouvrages de l'esprit', 46). Literary production is represented here as an exclusively commercial phenomenon, and the use of *peuple* to designate the public is related to this. Lough has shown that *peuple* does not invariably bear pejorative implications in this context (*Paris Theatre Audiences*, pp. 61–7), but they are evident here. Nothing is more characteristic of the discourse of taste than to equate the bad and the popular, but again the point is that La Bruyère's text contains no counter-term to give 'good taste' a social location.

The passages discussed above have all dealt with subjects of taste in cultural matters. Other kinds of taste are also ascribed by La Bruyère to particular classes of subject, but for clarity's sake it seems preferable to remain for the moment on the cultural level. The concern is still with the specific content conferred on the general notion of good taste by its discursive articulations. To recapitulate: I have argued that certain abstract values perform this function, as does the association of particular levels of taste with specific social positions, although, as we saw, there is a good deal of ambiguity in the latter area. What is now in question is the implicit definition of good taste in terms of attitudes to particular cultural institutions: bodies of texts and discourses, traditions.

When La Bruyère speaks of 'certains esprits' among whom one finds 'une prévention tout établie contre les savants, à qui ils ôtent les manières du monde, le savoir-vivre, l'esprit de société, et qu'ils renvoient ainsi dépouillés à leur cabinet et à leurs livres' ('Des jugements', 18), we should have no difficulty in recognizing the object of his criticism as the *honnête* discourse against the learned. 'Chez plusieurs, savant et pédant sont synonymes' ('Des jugements', 17). La Bruyère contests this discourse very much on its own terms, by the appeal to personal authority, that of 'personnages également doctes et polis' ('Des jugements', 18), all distinguished in various ways, some of royal blood. The examples of Ossat, Ximenes and Richelieu are adduced to show that statesmanship and learning are natural bedfellows. This is, in some sense, a restatement of the humanism of the Renaissance, but in contemporary terms, for instance those of *goût*. For 'il ne s'agit point si les langues sont anciennes ou nouvelles, mortes ou vivantes, mais si elles sont grossières ou polies, si les livres qu'elles ont formés sont d'un bon ou d'un mauvais goût' ('Des jugements', 19). La Bruyère imagines French going the way of Greek and Latin: if it did, would it then be pedantic in future centuries to read Molière and La Fontaine? There is a twofold perspective here: on language as constitutive of, and as itself charged with, value (*grossière* ou *polie*), and on value (*bon* or *mauvais goût*) as embodied in the works of individual authors. These are cited as representatives rather than producers of value, and this emphasis on the productive properties of systems is taken up again in 'Des ouvrages de l'esprit', 60. This is a difficult passage. While it may well not be the case, as has been suggested (originally by Julien Benda), that La Bruyère is representing thought as conditioned by language, the alternative interpretation, endorsed by Garapon and De Mourgues (namely, that this is a piece of special pleading aimed at justifying La Bruyère's own use of wit (*esprit*)), still lays considerable stress on to the collective force of language.[15] It is not any distinctive merit of his own, La Bruyère modestly implies, that gives rise to this kind of *esprit*: it is a natural result of trends taking place in the system of (literary) language itself. Like Althusserian history, this appears to be a process without a subject, only bearers. Other passages, of course, modify this emphasis, stressing the formative influence of important authors: see especially 'Des ouvrages de l'esprit', 40 and 42. In fragment 60 too, the discovery of the rhythmic resources of French is credited to Malherbe and Guez de Balzac. But there is no other mediating agency between the language-system and the works of authors produced within and by it, no cultural board of directors like Vaugelas's 'la plus saine partie de la Cour' to regulate linguistic and literary production.

It was implied in 'Des jugements', 19, that the ancient languages had produced works in good taste. These therefore enjoy a legitimate authority. La Bruyère bewails the lapse of centuries 'avant que les hommes, dans les sciences et les arts, aient pu revenir au goût des anciens et reprendre enfin le simple et le naturel' ('Des ouvrages de l'esprit', 15). Doric, Ionic and Corinthian columns are simple and natural in a way that Gothic arches are apparently not. The same holds good for literature as for architecture: imitation of the ancients is the only sure way to perfection. La Bruyère's sympathies are clearly on the side of the *Anciens* in their quarrel with the *Modernes*, and he refers to 'quelques habiles' who have intervened on the same side as he (Boileau and Racine, according to the *clefs*); ironically, he notes, their authority is repudiated because of their fidelity, in their own works, to the 'goût de l'antiquité', as a result of which they are accused of special pleading. Special pleading, however, is precisely what the *Modernes* go in for: 'Un auteur moderne prouve ordinairement que les anciens nous sont inférieurs en deux manières, par raison et par exemple: il tire la raison de son goût particulier, et l'exemple de ses ouvrages' (ibid.). *Goût*, attached to the ancients, is a perdurable standard; as the expression of an individual's opinion it is at best arbitrary, at worst self-interested.

Not that the ancients' taste is an inviolable standard. Corneille offers proof of this, in his successful handling of complex plots, which is one of the glories of his theatre even though 'il ne s'est pas assujetti au goût des Grecs et à leur grande simplicité' ('Des ouvrages de l'esprit', 54). La Bruyère here, for once, adopts the same position as Méré, namely that rules may be broken by those of superior intelligence, and tacitly echoes Molière's formulation that 'la grande règle de toutes les règles ... est ... de plaire'.[16] He does not, however, invoke *goût* to validate these happy faults.

This latter quality, it would appear from the same passage, is more characteristic of Racine. In him we find 'du goût et des sentiments'; Corneille, in contrast, offers 'des maximes, des règles, des préceptes'.

The significance of *goût* here may best be gauged from a study of the oppositional patterns in the passage. Not that the antithesis of the two writers is total. There is grandeur in Racine and pathos in Corneille, terror and pity in both. But there the resemblances end. 'Corneille nous assujettit à ses caractères et à ses idées, Racine se conforme aux nôtres; celui-là peint les hommes comme ils devraient être, celui-ci les peint tels qu'ils sont.' The validity of Racine's picture of human nature is confirmed by the subject's experience (he conforms to 'our' ideas): thus, while there is more in Corneille to inspire admiration and imitation, 'il y a plus dans [Racine] de ce que l'on reconnaît dans les autres, ou de ce que l'on éprouve dans soi-même'. As for their impact on the spectator, Corneille 'élève, étonne, maîtrise, instruit; l'autre plaît, remue, touche, pénètre'. Corneille's domain is 'ce qu'il y a de plus beau, de plus noble, et de plus impérieux dans la raison', Racine's 'ce qu'il y a de plus flatteur et de plus délicat dans la passion'. Then comes the antithesis between Corneille's maxims, rules and precepts, and Racine's *goût* and *sentiments*. Whereas the spectator is more intellectually engaged ('occupé') at a play by Corneille, the effect of Racine's is more emotional, leaving one 'ébranlé' and 'attendri'. Corneille, in fine, is more 'moral', Racine more 'naturel'.

However dubious some of these distinctions are in isolation (are there people like Mithridate or Roxane? Should people be like Rodogune and Horace?), they do, taken together, acquire coherence. Corneille works from outside the audience, promulgating in authoritative fashion the dictates of an external authority, with which he identifies himself. '*Ses* caractères' and '*ses* idées' are also those of Reason. But Racine enters into, reproduces, his audience's experience, both of themselves and of the people they recognize in his plays. Whereas Corneille's relations with the audience are authoritative, Racine's are semi-erotic: the words *plaît, remue, touche, pénètre, flatteur, délicat, ébranlé, attendri* are all suggestive in this way. The appeal, though, is not simply to private recesses of emotion, but to experience shared by each individual with all his or her fellow-spectators. Experience takes place at a pre-discursive level, *goût* and *sentiments* resisting the inscription of *maximes, règles, préceptes*.

In reality, Racine is just as discursive, no more 'natural' than Corneille, no less 'moral' if we stretch the word to mean 'ideological', referring to a set of presuppositions about human behaviour. What La Bruyère says here in connexion with Racine is very revealing of the unconscious subjection brought about by discourse, of its capacity to evoke the placing response analysed by Althusser, whereby the individual recognizes himself or herself as a subject in the discourse addressed to him or her.[17] It is this kind of recognition that *goût* is involved in, and helps to foster.

Here, La Bruyère's analysis converges with the objections to the theatre raised by Christian moralists such as Bossuet and Pascal, despite their difference of position. It is true that from the Christian moralists' viewpoint (and I am using the word 'moralist' here very much in the English sense, rather than as an equivalent of *moraliste*) Corneille is no less reprehensible than Racine, appealing as he does to the passions of pride and ambition as well as love. What La Bruyère describes as the effect of Racine's theatre on an audience holds good, according to these writers, for all plays. And it offers no grounds for congratulation. In plain English, if the expression is not too inappropriate, Racine and other playwrights excite concupiscence by their flattering representation of the passions. There is no merit in affecting our deepest emotional nature, for that is given over to corruption, except in the regenerate – who would, *ipso facto*, eschew attendance at the theatre.[18] The committed Christian La Bruyère does not, however, follow them all the way in this analysis: he notes the same psychological effects, but without condemning them. This discrepancy may be explained by the subjection of drama to a hegemonic secular court culture. Courtier spectators respond to the spectacle of love on the stage, in defiance, unconscious or otherwise, of Christian morality, for the same reason that they indulge in love affairs in ordinary life: which is partly that love, in a determinate cultural form, is an integral part of nobiliary ideology, even though it is at odds with the dominant religious ideology. And this is more or less admitted in the text. For Corneille is said not only to offer a personal vision, but at the same time to convey the dictates of a rational and objective moral order: 'ce qu'il y a de plus beau, de plus noble et de plus impérieux dans la raison'. His maxims and precepts must likewise be taken to be on the whole morally uplifting, except for the obvious sophistries put into the mouths of villains, for La Bruyère would otherwise surely have condemned him as a disseminator of falsehood. In short, Corneille is shown as the representative of official values, while Racine deals with the less creditable aspects of 'human nature', the truths of experience that conflict with the requirements of morality. The placing of *goût* on this latter side of the divide reveals its problematic, not to say adversarial, relationship to morality; the same relationship as emerges from *honnête* discourse, with its aversion to rules and resistance to the transcendent claims of the moral law.

One might question the validity, or at least the relevance, of this whole argument: namely, that *goût* in this passage bears a totally different sense from that which occurs in the other quotations discussed. Consequently, the conclusion pointed to here can in no way be integrated with those drawn from readings of other passages. For in these its meaning was broadly equivalent to 'discernment'. But there is no sense here of Racine's discernment being opposed to Corneille's lack of it. *Goût* here simply denotes a form of pleasure associated with a particular theatrical experience. It has nothing necessarily to do with the *bon goût* vindicated in 'Des ouvrages de l'esprit', 10; contrasted with *vivacité* in 'Des ouvrages de l'esprit', 11; ascribed, not unambiguously, to the monarch in 'Des grands', 42; domiciled in France in 'De la société', 71; denied to those who condemn operatic spectacle in 'Des ouvrages de l'esprit', 47.

This objection would be misconceived. The present work, as I have said, is not concerned with the aesthetic notion of 'good taste', with seventeenth-century French accounts of a supposed faculty of that name. It is concerned with the discursive and ideological relations reproduced in the use of the word *goût*. Even though it does not bear the same sense in this characterization of Racine as it does earlier in this very passage (where, in the phrase 'le goût des Grecs', it means 'style'), the different kinds of perception it alludes to can be brought into some kind of relation, as will be shown in the conclusion to this chapter. Besides, the response referred to by the word *goût* is logically prior to its evaluation as *bon* or *mauvais*, and it would be misleading to separate the judgmental from the affective senses, since the object and vehicle of the judgment is an affective reaction.

The ancients, we have seen, are in some sense a touchstone of the individual's taste. A rather similar pattern of thought is cited in 'Des ouvrages de l'esprit', 21, only to be repudiated by La Bruyère as hyperbolically laudatory. This runs 'On ne jugera à l'avenir du goût de quelqu'un qu'à proportion qu'il en aura pour cette pièce.' La Bruyère implies that such praise stinks of self-interest (it is uttered in the hope of being rewarded with a pension or an abbey); why not simply call a good book a good book? One could also agree that the utterance is an objectionable form of cultural blackmail, or that it is inappropriate to the book it is applied to. But this is the nub of the question. It is precisely the discourse of taste in itself that makes it possible to say this kind of thing; La Bruyère, in effect, does the same when equating the taste of the ancients with good taste. One remembers that the reasons put forward by the supporter of the *Modernes* were simply rejected out of hand as the effect of his 'goût particulier' ('Des ouvrages de l'esprit', 15). In short, the argument boils down to a confrontation between different discourses of taste, each affirming the validity of its own touchstone. The *goût des anciens* had a weight of tradition behind it, and the support of an educational system still wedded to the classics. But French was asserting its claims to autonomy, in the pedagogy, for instance, of the Jansenist *petites écoles*, where it was the primary medium, and to some extent the object, of teaching.[19] The *Modernes* also benefited from the anti-erudite consensualism of the discourse of *honnêteté*, tending at times, as we have seen in Méré, to pick on the supposed shortcomings of classical texts as a way of denting their authority. It was to be expected that modern works, even those produced by partisans of the ancients such as Racine, should eventually be given the status of touchstones. It is rather amusing to observe an echo of two of the 'phrases outrées, degoûtantes' quoted in this passage (*'C'est un chef-d'œuvre de l'esprit*; *l'humanité ne va pas plus loin'*, La Bruyère's italics) in Voltaire's eulogy of *Athalie* as 'le chef-d'œuvre de l'esprit humain'.

I shall move now from the area of language, literature and culture in the restricted sense to broader moral questions treated in terms of *goût*. People's taste changes, like so much else about them, while their basic deplorable moral condition remains the same ('De l'homme', 2). On the individual level, changes of taste seem to betoken a fragmented, therefore morally unreliable personality ('De l'homme', 6). The fleetingness of taste places it on a level inferior to morality and religion, whose domain is eternal truth ('la vertu seule, si peu à la mode, va au delà des temps', 'De la mode', 31; for the contrast between the pettiness of time and God's eternity, see 'Des esprits forts', 47). The wrongness of people's tastes, among other things, is presented, ironically, as a reason for rejecting this equation of real with lasting value: human beings are so radically faulty that they have less to lose from inconstancy than from stubbornness ('De l'homme', 157). Even if 'good taste' is a lasting value, as was suggested in La Bruyère's remarks on the ancients, the implication seems to remain that taste comes from a level of the personality more superficial than one's basic moral nature (although a quality analogous to 'good taste' is attributed to God in 'Des esprits forts', 43).

The tastes observed and evaluated by the *moraliste* can have a wide variety of objects. There can be tastes or fashions in people, irrespective of their intrinsic qualities ('De la mode', 4). One particular sense is noteworthy: that of 'sexual appetite'. In 'Des femmes', 32, medical discourse ('goût hypocondre') combines with a traditional image of female behaviour (the woman with her monkish lover seems to belong to the world of *fabliau*) to evoke the desired reaction, of bewilderment merging into scorn, towards women who transgress sexual codes, and in come cases class-taboos as well. In the passage immediately following ('Des femmes', 33) La Bruyère censures 'le nouveau goût qu'ont tant de femmes romaines' for stage-artistes of one sort or another, barbing his revulsion with a piece of racism. He returns to the charge in 'Des jugements', 16, where similar penchants on the part of men are also in question. These are linked to a change, which the context encourages us to see as a change for the worse, in the Romans' taste: their loss, due to the vanity and audacity caused by excessive power, of the 'goût du secret et du mystère'. Their degraded taste is juxtaposed with the ideal order of 'good taste' in the observation that 'leur goût n'allait qu'à laisser voir qu'ils aimaient, non pas une belle personne ou une excellente comédienne, mais une comédienne'.

An analogous juxtaposition between a particular taste and 'good taste', with a view to downgrading the former, occurs in 'De la mode', 2: 'La curiosité n'est pas un goût pour ce qui est bon ou ce qui est beau, mais pour ce qui est rare, unique, pour ce qu'on a et ce que les autres n'ont point. Ce n'est pas un attachement à ce qui est parfait, mais à ce qui est couru, à ce qui est à la mode.' The condemnation of *curiosité* is partly moral (the collector neglects to provide his daughters with dowries, his children with an education) and partly religious (some of these enthusiasms are virtually substitutes for religion). But there is an ideological strand running through it as well: it is, in effect and in parts, a protest against a specific kind of fetishism. Not, indeed, full-scale commodity fetishism, for not all these pursuits are concerned with commodities: the study of oriental languages, for instance. Nor are the *curieux* shown as acting in consciously economic terms: they refuse to sell when they could profit from doing so (un-consciousness of the economic wellsprings of one's action is, however, a characteristic effect of fetishism). One of them would not sell his favourite tulip-bulb for a thousand crowns, another could keep his family decently if he would only part with a few mouldy old busts. But this criticism of La Bruyère's is valid precisely because there is a market in such articles − into which all the numismatist's money, for instance, disappears. Moreover, many of these pursuits entail depriving objects of their use-value, or at least perverting their use. La Bruyère speaks of books that are never read, a magnificent house whose owner skulks in the attic, prints of no aesthetic merit. Value is an effect purely of the rarity of the object rather than its intrinsic quality or capacity to meet a genuine need. The need it does meet, which La Bruyère does not trouble to spell out, is of course the glorification of the possessor – in his own eyes and in other people's (all these *curieux* are trying to impress). As we saw, the collection of art objects had long served the purpose of glorifying the monarch – in France, since the time of Richelieu, at least.[20] But now it appears as the symptom of a privatization and fragmentation of culture. La Bruyère brings out this point by his stress on the specific languages proper to each hobby, represented as literally eccentric, marginal, violations therefore of *honnêteté*'s linguistic consensualism and hegemonism, its exclusion of technical vocabularies. For La Bruyère, collecting is a purely individualist activity; none of the collectors can see any point in the activity of the others; their distinctive idiolects are proof of this. The discourse of their hobby is solipsistic (talk of the harvest to a plum-grower, 'vous n'articulez pas, vous ne vous faites pas entendre'; mention other fruits, 'c'est pour lui un idiome inconnu') and totalitarian ('ne l'entretenez pas même de vos pruniers: il n'a de l'amour que pour une certaine espèce, toute autre que vous lui nommez le fait sourire et se moquer'). This sets it apart from the intersubjective and collective culture of *honnêteté*. It is interesting that in 'De la mode', 10, La Bruyère should bemoan the disappearance (giving quite different reasons) of 'les conversations légères, les cercles, la fine plaisanterie, les lettres enjouées et familières, les petites parties où l'on était admis seulement avec de l'esprit', of the whole way of life associated with the Hôtel de Rambouillet and that could be taken as embodying the spirit of *honnêteté*.

The fetishism takes the form of the subjection of men to things. They suffer from the gaps in their collections, to the paradoxical extent of being forced to abandon them, like the print-collector who lacks a single Callot. They are unable to resolve themselves to part with the fetish, like the house-builder and the collector of busts. At the extreme limit of subjection, they become the fetish: 'Vous le voyez planté, et qui a pris racine au milieu de ses tulipes'; 'il retrouve ses oiseaux dans son sommeil: lui-même il est oiseau, il est huppé, il gazouille, il perche'.

The passage is a remarkable combination of insight and enforced misperception. La Bruyère does not see the continuity that un-doubtedly existed between *honnête* culture and *curiosité* – a con-tinuity, indeed, that 'taste', with its wide range of applicability, could secure in discourse. *Curiosité* and connoisseurship, like *honnêteté*, serve as means for the individual to vindicate his social status; his possessions are both privately owned and, so to speak, held in trust for a whole class. And La Bruyère undermines his presentation of the *curieux* as eccentric and marginal by showing him as dominated by fashion and as implicated, as a buyer and seller, in a market structure. None the less he shows us enough of *curiosité* to justify his disquiet.

Through participating in *honnêteté*, one signifies one's privileged position in the system of production relations, or at least one's deference to those so privileged. The signifiers are material – dress, language, movement – but closely attached to the subject, so as to seem a part of him or her. They are actually perceived as non-material: *esprit*, *goût*, *honnêteté* are impalpable essences. The deliberate vagueness of the dominant cultural discourse, its appeal to the *je ne sais quoi*, to *sentiment*, to *goût* itself to back up its perceptions are a repression of the material and the concrete, of the real content of the social relations spiritualized by the discourse. *Curiosité* provokes discomfort from this point of view because, on the contrary, it foregrounds the material, detaches the signifier from the subject (the extreme case here is that of the man who lives in the garret of his splendid house). It signifies social relations more grossly, and it symbolizes the power of money to transform ('corrupt') them because it shows money as acting independently of the inner qualities of the subject. (The corrosive influence of money on public taste we have already seen in the case of Dioscore, above, pp. 150, 154; its similar effects on social relations are alluded to in 'Des biens de fortune', 1, 7, 19, and 'De quelques usages', 1, 10, 13.) In *honnêteté*, the subject's external attributes, produced to a significant extent by his or her social position, were taken as simply the accidents of a superior substance. *Curiosité*, as a widespread practice, is threatening because it reveals the material underpinnings that *honnêteté* has sought to conceal.

There are many other occurrences of *goût* in *Les Caractères* but not all are of equal interest. I want to conclude the discussion of particular texts with just three more examples.

The first of these is 'Du cœur', 1: 'Il y a un goût dans la pure amitié où ne peuvent atteindre ceux qui sont nés médiocres.' *Goût* means 'pleasure' here, but it is a pleasure valorized by the discourse and confined by it to certain privileged subjects: it counts also, then, as a 'good' taste. This celebration of sensibility obviously works by borrowing the categories of aristocratic ideology: but the connexions may be closer than that. It is quite probable that 'nés médiocres' has the further sense (not acknowledged by Garapon in his glossary) of 'not nobly born'. La Bruyère may well be saying that those not born to high rank are obliged to run their lives in terms of self-interest, which leads to the perversion of friendship: 'Il est doux de voir ses amis par goût et par estime; il est pénible de les cultiver par intérêt; c'est *solliciter*' ('Du cœur', 57).

In the last two examples, a particular taste is ascribed or denied to categories of subject with implications for the validity of existing social relationships. 'Des grands', 5, opens with the repudiation of a discourse that serves to legitimate them (it may be found, as Garapon points out in his note, in La Rochefoucauld's maxim 52). According to this, every station in life has its attendant goods and evils, inextricably intertwined, so that none is inherently preferable to any other; this creates a sort of *de facto* equality between them. La Bruyère sees through this: 'Celui qui est puissant, riche, et à qui il ne manque rien, peut former cette question; mais il faut que ce soit un homme pauvre qui la décide.' But, precisely because he lacks power, wealth, position, the poor man can never in practice exercise this discursive authority. This legitimation-discourse is self-interested; the pseudo-question it raises is answered by the person who has asked it; it serves, then, simply to reproduce the values embodied in that person: power, wealth, authority.

None the less, in the second paragraph of the passage, La Bruyère appears to be endorsing a modified version of the position criticized in the first. Objectively, in terms of 'peines' and 'avantages', there is no scheme of built-in compensations to equalize the lot of every class. Subjectively, however, there is a 'charme attaché à chacune des différentes conditions, et qui y demeure jusques à ce que la misère l'en ait ôté. Ainsi les grands se plaisent dans l'excès, et les petits aiment la modération; ceux-là ont le goût de dominer et de commander, et ceux-ci sentent du plaisir et même de la vanité à les servir et à leur obéir; les grands sont entourés, salués, respectés; les petits entourent, saluent, se prosternent; et tous sont contents.' Different tastes, distributed on a class basis, validate, therefore, the existing social relations. Over and above this, two readings of the passage quoted are possible: one would see the great and the small as human beings of essentially different types, with the tastes appropriate to their nature issued to them at birth and confirmed by upbringing; the other would see the tastes as developed in response to objective situations as a subjective compensatory mechanism. The phrase 'jusques à ce que la misère l'en ait ôté' militates in favour of the latter: the charms of subordination wear off under pressure from real hardship (a warning here to 'les grands'?), and the charms of nobility desert those who fall from power and favour. In line with this reading 'tous sont contents' at the end of the passage should doubtless be taken as ironic inasmuch as it rejects the complacency of the essentialist reading. None the less, the point is still that 'things inevitably work this way', that tastes will automatically adjust themselves to positions within the social structure so as to maintain it intact.

But this is true not only in respect of class but in respect of gender as well. In 'Des femmes', 49, La Bruyère exculpates men from responsibility for the ignorance of women. This is an anti-feminist move. He argues that men have never passed laws forbidding women to study; but law is of course unnecessary when more unobtrusive sanctions can be enforced. Of these, the generalization, the doxa, is one of the most powerful.

For La Bruyère, the ultimate truth of social activities is moral and religious: the behaviour of a social group is largely accounted for in terms of a set of ethical qualities or defects imputed to it as characteristics. Moral evaluation is in any case impossible to disentangle from the proposed explanations invoking objective conditions. Thus one reason put forward for women's ignorance is 'les distractions que donnent les détails d'un domestique', but behind this causation by objective circumstances is the ideological presupposition that household affairs are essentially the woman's responsibility. The picture that emerges from this passage is that women are themselves to blame for their failure to study, and this for a multiplicity of reasons, the majority of which are anchored in women's essential nature. The enumeration works in two ways: first, by overdetermining women's lack of education, making it unsurprising, and therefore acceptable; second, by suggesting that, among the multitude of explanations, there is one that will suit every individual case. Now one of these explanations is that women have 'un tout autre goût que celui d'exercer leur mémoire'. Women *don't like* having to remember things, just as the great *like* giving people orders, and other people *like* obeying them. Here, then, as in the previous example, we find a taste imputed to whole classes of human beings in such a way as to validate their existing social relationships with other classes.

The following remarks may perhaps serve as a conclusion to this study of La Bruyère's discourse of taste. The contradictions within it can best be approached via the distinction, recognized in his period, between the hegemonic-exclusive and the common culture. La Bruyère points to it himself, with satirical intent, in one of its manifestations: 'C'est déjà trop d'avoir avec le peuple une même religion et un même Dieu: quel moyen encore de s'appeler *Pierre, Jean, Jacques*, comme le marchand ou le laboureur?' ('Des grands', 23) Religion is the best example of a common cultural phenomenon, but the natural homeland of 'taste' is the hegemonic culture. The common people can be expected to show bad taste, and the court is the natural centre of good taste ('De la société', 71; 'Des grands', 42). This is the position constantly affirmed by writers on 'taste': cultural values are the appanage of an elite.

But La Bruyère lacks the true refinement defined by Dickens's Mrs General as seeming to be ignorant of the existence of anything that is not perfectly proper, placid and pleasant. It emerges from *Les Caractères* that the practice of taste goes on at all social levels. This state of things is somehow linked to the workings of money. The taste of 'the people' is there to be capitalized on by sharks like Donneau de Visé with his *Mercure galant*; it is corrupted by the mediocrity of writers like Dioscore. The taste for different *curiosités*, whether kinds of tulip, prints by Callot, or morocco-bound first editions, is supported by a thriving market that for the most part deals in futilities.

All this is no doubt undesirable. But surely the threat presented by this, in effect, 'bad taste' can be readily defused by the establishment of 'good taste' as the specific property of the hegemonic culture. It is true that La Bruyère does go some way towards doing this, and providing 'good taste' with a definite social context. It is, after all, a rarity (therefore one would incline to be suspicious of the majority taste); it is contrasted with *vivacité* and imagination, and allied to *bon sens* (this involves smuggling in nationalist cultural assumptions, but then France is of course the centre of 'good taste'). It is associated with respect for the literature of the ancients, and declared to be compatible with learning (these two propositions, of course, would be far from universally admitted). Moreover, it is to some extent socially placed. It is centred at court, for example, although the court is somewhat susceptible to infection from below. Court taste, however, is at least superior to city taste.

But the problem of 'taste' cannot be so cheaply resolved. *Les Caractères* contains no concept of the ideal subject of taste detailed enough to oppose to the mass practice of bad taste. This ideal subject takes the form, in other writers, of the *honnête homme*. Now it is quite true that La Bruyère sometimes uses this expression with unimpeachably serious intent,[21] and also that he defines *curiosité* in ways that contrast it unfavourably with the ethos of *honnêteté*. But he also defines the *honnête homme* as 'celui qui ne vole pas sur les grands chemins, et qui ne tue personne, dont les vices enfin ne sont pas scandaleux' ('Des jugements', 55). This effectively undercuts the whole authoritative ideal enunciated by writers like Faret and Méré. What is more, it dissociates 'taste' from the total social practice to which the term *honnêteté* refers. In La Bruyère, 'taste' is essentially linked with literature and the arts. This fact, and the absence of the subject from his discourse of taste, are interconnected.

Various heterogeneous reasons can be assigned to this relative devaluation of *honnêteté*. Doubtless La Bruyère's own social origins in the professional and official middle classes distance him from the residual military aristocraticism of *honnêteté*. Secondly, the prominent role of Christian ethics in *Les Caractères* diminishes the scope of the autonomous discourse of *honnêteté*, with its tendency to substitute itself for or privilege itself above morality. Méré thinks that any old fool can be an *homme de bien*, but it takes something extra to be an *honnête homme*.[22] La Bruyère reverses the valuation: 'On connaît assez qu'un homme de bien est honnête homme; mais il est plaisant d'imaginer que tout honnête homme n'est pas homme de bien' ('Des jugements', 55). Thirdly, the increasing commercialization of certain areas of culture, hiving off the potential commodity from the non-commodity, dismantles the totality of *honnêteté*. The dissemination of literary and other cultural objects as commodities exempts the subject from the positive sociocultural vetting that determines access to the privileged gathering where, according to *honnête* discourse, all value resides. It no longer appears natural that forming an opinion about Virgil should have anything to do with one's ability to cut a dash in society or divert an aristocratic lady with one's conversation. It may seem more natural to associate it, at the risk of being branded a pedant, with a measure of classical learning.

Alongside these silences and reservations about *honnêteté*, there are arguably reservations about 'good taste' itself. It frequently appears, after all, as objectionably authoritative: to exclude, as 'taste' inevitably does, seems tantamount to repressing. The 'taste'-discourses cited by La Bruyère are totalitarian. It is simply not allowed to like anything Cliton the epicure has rejected, or whatever does not conform to the officially accepted models in art (Racine, Lulli, Le Brun). The affirmation of one's own taste or that of one's particular set of associates closes off discussion.[23] It can be a proof of ingratitude, even, perhaps, of self-interest, as with the disgruntled courtiers. It can operate so as to exhaust the individual's response in areas, such as religion, where practical action is required. This, too, seems to validate the confinement of 'taste' to a limited, albeit important, sphere, quite against the tendency of the discourse of *honnêteté*, which represents it as applying in every kind of social activity. Indeed, even though La Bruyère accepts the validity of the equation, structurally crucial in the discourse of taste, between the popular and the contemptible, he treats it as essentially superficial. The common people who have 'un bon fond, et ... point de dehors' are ultimately preferable to the grandees who are all *dehors* ('Des grands', 25). This does not mark a quasi-revolutionary self-*déclassement* and alignment with the oppressed; its significance is rather as a critique of the ruling-class ideology that privileges as essential what La Bruyère declares to be superficial.

If 'taste', then, is not pre-eminently situated in some circle, real or ideal, of 'persons of taste', where, if anywhere, is it located in concrete terms? La Bruyère in effect adumbrates a twofold answer. Firstly, 'taste' reflects a quality: the *point de perfection*, inherent in the object. Obviously, the *honnête* discourse of taste would also claim to detect an intrinsic quality. But its recognition was closely linked to the postulation of a subject of taste of a quite definite kind: one conversant, for instance, with the dictates of *honnêteté* and the *bienséances*. What might pass, in Méré's strictures on Virgil, say, as mere pedantic niggling, is really a requirement of the discourse's need continually to re-establish the priority of the subject of taste over the object. With La Bruyère, it is rather the privileged object, the Greek or Latin text, Molière or La Fontaine, that constitutes the point of reference in assertions of value.

Yet the value of the object does not exist in total independence of any observer. There is, after all, one judge whose verdict in matters of taste is unimpeachable: the public. In the preface of his *Discours de réception à l'Académie française* La Bruyère opposes 'le jugement de la cour et de la ville, des grands et du peuple' to the so-called 'taste' of his adversaries, with their contempt for the public (p. 501). Significantly, these diverse social groupings are simply lumped together; there is no sense of a process of fusion or incorporation similar to that by which middle-class intellectuals were admitted into nobiliary society under the collective label of *les honnêtes gens*. These cultural judgments are presented as being all the more authoritative for having been reached in apparent isolation. In 'Des jugements', 61, the public is firm as a rock, resistant to the influence of 'la puissance, les richesses, la violence, la flatterie, l'autorité, la faveur'. A satirical or anecdotal work circulated in manuscript (as its partisans might claim, among 'persons of taste'), however mediocre, can enjoy a tremendous reputation; publication, however, is liable to cut it down to size ('Des ouvrages de l'esprit', 5). In other words, 'taste' has been transported from the hegemonic to the common culture.

Well, not that common. It is obvious that the *peuple* whose judgment is cited with approval in the preface to the *Discours de réception* are *peuple* in the respectable sense; whereas the *peuple* in 'De la société', 1, with their deplorable sense of humour, are the common people and no mistake. All the same, the notion of the public as authoritative in matters of taste marks a certain emancipation of culture from aristocratic hegemony, precisely because it diminishes the influence of the personal relations of authority that help to support the aristocratic social structure.

And yet we saw, with reference to 'De la mode', 2, and its dissection of *curiosité*, that impersonal cultural relations go with the commercialization of culture and the fetishism of the cultural object; all of which was represented as undesirable. None the less, on La Bruyère's showing it appears to be inescapable. Indeed, the privileging of *le goût des anciens* is itself a form of fetishism, ignoring as it does (as the discourse of *honnêteté* did not) the role of the subject in the determination of cultural values. It is easy to see, however, that from La Bruyère's point of view, the supposed 'taste' of his *Moderne* adversaries appears as mere self-aggrandizement and disrespect for legitimately constituted authority. (Doubtless, the anti-feminism perceptible at several points in *Les Caractères* is connected with La Bruyère's alignment with the *Anciens*: Boileau also combines the two attitudes, and, as Françoise Escal notes (in Boileau, *OC*, p. 927), the satire 'Des femmes' contains various gibes at the *Modernes*, one of whose principal spokesmen, Perrault, responded to it with an *Apologie des femmes*.)

The mutability of taste in the cultural sphere is, as we have seen, a source of disquiet to La Bruyère. None the less, while he can see taste as being corrupted, and as vulnerable to the perversity of the *Modernes*, he is preserved from any more radical anxiety about the stability of the values he upholds by the assumption that human nature and the social order are alike immutable. They are kept in place partly by what appears to be a natural distribution of tastes of a rather different sort: the taste for exercising or deferring to authority, women's aversion from taxing their memories, which discourages them from study (although here La Bruyère rather lets the cat out of the bag by admitting that women's ignorance is an advantage from the male point of view). This moral and political, in short ideological, order of tastes imputed to different categories within society offers some kind of defence against the vagaries of taste in the cultural sphere. These, however, are linked, as obscurely emerges from the text of *Les Caractères*, to the workings of a market that will refuse to be moralized away.

La Bruyère's discourse of taste highlights certain crucial structural features of the notion. It is all very well to celebrate the value of 'good taste', to associate it with other valorized abstract qualities, reason, good sense, the 'natural', and so forth. But in order to exert a practical effect, these abstractions require to be provided with a concrete content, in the form of specific attitudes, (ideological) modes of recognition; and this means, in the last analysis, acknowledging the authority over 'taste' of a privileged category of subject that embodies these attitudes and forms of recognition. In La Bruyère this subject is absent or at best dispersed as a series of isolated qualities (learning, good sense, moral worthiness, and so forth), which the discourse never manages to unite. This is doubtless an unconscious lack: La Bruyère may know exactly what he means by a 'person of taste'. But if so, he does not let on. Nor does he make it quite comfortable to assume that the person he means is the good old *honnête homme*. His discourse of taste can certainly be placed *ideologically*: Christian-moralist, anti-feminist, politically conservative, traditionalist (pro-*Anciens*), classicist. But it does not profit from appealing to a determinate *social* backing, except in so far as that can be provided by the 'public'. It is of course because of its lack of an ideological alignment with any specific social group, and because of the reservations and ironies inherent in its deferences to authority, that *Les Caractères* reveals more than any other text here studied of the complexities and contradictions of ideological experience in late seventeenth-century France. That it does so partly reflects the individual social situation of La Bruyère, as a *bourgeois* (in the seventeenth-century sense) and humanist man of letters brought into contact wth the court-aristocratic culture embodied in the Condé household, and both impressed by and suspicious of the values of that culture. But beyond that the ambiguities of *Les Caractères* bear the mark of the contradictions in the situation of the non-commercial middle classes within the *ancien régime*, economically independent of the aristocracy, but dependent (through the *rentes* and through the holding of offices)[24] on the monarchy that supported the aristocracy; ideologically dependent on the aristocracy ('Nous devons les honorer, parce qu'ils sont grands et que nous sommes petits, et qu'il y en a d'autres plus petits que nous qui nous honorent', 'Des grands', 52); excluded from aristocratic culture, but with cultural traditions of its own; lacking any autonomous consciousness; merged in this composite formation, the public, yet distrustful of it because of its inherent subjection to purely commercial pressures that menace traditional cultural values. But to give these determinations their full scope is not necessarily to deny to La Bruyère the tribute due to an impressive honesty.

7

BOILEAU: TASTE AND THE INSTITUTION OF 'LITERATURE'

It is almost axiomatic to associate Boileau with 'taste'. According to Bray, he is the representative of French classical literature's phase of Taste, as Ronsard and Chapelain embodied the earlier phases of Imitation and the Rules. Mornet pays tribute to the excellence of Boileau's own taste, almost invariably confirmed by posterity. Litman observes that 'il possédait un goût très sûr pour la grande poésie de l'antiquité dont la splendeur ne pouvait s'expliquer par les règles de l'art'.[1] The last remark suggests how easy it is, while accepting the relative originality of Boileau's recourse to the notion of the sublime, to draft him into the chorus of seventeenth-century witnesses to the role of the ineffable, the mysterious, the non- or supra-rational in art. But to seek to harmonize Boileau's *sublime* with Bouhours's *je ne sais quoi* or Méré's *agrément*, on the grounds of their impalpability and elusiveness, is to obscure the specificity of Boileau's position. Certainly, no common discourse of taste provides a reason for doing so. The mere collation of textual formulae is not enough here; two texts may resemble each other as to terminology and even in substantive propositions while differing radically on the discursive level. The values they appeal to may be formally the same, but they may be appropriated to quite different categories of subject. The discourses of 'taste' studied up to now constitute their subjects in a quite specific way, by reference to the figure of the *honnête homme* and to the aristocratic culture that supports it. In Boileau, the subject of the 'taste'-judgment is quite differently defined.

The obvious place to begin the examination of Boileau's discourse of 'taste' is with the Longinian works; so I shall start instead with the poems. One of the targets of the satire 'Des femmes' is the *précieuse* who makes her house a haven for unpopular authors: 'Au mauvais goust public la Belle y fait la guerre.'[2] Very similar is the line from the portrait of the marquis in the ninth epistle who sets up as a literary critic: 'Il rit du mauvais goust de tant d'Hommes divers' (line 97; *OC*, p.135). Both *précieuse* and marquis are consciously

171

opposed to a majority 'bad taste'. In the second case this is further defined not only by the numerical weight but by the variety of its upholders. It is eminently clear from the context that this minority 'good taste' is a sham. The *précieuse* likes Cotin and Chapelain, and their badness is almost a central presupposition of Boileau's discourse. The marquis is nice but stupid; he goes to the opera to listen to the words, and is quoted as a particular instance of the general folly of belying one's original nature. The language in her case is especially loaded. She is mocked by the mock-heroic: this fair warrior is a figure from the 'heroic women' discourse of the earlier part of the century, is in other words dated and incongruous. As a woman, the implication is, she had better be a 'Belle' in earnest and keep out of matters she doesn't understand. The stupid marquis is a comic stereotype.[3]

That the taste of the multitude is bad goes without saying in certain contexts. But Boileau's apparent endorsement of it here is obviously ironical. He places it in the mouths of a *précieuse* and an aristocrat. Now I have argued that the discourse of good taste can foster nobiliary ideological dominance, and can also privilege the natural good judgment of women against the book-learning of scholars. True, many so-called *précieuses* (those of Mademoiselle de Scudéry's circle, for instance) were bourgeois in origin.[4] But this is not quite the point. It is also true that, although characters in poems are not real people but discursive constructs, they can be recognized as real, and if Méré, Saint-Evremond, or La Rochefoucauld were to recognize these two, they would probably condemn them as well: the marquis, for instance, has so far forgotten his rank as to act the pedant.[5] None the less, both marquis and *précieuse* could recognize themselves in the discourse of 'good taste' upheld by these writers, as members of the minority enlightened enough to dissent from the vulgar herd. Boileau intends to enforce a contrary recognition of the minority taste as bad. This is particularly clear if we look at his more extended discussions of literary judgments, as in the 1701 preface to his collected works. He begins by taking leave of the public with thanks for having bought his works in such quantities and attributes his success 'au soin que j'ay pris de me conformer toûjours à ses sentimens, et d'attraper, autant qu'il m'a esté possible, son goust en toutes choses' (*OC*, p. 1). *Goût*, like God, is on the side of the big battalions. The reward for a poet of being good alike at grave and gay is that 'Son livre aimé du Ciel et cheri des Lecteurs, / Est souvent chez Barbin entouré d'acheteurs' (*AP* I. 77–8; *OC*, p. 159). The alternative is the nightmare vision of (bad) books rotting away in the bookseller's or being torn up and used for wrapping groceries.[6] The equation of commercial success and artistic merit is justified as follows:

Un ouvrage a beau estre approuvé d'un petit nombre de Connoisseurs, s'il n'est plein d'un certain agrément et d'un certain sel propre à piquer le goust general des Hommes, il ne passera jamais pour un bon ouvrage, et il faudra à la fin que les Connoisseurs eux mesmes avoüent qu'ils se sont trompés en luy donnant leur approbation.   (*OC*, p. 1)

It should be obvious that this position is diametrically opposed to that of Méré, Saint-Evremond, and (for once) La Bruyère. It is the majority verdict that is authoritative, not that of a chosen few. These writers of course usually talk of 'les gens de (bon) goût' rather than 'les Connoisseurs', but this is immaterial; Boileau could hardly have spoken of 'les gens de goût' in this context without committing himself to the very position he is refuting. He agrees with them on the potential opposition between minority and majority taste but reverses the valuation they place on them. The minority cannot claim special authority on the basis of special knowledge, or a special faculty of discernment, the existence of which is not even acknowledged here.

Jules Brody observes that the abbé Guéton thought that what Boileau meant, or should have meant, by 'public' in this context was 'tous les connaisseurs', and that, whereas Boileau corrected others of Guéton's notes, he allowed this one to stand.[7] But the argument from silence cuts both ways. If by 'public' Boileau had meant 'tous les connaisseurs', as distinct from a minority of them, why on earth did he not say so? Besides, this interpretation makes nonsense of the preface as a whole. The point of departure is Boileau's gratitude to the public for buying 'tant de fois des ouvrages si peu dignes de son admiration' (*OC*, p. 1). It would be both naive and question-begging to assume that only connoisseurs have bought his works, and churlish to thank only those connoisseurs who have bought them. The fundamental presupposition is that the economic facts of literary consumption reflect general human values. A good book is one that pleases 'le goust general des Hommes'.

Boileau veers into the discourse of mystery by his assertion that the 'agrément' and 'sel' by which this taste is gratified consists in 'un je ne scay quoy qu'on peut beaucoup mieux sentir, que dire' (*OC*, p. 1). But he veers immediately out again by proceeding to define them as the effect of a combination of 'pensées vraies' and 'expressions justes'. The mind is constantly full of nebulous ideas of the truth, and is therefore delighted to encounter 'quelqu'une de ces idées bien éclaircie, et mise dans un beau jour' (*OC*, p. 1). The locus of literary pleasure is thus 'l'Esprit de l'Homme' as such, not a particular type of mind. One is part of the public through the economic act of purchasing a book, but in the last instance through one's basic humanity. It is true that Boileau remarks in the ninth reflection on Longinus that 'tout le monde ne peut pas juger de la justesse et de la force d'une pensée'. But there he is contrasting this kind of judgment with the universal instinctive perception of linguistic register: 'il n'y a presque personne ... qui ne sente la bassesse des mots' (*OC*, p. 532). But even if truth-judgments are allowed to belong to a higher order of difficulty, the fact remains that the 1701 preface refers truth to a universal order of human value in which everybody is admitted to participate.

For this reason, Boileau argues, the ideational content of poetry must be universally accessible:

Qu'est-ce qu'une pensée neuve, brillante, extraordinaire? Ce n'est point, comme se le persuadent les Ignorans, une pensée que personne n'a jamais euë, ni dû avoir. C'est au contraire une pensée qui a dû venir à tout le monde, et que quelqu'un s'avise le premier d'exprimer.   (*OC*, p. 1)

Boileau's own examples of the wrong kind of thought come from Théophile and Benserade, and while in the latter case he is probably venting a grudge (see *OC*, p. 861, n. 3), the former example suggests that his theory is directed at the poetry of the early part of the century, with its fondess for the conceit. But it also clashes with a tendency in taste-discourse to prize difficulty of access as a compliment paid by the author to the reader of taste, a connotative signifier of the distinction between the exceptional and the 'common' reader – take the following remark of Saint-Evremond's: 'Les choses communes font regreter le tems qu'on met à les lire; celles qui sont finement pensées, donnent à un lecteur délicat le plaisir de son intelligence et de son goût' (*L* II, 368).

The appeal to consensual judgments as authoritative is taken up in Boileau's conclusion:

Puis donc qu'une pensée n'est belle qu'en ce qu'elle est vraye; et que l'effet infaillible du Vray, quand il est bien énoncé, c'est de frapper les Hommes; Il s'ensuit que ce qui ne frappe point les Hommes, n'est ni beau, ni vray, ou qu'il est mal énoncé; et que par consequent un ouvrage qui n'est point goûté du Public, est un très-méchant Ouvrage.   (*OC*, p. 3)

The public is thus equated with 'les Hommes' in general and constituted as the source of true value-judgments. A good book may fail for a time, owing to intrigue or envy, but in the end it will triumph.

The mature judgment of the public reflects man's natural orientation to truth: 'l'effet infaillible du Vray ... est de frapper les Hommes'.

How much difference is made by the phrase I have just omitted: 'quand il est bien énoncé'? Brody would presumably take it as crucial, since he argues that Boileau is here concerned with an 'esthetic' truth (*Boileau and Longinus*, p. 136). I am not sure what 'esthetic truth' may be, but whatever it is, it is not what Boileau means by '[le] Vray'; he is using the word in a perfectly ordinary sense. He distinguishes quite clearly between the truth-content of an utterance and its expressive qualities. Truth-content is reflected in consensus. The basis of a *bon mot* is 'une chose que chacun pensoit', which is then expressed 'd'une maniere vive, fine et nouvelle'. Similarly, Louis XII's epigram 'Un Roy de France ne venge point les injures d'un Duc d'Orléans' is striking because it conveys 'une vérité que tout le monde sent' in a memorable form (*OC*, p. 2). The truth that makes an impact on the reader is not aesthetic but moral, in the broad sense; it is the manner of its utterance that comes in for aesthetic judgment.

The infallibility of the literary effect deserves attention. If we are struck by a line of poetry, we can be sure (at least provisionally, until the public has made up its mind) both that it contains a truth and that it expresses it well. If we are not, we can be sure that the idea expressed is not true, or that it is badly expressed. Indeed, matters can be simplified still further. In order to know that something is badly expressed, we must have an idea at least of what that something is; and knowing that a line of poetry that fails to strike us is deficient either in truth or in expressiveness, we should be able to tell whether it is badly expressing a truth, skilfully expressing what is false, or inept in both conception and execution. And in making these judgments, we are simply participating in a general human rationality (which, admittedly, only the definitive verdict of the public can fully embody). It is difficult, on this showing, to find room for a specific category of 'good taste', still less to see it as the privilege of a minority.

Again, in the preface to the *Epistres nouvelles* (1698), Boileau asserts that 'le Public n'est pas un Juge qu'on puisse corrompre, ni qui se regle par les passions d'autruy'; it is in consequence quite unaffected by authorial defences of bad works or by hostile criticism of good ones (*OC*, p. 138). Indeed, the public takes on the role of the poet's super-ego: although he has taken as much care over the eleventh satire as over the rest of his writings, Boileau concedes that 'je ne sçaurois pourtant dire si elle est bonne ou mauvaise: car je ne l'ai encore communiquée qu'à deux ou trois de mes plus intimes Amis ... C'est donc au Public à m'apprendre ce que je dois penser de cet ouvrage' (*OC*, pp. 4–5).

That Boileau shifted the locus of 'good taste' from the select minority to the public as a whole has of course been pointed out before, by J.-B. Barrère for instance, although he tends to talk as if, in doing so, Boileau was selling the pass.[8] But this displacement should not be read as a mere vicissitude befalling the essential concept of 'taste' but as the substitution of one taste-discourse, postulating a different kind of subject, appealing to different values, for another. The social determinants and implications of this shift are examined below.

But who does Boileau mean by 'the public'? In the simplest sense, he means the people who buy books. But the definition is more specific than that. Taking up the cudgels on behalf of Boileau, Arnauld affirms in a letter to Perrault, one of the severest critics of the satire 'Des femmes', that 'on doit avoir du respect pour le jugement du Public; et quant il s'est declaré hautement pour un Auteur ou pour un Ouvrage, on ne peut guére le combattre de front, et le contredire ouvertement, qu'on ne s'expose à en estre mal-traité' (Boileau, *OC*, p. 586). Perrault, then, should know what to expect since the poem has been well received 'dans le monde, à la Cour, à Paris, dans les Provinces' and even abroad (*OC*, p. 587). Arnauld divides up the audience socially, but the verdicts of different groups confirm rather than clash with one another. He also brings in 'les bons Connoisseurs' and 'tout ce qu'il y a des gens d'esprit à la Cour et à Paris' (*OC*, p. 587). But these simply ratify, indeed in some sense represent, the judgment of the public: they do not contradict it, nor are they shown as leading it. The 'divisive' move by which the connoisseurs are distinguished from the public as a whole and the public itself broken down into its social constituents is cancelled by the 'inclusive' move that fuses all their verdicts together in a consensus. Its function here is therefore not the same as in the *honnête* discourse of taste.

Boileau himself endorses this definition of the public, accusing his poetry of misplaced optimism as to its reception:

> Vains et foibles Enfans dans ma vieillesse nés,
> Vous croyés sur les pas de vos heureux Aisnés,
> Voir bien-tost vos bons mots passant du Peuple aux Princes,
> Charmer également la Ville et les Provinces.
>
> (*Epistre* X, lines 7–10; *OC*, p. 141)

Again, literary response is seen as transcending social barriers, whether of class or of region. This 'aggregative' discourse recurs, in more nuanced form, in the epistle to Seignelay: 'Sçais-tu pourquoy mes vers sont lûs dans les Provinces, / Sont recherchez du peuple, et receus chez les Princes?' (*Epistre* IX, lines 47–8; *OC*, p. 134). The explanation, says Boileau, is the moral soundness of his poetry:

> C'est qu'en eux [mes vers] le Vrai du Mensonge vainqueur
> Partout se montre aux yeux et va saisir le cœur:
> Que le Bien et le Mal y sont prisez au juste,
> Que jamais un Facquin n'y tinst un rang auguste.
>
> (lines 53–6; *OC*, p. 134)

This helps to clarify the meaning of 'truth' in the 1701 preface as essentially or predominantly moral truth. The view of literary judgment expounded there is largely shaped by Boileau's moral conception of his poetry. The addressee of his poetic discourse is not the discerner, in the manner of Méré, of what is appropriate in each and every worldly situation, but the moral, and therefore universal, subject. The coincidence of Boileau's attitude with Arnauld's is deeply significant, as is the obvious contrast with Saint-Evremond's amoralism, articulated, as we have seen, with the notions of 'taste' and *délicatesse*.

But the conception of the public as an aggregate of different social and regional groups is countered by two rival tendencies: the proscription of certain tastes by their ascription to particular social categories of subject and the association of social authority with cultural authority. There is, to begin with, a systematic identification of popular, as distinct from public, taste as bad. The craze for burlesque violated all stylistic decorum, the precept that 'Le stile le moins noble a pourtant sa noblesse' (*AP* I. 80; *OC*, p. 159). Instead, 'Le Parnasse parla le langage des Hales' (*AP* I. 84). The proper place for the burlesque is among '[les] Plaisans du Pont-neuf' (*AP* I. 97), the puppeteers and mountebanks (see *OC*, p. 990, n. *e*). The Pont-Neuf reappears as a locus of popular taste in the injunction to playwrights to leave dirty jokes to the lackeys who hang about that area (*AP* III. 424–8; *OC*, p. 179). The purpose of comedy is not 'd'aller dans une place, / De mots sales et bas charmer la populace' (*AP* III. 403–4). The open space of the street connotes indiscipline, the rule of the body and its lower appetites, which find linguistic expression in 'saleté' (*AP* III. 425), and 'mots sales et bas'.[9] The theatre, by contrast, is hygienic, respectful of social hierarchy, keeping popular elements in the audience literally in their place, under the eyes of their superiors.[10]

Among the non-popular classes, no group can claim a monopoly of good taste. The infection of the burlesque spread geographically and socially, from Paris to the provinces, from 'clerc' and 'Bourgeois' to 'Princes' (*AP* I. 87–8; *OC*, p. 159). Again, the public is broken down into its social constituents and then re-united, only this time by its (temporary) bad taste. If the upper classes did not initiate the craze, they cannot claim much credit for having borrowed it from their inferiors. And when Reason put a stop to the taste for conceits and wordplay, the last pockets of resistance were to be found at court (*AP* II. 130–2; *OC*, p. 166). On the other hand, it was the court that first abandoned the burlesque (*AP* I. 91–4; *OC*, p. 159). And a person like Condé (the 'prince non moins considérable par les lumières de son esprit que par le nombre de ses victoires') embodies both social and cultural authority.[11] None the less, cultural authority in the last resort remains with the public as a whole, and though this excludes the popular masses, it contains middle-class as well as aristocratic elements.

To attribute Boileau's practical deference to the public to avariciousness would be not only cynical but erroneous. He took no payment from booksellers for his own work.[12] But he was conscious of the economic basis of literary activity, as the *Art poétique* shows:

> Travaillez pour la gloire, et qu'un sordide gain
> Ne soit jamais l'objet d'un illustre Ecrivain.
> Je sçai qu'un noble Esprit peut, sans honte et sans crime,
> Tirer de son travail un tribut legitime:
> Mais je ne puis souffrir ces Auteurs renommez,
> Qui dégoûtez de gloire, et d'argent affammez,
> Mettent leur Apollon aux gages d'un Libraire,
> Et font d'un Art divin un métier mercenaire.
> (IV. 125–32; *OC*, p. 183)

Commercial values come under bombardment from no fewer than three positions gestured at in the language: nobiliary ('gloire'), monarchical ('tribut'), and mytho-theological ('Apollon', 'divin'). The poet, like the nobleman, may not engage in lucrative activity without *dérogation*. Boileau is alluding here to a decisive shift in, to use Terry Eagleton's term, the literary mode of production (*Criticism and Ideology*, pp. 45–8). H.-J. Martin notes that, from the mid-1660s on, booksellers' *privilèges*, hitherto confined to ten years at most, were more and more often extended, thus boosting the profitability of individual titles. Realizing this, authors showed an increasing propensity to haggle over the sale of potentially lucrative works, even going so far as to demand a share in the profits. In this golden age of vulgarization, as Martin calls it, it was getting easier to make a living from literary hack-work, churning out treatises on *honnêteté* or La Bruyère-style observations on men and manners, not to mention novels, lists of useful addresses, and cookery books. The booksellers, of course, complained of authors' cupidity in terms that curiously resemble Boileau's fulminations: 'L'art de composer est pour ainsi dire devenu un métier pour gagner sa vie.'[13] From the authors' point of view, this development was just as well, since although the backing of the great was still a powerful aid to literary success, it would appear that they were becoming less willing to act directly as patrons, and that a 'servile address' to them (as Johnson defined 'dedication') was less likely to earn a reward (Martin, *Livre, pouvoirs et société*, vol. II, p. 913).

Boileau is hostile to this commercialization of literature. His admission that 'un noble Esprit' may legitimately make money from writing was very likely prompted by concern for the susceptibilities of Racine, who did receive payment for his tragedies.[14] But the word 'illustre' suggests that disinterestedness is an additional sign of the difference between the great and the mediocre writer, a matter to which I shall return.

Ideally, for Boileau, the financial situation of poetry is comparable to that of the noble art of war, where financial gain comes by accident: 'Aux plus savans Auteurs, comme aux plus grands Guerriers / Apollon ne promet qu'un nom et des lauriers' (*AP* IV. 177–8; *OC*, p. 184).[15] In one of his surveys of the history of poetry, Boileau traces its deterioration into a commodity:

> Mais enfin l'Indigence amenant la Bassesse,
> Le Parnasse oublia sa premiere noblesse.
> Un vil amour du gain infectant les esprits,
> De mensonges grossiers soüilla tous les écrits,
> Et par tout enfantant mille ouvrages frivoles,
> Trafiqua du discours, et vendit les paroles.
>
> (*AP* IV. 167–72; *OC*, p. 184)

Again the commercialization of poetry appears as a derogation from nobility. But there seems to be a contradiction between this passage and the 1701 preface. There, the purchase and sale of literary works was the medium in which the public judgment, and through it the universal order of truth, was expressed. Here, it is a betrayal of the nature of poetry and a breeding-ground of lies.

What is required in order to reconcile these two perspectives is the existence of a book trade, and therefore a general public, in which the author shall not, however, be implicated. On the other hand, as Boileau himself acknowledges, authors have to live. The solution he points to is royal patronage:

Et que craindre en ce siecle, où toûjours les beaux Arts
D'un Astre favourable éprouvent les regards,
Ou d'un Prince éclairé la sage prévoyance
Fait par tout au Merite ignorer l'indigence?

(*AP* IV. 189–92; *OC*, p. 184)

The economic attachment of poetry to the monarchical order thus authenticates and purifies the relation between the poet and his audience. It further endorses the poet's claim to quasi-nobiliary status by annulling his dependence on direct financial gain. The role of the monarchy as a preservative against the commercialization and capitalization of literature was to be pointed to in 1685 by the booksellers of Paris, explaining why their prices were higher than those of Lyons: in the good old days authors had actually contributed to printing costs out of the money they received from the Crown in the form of pensions and gratifications (Martin, *Livre, pouvoir et société*, vol. II, p. 915).

To summarize: Boileau has displaced the aristocratic values of a minority good taste by the universal values of a 'public' culture. By the same token, the locus of repression of the discourse of taste has been shifted downwards. It no longer predominantly functions, as in Méré, Saint-Evremond, or La Rochefoucauld, to sustain aristocratic hegemony among the privileged strata in general (including the upper bourgeoisie and the *noblesse d'épée*). That hegemony is to some small extent admitted in cultural matters, but Boileau refuses to identify the non-aristocratic with the popular. Rather, the non-popular classes are brought together in the notion of the public. The poet depends on their verdict, but not in any squalid financial sense, for his economic welfare is secured by an all-pervasive monarchical cultural apparatus.

The relation between author and public pivots on the literary work. Work and author are, moreover, inseparable. These assumptions appear self-evident, but their implications for Boileau repay consideration. Certainly, his use of the notion of taste is focused on this composite of work and author, as a passage like the following makes clear:

Lors que des Ecrivains ont esté admirez durant un fort grand nombre de siecles, et n'ont esté méprisez que par quelques gens de goust bizarre, car il se trouve toûjours des gousts dépravez, alors non seulement il y a de la temerité, mais il y a de la folie à vouloir douter du merite de ces Ecrivains. Que si vous ne voyez point les beautez de leurs ecrits, il ne faut pas conclure qu'elles n'y sont point, mais que vous estes aveugle, et que vous n'avez point de goust. Le gros des Hommes à la longue ne se trompe point sur les ouvrages d'esprit. Il n'est plus question, à l'heure qu'il est, de sçavoir si Homere, Platon, Ciceron, Virgile, sont des hommes merveilleux; c'est une chose sans contestation puisque vingt siecles en sont convenus: il s'agit de sçavoir en quoy consiste ce merveilleux qui les a fait admirer de tant de siecles; et il faut trouver moyen de le voir, ou renoncer aux belles lettres, ausquelles vous devez croire que vous n'avez ni goust ni génie, puisque vous ne sentez point ce qu'ont senti tous les hommes.   (*OC*, pp. 524–5)

Not only individual writers can be a touchstone of 'taste': the same applies to certain privileged passages. No one, says Boileau, can hear the words of Genesis, 'Que la lumiere se fasse; et la lumiere se fit', without a pleasurable feeling of exaltation, the sign of the sublime: should there be 'quelque Homme bizarre' who does not feel it, 'il ne faut pas chercher des raisons pour luy monstrer qu'il y en a; mais se borner à le plaindre de son peu de conception, et de son peu de goust, qui l'empesche de sentir ce que tout le monde sent d'abord' (*OC*, p. 546). The 'douceur majestueuse' of these words 'frappe ... agreablement l'oreille de tout homme qui a quelque delicatesse et quelque goust' (*OC*, p. 556).

Boileau instantiates the observation that 'il se trouve toûjours des gousts dépravez' (*OC*, p. 524) by citing the Emperor Hadrian, whose 'goût bizarre' led him to prefer the writings of 'un je ne sai quel Poëte' to those of Homer, and who refused to believe that 'tous les hommes ensemble, pendant près de vingt siecles, eussent eu le sens commun' (*OC*, p. 309).[16] Another case is Perrault, insensitive to Pindar's lyric discontinuities, unaware of the rule that the rules are sometimes there to be broken – as one would expect from 'un Homme sans aucun goust, qui croit que la Clelie et nos Opera sont les modeles du Genre sublime; et qu'une espece de bizarrerie d'esprit rend insensible à tout ce qui frappe ordinairement les Hommes' (*OC*, pp. 227–8).

The repressive aspect of the discourse of taste here is plain to see: one's response to a particular historically-constituted corpus of texts becomes the touchstone of one's normality, of one's humanity, even – what sort of human being are you if you can't respond to what all other human beings have responded to? These passages are evidently linked to the 1701 preface by their common emphasis on the consensual basis of literary judgments; here, however, the consensus is extended backwards in time, invoking an eternal ahistorical human nature as the basis of literary and other judgments.

So what does 'taste', if one has it, subject one to, apart from this assumption of an unchanging human nature? The *honnête* discourse of 'taste' calls on the subject to know his or her place, a specific position, largely constituted by the transindividual factors of class and gender, within a network of potential relations with other people. But Boileau's 1701 preface implicitly identifies good taste with 'le goust general des Hommes' (*OC*, p. 1), which is in turn defined in relation to a universal order of truth. And the ninth epistle suggests, as we saw, that Boileau's universal appeal is grounded on his respect for moral truth. Moral values dissolve the class barriers between the various subjects who perceive them, for they are supposedly binding on all and sundry.

But 'taste' in Boileau promotes another kind of recognition: of the exceptional, privileged status of particular utterances, texts, authors, not of poets and poetry, even ancient poetry, in general. Boileau specifically states that his vindication of the ancients applies only to a few outstanding writers, not to the corpus of ancient literature as such (*OC*, pp. 526–7). Moreover, the distinction between good and bad literary works is built into Boileau's doctrine of the public as arbiter of 'taste'. The favour that it bestows on some works is significant only by contrast with its indifference or hostility to others. The crowds flocking to buy a good book count for something only if there are also piles of unsold, and therefore negligible, works left on the booksellers' shelves. To be an exception thus means something quite different depending on one's position in culture. The reader or critic who stands out against the majority is exposed as a freak, as 'bizarre'. But only the poet who stands out from the majority is worthy of consideration. In any other art or craft mere competence is respectable, 'Mais dans l'Art dangereux de rimer et d'écrire, / Il n'est point de degrez du mediocre au pire' (*AP* IV. 31–2; *OC*, p. 180). Poetry is thus a different kind of art from any other, and the poet a different kind of person from his readers.

It will be seen that Boileau sometimes makes the same observations as the *honnête* discourse of 'taste', but attaches different valuations to them. For example, both he and his implicit adversaries agree that the 'taste' of a minority with pretensions to special knowledge or insight may differ from that of the majority; but they draw contrasting inferences from this. Much the same is true here. Saint-Evremond also perceives the discontinuity between poetic and ordinary language, but from the point of view of the *honnête homme* for whom this is one more sign of poetry's essentially subordinate role: it exists for his pleasure, not as an object of his veneration (*OP* IV, 112). For Boileau, the difference between ordinary and poetic language is a sign of the transcendent status of great poetry and poets, a status to be acknowledged by all alike, irrespective of their claims to *honnêteté*.

What is the poet's privilege founded on? Truth is accessible to all, in the sense that when it is well expressed we cannot but be struck by it. But it is the poet's privilege to give it memorable expression. Equally, reason and good sense are universal qualities, not confined to a handful of individuals, but it is not given to everyone to embody them in poetry:

> Tout doit tendre au Bon sens: mais pour y parvenir
> Le chemin est glissant et penible à tenir.
> Pour peu qu'on s'en écarte, aussi-tost l'on se noye.
> La Raison, pour marcher, n'a souvent qu'une voye.
>
> (*AP* I. 45–8; *OC*, p. 158)

As Brody points out, *raison*, as used by Boileau in the *Art poétique*, denotes 'a kind of privileged faculty' (*Boileau and Longinus*, p. 65). 'The means to the right conduct of *la raison* itself', as Brody further observes, 'are left in question', which 'stirs the suspicion that *le bon sens*, rightly used, is a good "sense", a kind of sensitivity, having more to do with practised taste than with ratiocination' (p. 67). 'Taste' here is Brody's word rather than Boileau's, but he is not unjustified in using it, or in suggesting that the kind of knowledge denoted by Boileau's use of *savoir* is 'functionally close' to *génie*, *talent*, *secret* and *goût* (p. 51): only the subject of this taste is not the consumer of the work but its producer.

For the reader, then, 'taste' consists in recognizing this exceptional ability of the great poet and admitting his claims to mastery of the order of discourse. It is Perrault's lack of taste that prevents his seeing that the ordinary rules of discursive continuity may be legitimately broken in the ode (*OC*, pp. 227–8). This is a 'mystere de l'Art' – that is, for everyone else it is mysterious, but for the great poet it is a liberty he knows how to take. 'Taste' is a kind of trust in his superior knowledge. It is precisely this kind of trust that the *honnête homme* refuses when he takes it upon himself, in the name of his own 'good taste' and of the *bienséances*, to find faults in Virgil.

The antithesis between Boileau's conception of taste and the *honnête* conception takes striking form in a struggle for control of the key term *pédant*. The role of this label in excluding the learned humanist from a position of cultural authority has already been discussed. The *honnête* representation of a pedant can be found in Perrault, who, according to Boileau, believes that 'un Pédant ... est un sçavant nouri dans un Collége, et rempli de Grec et de Latin, qui admire aveuglément tous les Auteurs anciens', both in literary and in scientific matters (*OC*, p. 515); whereas it is in fact

un homme plein de luy-meme, qui, avec un mediocre sçavoir décide hardiment de toutes choses ... qui blâme tous les Auteurs anciens ... qui trouve,
à la verité, quelques endroits passables dans Virgile; mais qui y trouve aussi
beaucoup d'endroits dignes d'estre siflez: qui croit à peine Terence digne du
nom de joli; qui au milieu de tout cela se pique surtout de politesse: qui tient
que la plûpart des Anciens n'ont ni ordre, ni œconomie dans leurs discours:
En un mot, qui compte pour rien de heurter sur cela le sentiment de tous les
hommes.   (*OC*, pp. 515–16)[17]

But what is the authority for this 'relexicalization'?[18] Well, this
depiction of a pedant corresponds, says Boileau, with Régnier's, and
he is, by common consent, the French poet with the keenest insight
into men and manners apart from Molière.

   'By common consent': the relexicalization that damages the elitist
discourse is validated by an appeal to the consensual discourse. In
other words, Boileau is begging the question. But this is not said in
order to blame him, rather to underscore the irreducibility of this
ideological confrontation.

   The 'anti-pedant' discourse and its concomitant aristocraticism
are turned against its upholders elsewhere, in a passage of the tenth
satire that Boileau later discarded. The *précieuse* likes Chapelain, but
in the original version she likes Perrault as well. But she has to account
for his unpopularity:

> Elle en accuse alors nostre Siecle infecté,
> Du pedantesque goust qu'ont pour l'Antiquité
> Magistrats, Princes, Ducs, et mesme Fils de France,
> Qui lisent sans rougir et Virgile et Terence.
>
> (*OC*, p. 929, n. *az.*)

The point is not, of course, that Virgil and Terence are good because
the right sort of people read them, but that it is absurd to accuse the
leaders of French society of pedantry. They, the implication is, are
perfectly happy to accept the verdict of the centuries without pluming
themselves on their superior discernment.

   What are the effects of this reorientation of the notion of taste?
In the first place, the relative devaluation of the individual subject,
whose voice now merges in the chorus of the ages, and its corollary,
the increased importance of the order of values external to but
acknowledged by him or her. Secondly, the liberation of culture,
poetry in particular, from aristocratic hegemony. The two, of course,
are connected, for aristocratic hegemony finds ideological expression
in the notion of the individual whose superior discernment sets him off
from the common herd. Boileau's poet does more than occasionally

strike a chord that gratifies the ear of the *honnête homme*. He has special access to values to which the *honnête homme* is subject along with everybody else: truth, reason, that kind of grandeur which goes by the name of the sublime.

It is not, perhaps, surprising that Boileau should have represented, and celebrated, poetry as a kind of alternative nobility (the gift for it comes by birth; it is not exercised for profit). To do so of course reinforces the ideological prestige of the nobility proper but it simultaneously confines its authority to its rightful social and political sphere. On his own territory, the poet owes no allegiance to any one sectional group. His splendour does not come from isolation, but from his subjection only to *collective*, consensual authority.

But this discourse is tenable only because of the existence of such an authority: an identifiable but impersonal public. Personal cultural influences are certainly recognized in Boileau: if Condé tells you that the ending of a poem is wrong, you had perhaps better think about changing it. And the would-be poet needs friends honest enough to give him good advice about his efforts (*AP* I. 186–207; *OC*, pp. 161–2). But the opinion of two or three close friends can be no substitute for the judgment of the public, as Boileau himself implies (*OC*, pp. 4–5). There is in all this a curious anticipation of Rousseau's substitution of the impersonal authority of the collective sovereign for relations of personal dependence.[19] And this on second thoughts is not so curious. Rousseau's political theory is one of the classic statements of a bourgeois democratic ideal. Boileau's doctrine of the public is, relatively speaking, pre-bourgeois to the extent that it admits the middle classes (especially the professional strata to which he himself belonged) as cultural interlocutors.

It could be argued very generally that this substitution of impersonal for personal relations of domination is characteristic of the transition from feudalism or feudal-absolutism to capitalism. Social formations of the former type depend on multiple networks of interpersonal relations, based on kinship, clientage, personal attachment, and so on. The peasant pays no dues to lords in general, only to his lord, who in turn owes protection only to his own dependants. Capitalist relations, speaking in the abstract, are impersonal: as long as someone buys this product, operates this machine, manages this plant, and does so competently where it matters, the system can work. Similarly, for Boileau, as long as his poems don't end up being read for the entertainment of lackeys hanging around the Pont-Neuf, it doesn't much matter who reads them. By buying them, one has staked out at least a preliminary claim to a share in the collective authority of the public.

This, of course, is unduly schematic. In real life, Boileau was necessarily involved in personal cultural relations. He had friends in high places, such as Mme de Montespan (without whose intervention he would probably not have been appointed royal historiographer, Adam, *Histoire*, vol. III, p. 153) and the chancellor Pontchartrain. And no doubt he enjoyed his forays into high society, as described by Clarac (pp. 94–5), and being accepted as an *honnête homme* by the likes of Bussy-Rabutin.[20] But his most significant links with a group, intellectually speaking, were with the serious and scholarly *Académie de Lamoignon* to which Rapin, Pellisson, Claude Fleury and Bossuet all lectured (*OC*, pp. xv–xvii). Lamoignon's circle was hostile, as Adam notes, to the cultural influence of women and aristocrats (*Histoire*, vol. III, p. 136).

Boileau's grounding of 'taste' in a broadly-based consensus presupposes a wider audience for poetry than the few *habitués* of even the most cultured salon. The 'taste' that recognizes the pre-eminence of certain writers thus rests upon what Boileau in principle objects to – the commercialization of the book. Only by the operations of a market can literature escape the control of small select audiences and individual patrons: personal influences that help to sustain, in the cultural sphere, the traditional social hegemony of the aristocracy.

At first sight, 'taste' in Boileau seems merely to generate tautologies; it tells us that great writers are great. And the concept, in some ways, has only a marginal significance in his work. He never attempts to say what taste is, only that certain people lack it. None the less, taste-statements carry a sizeable ideological burden. 'Taste' recognizes, so to speak, the universal recognizability of the *merveilleux* embodied in the works of great writers, and thus helps to foster the presuppositions of an unchanging human nature and universal human values, which the *Modernes* were beginning to question. Where literature is concerned, these values are manifested only gradually, as the witnesses to a writer's greatness slowly accumulate over the centuries. But their contemporary realization is at its fullest in the public, due allowance being made for temporary misjudgments. The verdict of the public tends towards the status of a universal norm. This is true as regards both sublimity and (moral) truth, although it has to be said that there is a contradiction between these two values. The sublime is defined in terms of power: 'cet extraordinaire et ce merveilleux qui frape dans le discours, et qui fait qu'un ouvrage enleve, ravit, transporte' (*OC*, p. 338), 'une certaine force de discours, propre à eslever et à ravir l'Ame, et qui provient ou de la grandeur de la pensée et de la noblesse du sentiment, ou de la magnificence des paroles, ou du tour harmonieux, vif et animé de l'expression', or from all three of these qualities together (*OC*, pp. 562–3). Although the verb *frapper* is also used in the 1701 preface to describe the impact of truth upon the mind, no mention is made of truth in these definitions of the sublime, and great authors are praised for their *merveilleux* qualities rather than for their truthfulness. That the sublime is non-moral in nature is clear from at least one of Boileau's examples, the exchange from Corneille's *Médée*: 'Contre tant d'ennemis que vous reste-t-il?' – 'Moy'; where what is held up to admiration is Médée's Satanic self-assertion, 'la fierté audacieuse de cette Magicienne, et la confiance qu'elle a dans son Art' (*OC*, p. 549).[21] But this is by the way.

By ratifying a consensus extended in time, 'taste' lends validity to its synchronic equivalent, the consensus extended in space, diffused throughout the various social strata possessed, in differing degrees, of power and wealth – *rentiers*, officials, professional men, respectable merchants, alongside the dominant class proper, the seigneurial landowners and their spearhead, the court aristocracy. In other words, it gives ideological expression to the 'class front' that was the basis of French absolutism (Porchnev, *Les Soulèvements populaires*, p. 292). The importance attached to the public is an instance of this, but also an unconscious tribute to the increasing penetration of the French economy by capitalism.

But the commercialization of literature, the commodification of the poem, is perceived by Boileau as inimical to the production of true poetry, as degrading the poet from the exceptional status that the public is supposed, in virtue of its 'taste', to recognize. As we have seen, for Boileau the remedy lies in royal financial support, which, by removing the writer from sordid involvement with money matters, assures his 'nobility' and independence. Moreover, the great monarch is a positive source of poetic inspiration: 'Un Auguste aisément peut faire des Virgiles' (*Epistre* I, line 174; *OC*, p. 107). And it is the monarchy that consolidates, and benefits from, the class front.

In a sense, then, 'taste' promotes a system of values and assumptions that contributes to the reproduction of the existing socio-economic order. I say 'in a sense', however, because it is only fair to add that Boileau's own assent to the regime he lived under was far more qualified than the foregoing would suggest. His Jansenist sympathies are well known. Adam points out that the Lamoignon circle was something of an oppositional group (*Histoire*, vol. III, p. 115), with a tendency to turn away from modern society and look nostalgically back at the noble simplicity of Homeric and biblical times (ibid., p. 142). Boileau's own last poem, the satire 'L'Equivoque', was banned. And the poetry is perhaps the most powerful indication of the tensions in his attitude towards the regime. So far from being a source of inspiration, the glories of Louis's reign seem to affect Boileau with writer's block. When he tries to write heroic verse, he finds himself sterile: but 'quand il faut railler, j'ai ce que je souhaite; / Alors certes alors, je me connois Poëte' (*Satire* VII, lines 33–4; *OC*, p. 38). The opposition between the satiric and the heroic or dithyrambic is made plain at the beginning of the eighth epistle:

> Grand Roy, cesse de vaincre, ou je cesse d'écrire.
> Tu sçais bien que mon stile est né pour la Satire:
> Mais mon Esprit contraint de la desavoüer,
> Sous Ton regne étonnant ne veut plus que loüer.
>
> (lines 1–4; *OC*, p. 130)

The heroic is the death of satire, of Boileau himself as a writer: 'Moi, qui sur Ton nom déjà brûlant d'écrire / Sens au bout de ma plume expirer la Satire' (*Epître* I, lines 177–8; *OC*, p. 107). Satire may disappear, but the heroic never arrives to take its place. The fourth epistle ends with the promise of authentic heroic verse: 'Assuré des beaux vers dont Ton bras me répond, / Je T'attens dans deux ans aux bords de l'Hellespont' (lines 171–2; *OC*, p. 117). Two years later, in 1674, the *Art poétique* appears, with the declaration that its author, 'nouri dans la Satire, / N'ose encor manier la trompette et la lyre' (IV. 223–4; *OC*, p. 185). When he does go all out for the heroics, in the *Ode sur la prise de Namur*, he still feels impelled to sign it with a last flourish of satire, a side-swipe at Perrault (line 170; *OC*, p. 234), and the discarded second stanza hit out at Perrault again and at Fontenelle (see *OC*, p. 1023, n. *a*).

'Taste', in Boileau, to recapitulate, serves to liberate both reader and poet from the domination of the exclusive culture of self-labelled *honnêteté*, with its seigneurial, nobiliary and court connexions. It installs, on the contrary, an inclusive ideal of the public. It restores classical scholarship and the humanist tradition to favour. It sanctions, in some ways reluctantly, the operation of a literary market, and with it, by implication, the growing influence of capitalist attitudes and activity. By celebrating Augustan-style patronage of poetry, it endorses the cultural policy of the Ludovician regime. It does not, however, help to resolve the contradictions in Boileau's own position as both official propagandist and satirist.

CONCLUSION

In chapter one I outlined some of the social and cultural divisions within the *ancien régime* that the discourse of taste could be seen as incorporating. In succeeding chapters I have tried to show how varieties of the discourse construct themselves by allusion to these. I shall now try to tie together the general picture of seventeenth-century French society and the conclusions of the individual studies.

The discourse of taste provided a sphere in which major transformations in seventeenth-century French society could be negotiated, assimilated, resisted. These transformations were taking place at several levels of the social process, in the relationships between the dominant and the subordinate classes, between different fractions of the dominant class, between the dominant class and the state. On the first of these levels, patterns of surplus-extraction were being modified so that in certain regions proto-capitalist agrarian production (essentially, large-scale tenant farming) was being combined with traditional feudal forms of production and grafted onto the social and institutional heritage of feudalism. That that heritage remained substantially intact for the duration of the *ancien régime* is not surprising, given that these changes in the form of production were in part a response to the aristocratic landowners' need to levy rent effectively, and thus contributed to maintaining their social dominance. As a result, those who moved into land ownership from outside the nobility – from legal, bureaucratic, or mercantile backgrounds – tended to legitimize and lubricate the move by assimilating aristocratic culture and ideology. So that the dominant class of landowners, even though partly dependent on capitalist forms of rent, continued to wear the appearance of a feudal nobility, and within the class as a whole the nobility proper continued to exercise cultural and ideological dominance.

Yet the content of its culture and ideology were changing under pressure from the state. Briefly, the state was both weakening the nobility and sustaining it, albeit on terms more favourable to the state.

Conclusion

The political defeat of the magnates was accompanied by an intensification of fiscal pressure on the popular masses, in direct competition with the landowners' need to extract rent from them. Yet at the same time, the Crown was ready to subsidize the great aristocrats, helping thereby to preserve, in the name of overall social hierarchy, their pre-eminence within French society. The upshot of this process was a redefinition of the nobility's collective self-image in keeping with its increased subordination to, and dependence on, the state. New discourses of distinction were generated, principally that of *honnêteté*, which fostered codes of behaviour that were deemed suitable for individual self-advancement in the world of the court. But these codes contributed also to the growth of new forms of social interaction and of solidarity among the higher echelons, not merely of the *noblesse d'épée*, but of the dominant class as a whole. For while, in certain forms of the discourse of *honnêteté*, new *honnête homme* is but old *gentilhomme* writ large, in others the new criteria of value tend to displace, and not merely cohabit with, the old ones. Thus birth and military prowess can be subordinated to elegance of manners and speech. And this process facilitated the admission into the world of the nobility proper of individuals and families whose economic position put them squarely within the dominant class of seventeenth-century French society, but whose antecedents were not those of the *noblesse d'épée*. As I have argued, following Carolyn Lougee, the role of women in the salons was crucial in this process of negotiation, a negotiation in which acceptance of traditional aristocratic hierarchies within the dominant class was the trade-off for new members of the class (in virtue of economic criteria) to bring about their cultural assimilation.

'Taste' mattered in all this because it could be represented as, essentially, the knowledge that pertains to *honnêteté*, and that distinguishes the *honnête homme* and his female counterpart from the popular masses and everything that smacks of their way of life. But 'taste' also had a specific role to play. A certain literary culture was one of the attributes of the new model courtier, and it provided material for the new forms of social interaction to which I have referred. But literary and artistic culture were also among the forms in which the absolutist state was seeking to command assent from the dominant class. 'Good taste' could be the name of the response that internalized that process, that accepted the authority of newly-constituted speech norms, that recognized the distinctive and superior character of French culture and rejected the pretensions of Italy and Spain. But again, in a marginal figure like Saint-Evremond, 'taste' could serve to condemn those norms in the name of a purer, if unreal, courtly culture. In either case, 'taste' conceives itself as essentially a courtly ideal, and thus registers and naturalizes the transformation of the nobility into a court aristocracy supported by and supporting the absolutist state.

The taste-judgment was held to be spontaneous, the fruit either of an innate gift or of a process of learning so internalized as to promote an automatic response that goes beyond the conscious and systematic application of rules; and thus 'taste' offered a discursive space in which the *noblesse d'épée* could recognize its own difference from and superiority to the *robe*, the group that had hitherto laid claim to proprietorship over cultural standards, but that could now be condemned in the name of 'taste' as deficient in *honnêteté* and sunk in pedantry. The *honnête* discourse of taste thus helped to preserve nobiliary hegemony within the dominant class. Again, women were important in this process, both as real agents and as objects of representation. For 'taste' belongs in a certain notion of women's innate qualities – a notion founded on women's real exclusion from institutions of knowledge – that can be mobilized in support of this exclusion of the 'pedantic'. At the same time, the response of women from the dominant class to their exclusion from the learned culture was to promote, in the salons, the new *mondain* approach to culture and knowledge in which 'taste' played such an important role.

All this applies to what may be called the *honnête* discourse of taste. Yet, by reason of its very potency, a term privileged by and within a discourse can be coveted and appropriated from other positions than those the discourse upholds. Thus Boileau uses the notion of 'taste' to vindicate the authority conferred by a historical consensus on the ancients, against the image of an enlightened minority setting itself apart from the public and calling the authority of the ancients into question. So, albeit less explicitly, does La Bruyère; and both writers show, furthermore, a tendency to uphold the authority of a more broadly-defined public than the court and the *grand monde* of *honnête* discourse, mingled with a certain troubled awareness that the commercialization of culture by which that public is constituted is in some sense inimical to true cultural values.

These readings of taste-discourse have, I think, certain implications beyond the merely literary-historical. If one thinks of 'taste' as essentially a philosophical concept, then the notion is readily appropriable as a means of thinking about our own culture. But the whole contention of this book is that 'taste' in seventeenth-century France was not a philosophical concept directed at purely speculative truth; rather, discourses of taste meshed with divergent and conflicting representations of society. 'Taste' designates various modes of 'recognition' of cultural difference, and through that of social difference, always in terms of superiority/inferiority. And, beyond the discrepancies between different discourses, there are crucial common elements that enable us to say that taste-discourses contribute on the cultural level to the reproduction of the dominant social relations. For it is not enough to say that 'taste' was rooted in a minority social group, as if one were saying, as a mere matter of fact, that a minority of the population have BMWs. 'Taste' was rooted in the *relation* of that minority to the rest of the population, a relationship of the dominant class to the popular masses, and in an internal relationship between different groups within the dominant class. It is in the latter area that the discourse allows a certain play, allows for different representations of culture; while in the former, in their exclusion of all that is 'popular' or 'vulgar', the different discourses coincide.

Discourses of taste, then, may faithfully record individuals' perceptions of the society in which they lived: but these perceptions should not be taken as *descriptions* of a real state of affairs. They are rather, as I have argued, 'recognitions' that position the subject with regard to real social relations. It seems to me that these social relations cannot be stripped away to reveal cultural or transcultural values in a pure state. Our relationship to the values of the discourse of taste cannot – or should not – be one of unproblematic and admiring appropriation. At least, this appropriation involves taking on, as I have tried to show, a sizeable ideological baggage of assumptions; assumptions that can of course be deeply reassuring but that, in my view, should be resisted. Such considerations can affect the way we read seventeenth-century French texts: they do not imply a root-and-branch rejection of them. As 'cultural treasures', in Walter Benjamin's phrase, they should perhaps be regarded with suspicion – their place within our culture, the kind of pleasures we get from them, need detached examination – but that they can provide intense pleasure and that the study of them can be immensely satisfying I would be the last person to deny. The point of this book has not been to pass some kind of global judgment on the dominant culture of seventeenth-century France – as, that it was a bad thing because it upheld aristocratic hegemony, or a good thing because it offered more positive representations of women. Rather, the point is that global evaluation, and the hiving-off of particular aspects of the culture as touchstones by which, as a whole, it is to be judged, are alike futile precisely because of the inextricable links between apparently discrete practices, the

Conclusion

connexions between sophisticated cultural perceptions and basic social modes of exploitation. And this is not simply a point of literary history, but an invitation to consider how, within our own culture, the judgments and norms we spontaneously apply are likewise the product of our implication in social relations of dominance and subordination.

NOTES

1. 'Taste' and history

1 Raymond Naves, *Le Goût de Voltaire*; see especially pp. 508–12.

2 Pierre Bourdieu, *La Distinction: critique sociale du jugement*, pp. 75–7.

3 There is important work on the sociology of taste in seventeenth-century France in, for instance, John Lough, *Paris Theatre Audiences in the Seventeenth and Eighteenth Centuries*, and Anthony Blunt, *Art and Architecture in France, 1500–1700*.

4 Jean V. Alter, *Les Origines de la satire antibourgeoise en France*, vol. II, *L'Esprit antibourgeois sous l'ancien régime: littérature et tensions sociales*, p. 110.

5 La Bruyère, *Les Caractères ou les Mœurs de ce siècle*, 'De la mode', 2.

6 Alter, pp. 111–12.

7 Montchrétien, *Traité de l'œconomie politique*, p. 60.

8 Alter, p. 183.

9 See Raymond Williams, *Marxism and Literature*, pp. 149–50, and Paul Oskar Kristeller, 'The Modern System of the Arts'.

10 Molière, *La Critique de l'Ecole des femmes*, scene vi; Racine, *Bérénice*, Préface; Boileau, *L'Art poétique*, III, lines 25, 245; Méré, *Des agréments*, in *Œuvres complètes*, ed. Ch.-H. Boudhors, vol. II, pp. 9–53; La Bruyère, *Les Caractères*, 'Des ouvrages de l'esprit', 54.

11 This interpretation of classicism is powerfully developed in E. B. O. Borgerhoff, *The Freedom of French Classicism*, and Jules Brody, *Boileau and Longinus*.

12 I use the word 'subject' henceforth in the sense of the person who performs an action, experiences a state, etc., and, except where the context excludes ambiguity, not in the more usual sense of 'topic'.

13 Daniel Mornet, *Histoire de la littérature française classique*, p. 97.

14 Christoph Strosetzski, *Rhétorique de la conversation*.

15 Jean-Pierre Dens, *L'Honnête Homme*, p. 139.

16 Louis Althusser, 'Idéologie et appareils idéologiques d'Etat', p. 122.

17 H. Frank Brooks, 'Taste, Perfection, and Delight in Guez de Balzac's Criticism'.

18 Raymond Williams, *Politics and Letters*, pp. 334–6.

19 Emile Benveniste, *Problèmes de linguistique générale*, vol. I, pp. 238–42.
20 See Odette de Mourgues, *Two French Moralists*, p. 4.
21 Descartes, *Discours de la méthode*, in *Œuvres philosophiques*, vol. I, p. 568.
22 Méré, *Lettres*, vol. I, pp. 218–19.
23 Anne Le Fèvre (Mme Dacier), *Le Plutus et les Nuées d'Aristophane*, Préface (no pagination).
24 The value of imitation is asserted in *Des causes de la corruption du goût*, pp. 14–15; compare La Bruyère, *Les Caractères*, 'Des ouvrages de l'esprit', 15, and Boileau, *L'Art poétique*, II. 26, 168; III. 415–20. The appeal to particular authors, works or passages as 'touchstones' of taste, can be found in *Des causes de la corruption du goût*, pp. 208, 319, and in Boileau, *Réflexions sur Longin*, VII, in *Œuvres complètes*, edited by Antoine Adam and Françoise Escal, Bibliothèque de la Pléiade, pp. 524–5. (References to this edition hereafter will be given where possible in parentheses in the text, using the abbreviation *OC*.) The significance of this kind of argument is discussed below, pp. 16–17; and for the broader cultural significance of La Bruyère's and Boileau's views on taste and related matters, see chapters 6 and 7.
25 See *Les Caractères*, 'De la société', 71; and *L'Art poétique*, III. 401–4; these passages are discussed below, pp. 151, 177.
26 Boileau to Brossette, 12 March 1707, in *OC*, 707. On Anne Le Fèvre's life and career, see Enrica Malcovati, *Madame Dacier*.
27 *Des causes de la corruption du goût*, p. 223.
28 Bouhours, *La Manière de bien penser dans les ouvrages d'esprit*, pp. 515–17.
29 See below, p. 62.
30 *La Manière de bien penser*, pp. 460, 530, 532, 545.
31 Jean Frain du Tremblay, *Discours sur l'origine de la poésie, sur son usage et sur le bon goût*, p. 116.
32 Stephen Heath, *The Sexual Fix*, p. 120.
33 Terry Eagleton, *Literary Theory*, p. 26. The Althusserian theory of ideology alluded to here is developed in the essay 'Idéologie at appareils idéologiques d'Etat' already referred to, where Althusser goes significantly beyond the positions earlier worked out in *For Marx* (see pp. 232–5 of the latter work in particular). For a powerful restatement of the Althusserian theory, see Diane Macdonell, *Theories of Discourse*.
34 Walter Benjamin, 'Theses on the Philosophy of History', VII (in *Illuminations*, p. 258).
35 E. P. Thompson, 'Eighteenth-Century English Society: Class Struggle without Class?', p. 157.
36 Dens, *L'Honnête Homme*, p. 14.
37 Domna C. Stanton, *The Aristocrat as Art*, p. 71.
38 Robin Briggs, *Early Modern France*, p. 59. Mousnier's views on social

stratification in the *ancien régime* are clearly set out in his *Les Hiérarchies sociales de 1450 à nos jours*.

39 Thus Georg Lukács, *History and Class-Consciousness*, pp. 55–9; he is followed by Eric Hobsbawm, 'Class-Consciousness in History', in *Aspects of History and Class-Consciousness*, edited by I. Mészáros, pp. 7–11.

40 G. E. M. de Ste.-Croix, *The Class Struggle in the Ancient Greek World*, p. 43.

41 Marx, *Capital*, vol. III, p. 927.

42 P. J. Coveney, in his introduction to *France in Crisis*, pp. 25–6.

43 Roland Mousnier, 'Recherches sur les soulèvements populaires', p. 107.

44 Rodney Hilton, 'A Note on Feudalism', in *The Transition from Feudalism to Capitalism*, edited by Rodney Hilton, p. 30; but see Ste.-Croix, pp. 267–9 for a critique of the concept 'feudal'.

45 See G. A. Cohen, *Karl Marx's Theory of History*, p. 65.

46 Pierre Goubert, in *Histoire économique et sociale de la France*, edited by F. Braudel and E. Labrousse, 4 vols., vol. II, pp. 130–1, 125. This volume (the only one in the series referred to) will hereafter be cited as *HESF*.

47 *HESF*, 125–6, 573.

48 Robert Mandrou, *La France aux XVIIe et XVIIIe siècles*, p. 72.

49 *HESF*, 135–7.

50 Pierre Goubert, *L'Ancien Régime*, vol. I, p. 100.

51 Marc Bloch, *Les Caractères originaux de l'histoire rurale française*, vol. I, pp. 98–105.

52 Bloch, vol. I, pp. 140–47; the process is described in detail with reference to Poitou by Jean Jacquart, in *Histoire de la France rurale*, edited by G. Duby and A. Wallon, 4 vols., vol. II, p. 130. This volume will be referred to hereafter as *HFR*.

53 Two varieties of sharecropping are described by Jacquart in *HFR*, 127–31. See also *HESF*, 142–4.

54 Marx, *Capital*, vol. III, p. 939.

55 See *HESF*, 143; and Goubert, *L'Ancien Régime*, vol. 1, pp. 137–8, where extracts from a sample contract are given.

56 *HESF*, 144–5; *HFR*, 126. See also Jacquart, *La Crise rurale en Ile-de-France*, pp. 130–1.

57 Jacquart, *La Crise rurale,* p. 152.

58 *HFR*, 126.

59 *HESF*, 145.

60 *HESF*, 586–87, 584–85. *Rentes constituées* are described p. 581.

61 Marx, *Capital*, vol. III, p. 935.

62 Patricia Croot and David Parker, 'Agrarian Class Structure and Economic Development', p. 45.

63 Goubert, *L'Ancien Régime*, vol. I, pp. 106–7; *HESF*, 89, 107.

64 *HESF*, 145, 587; Jacquart, *La Crise rurale*, pp. 151–2, 347–8, 755–6.

65 For the relative importance as income-sources of *réserve* and *censives*,

see Jacquart, *La Crise rurale*, pp. 83−5, 416, 441; for the leasing-out process, see pp. 130, 435−8; for the 'pre-capitalist' aspect of the growth of big farming, see pp. 348, 755−6, and *HESF*, 145.

66 Jean Meyer, *La Noblesse bretonne au XVIIIe siècle*, vol. II, pp. 888, 891. The burden of seigneurial dues was heavier in Brittany than in any other province, and seigneurial revenues bulked larger in the income of the Breton nobility than in that of their counterparts elsewhere (Meyer, vol. II, pp. 651, 655).

67 Jean-Pierre Labatut, *Les Ducs et pairs de France au XVIIe siècle*, pp. 296−8.

68 *HFR*, 146.

69 Goubert, *L'Ancien Régime*, vol. I, p. 176; see *L'École des femmes*, I.i. lines 166−72, and *Les Caractères*, 'De la ville', 10.

70 Mousnier, *La Vénalité des offices*, pp. 539−40, 490.

71 *HESF*, pp. 581−2.

72 See A. D. Lublinskaya, *French Absolutism: the Crucial Phase*, pp. 103−45, for the first part of the seventeenth century; and for the second half, see Goubert, *Louis XIV et vingt millions de Français*, pp. 20−4, and Mandrou, *La France aux XVIIe et XVIIIe siècles*, pp. 81−91.

73 Briggs, p. 54.

74 Mandrou, p. 84.

75 Briggs, pp. 55, 134.

76 On these trends, see Jacquart, *La Crise rurale*, pp. 753−7.

77 Lublinskaya, 'The Contemporary Bourgeois Conception of Absolute Monarchy', p. 70.

78 See Goubert, *L'Ancien Régime*, vol. I, pp. 178, 219.

79 Robert Brenner, 'Agrarian Class Structure and Economic Development in Pre-Industrial Europe', p. 68.

80 Pierre Léon, in *HESF*, 622−6; and La Bruyère, *Les Caractères*, 'Des biens de fortune', 7, 14−17.

81 Goubert, *L'Ancien Régime*, vol. I, pp. 177−8.

82 Labatut, pp. 239−74, especially pp. 239−45, 252−3, 270−4.

83 *HESF*, 582−3.

84 Labatut, p. 271.

85 Tallemant des Réaux, *Historiettes*, edited by A. Adam, Bibliothèque de la Pléiade, 2 vols., vol. I, pp. 458, 440.

86 For the terms 'residual' and 'emergent', see Williams, *Marxism and Literature*, pp. 121−7.

87 See the discussion of *agrément* and *beauté* in Méré, *Œuvres complètes*, vol. II, pp. 37−8. This edition is referred to hereafter as *OC*, and references will be given where possible in parentheses in the text. The *beauté/agrément* distinction is discussed below, pp. 101−2.

88 See Saint-Evremond, *Lettres*, edited by René Ternois, 2 vols., vol. I, p. 25, and La Bruyère, *Les Caractères*, 'Des femmes', 32, 33 (these latter passages are discussed below, pp. 160−1).

89 I base this enumeration of 'elite cultures' on Peter Burke, *Popular Culture in Early Modern Europe*, p. 24.

90 There is a very good account of learned anti-feminist theories in Ian Maclean, *Woman Triumphant*, chapter 1.

91 Marc Fumaroli, *L'Age de l'éloquence*, pp. 430—2.

92 Baldassare Castiglione, *The Book of the Courtier*, translated by Sir Thomas Hoby, Everyman's University Library, pp. 36—7. The Renaissance translation has been chosen as having an appropriate feel in this context.

93 Nicolas Faret, *L'Honneste Homme ou l'art de plaire à la cour*, edited by M. Magendie, pp. 85, 95.

94 See below, pp. 48, 100—1.

95 Carolyn C. Lougee, *Le Paradis des Femmes*, pp. 113—18. (It was possible in France to enjoy noble status without the possession of a title, *chevalier, baron, comte*, etc. This being so, one might be from an old noble family — i.e. one that had been noble for four generations — and not have a title, while a titled nobleman whose family had recently risen to prominence might still not enjoy 'old' nobility. Hence the apparent discrepancy in the figures for the two categories.)

96 Ruth Kelso, *Doctrine for the Lady of the Renaissance*, pp. 33—6.

97 Lougee, p. 29. On relexicalization, see Roger Fowler, *Literature as Social Discourse*, pp. 147—50.

98 Roger Lathuillère, *La Préciosité*, vol. I, p. 537.

99 Somaize, *Dictionnaire des précieuses*, edited by Ch.-L. Livet, 2 vols., vol. I, p. 219.

100 Henri-Jean Martin, *Livre, pouvoirs et société à Paris au XVIIe siècle*, p. 544.

101 Lougee, pp. 27—9; Strosetzski, *Rhétorique de la conversation*, pp. 142—3, where the point is made that in this context 'la *femme* ... servait toujours de *représentante du type des non-initiés, de ceux qui n'avaient pas de connaissances préliminaires*', and thus as a model for the *honnête homme* 'qui sait un peu sur tout, mais pas plus que l'essentiel' (p. 142, his italics).

102 Fumaroli, pp. 608—11.

103 Fumaroli, p. 674; Martin, p. 543.

104 Domna C. Stanton, 'The Fiction of *Préciosité* and the Fear of Women', p. 126.

105 Stanton, *The Aristocrat as Art*, p. 135.

106 The desirability of noble birth is asserted by Castiglione, pp. 31—5; he is echoed by Faret, pp. 9—11. The disappearance of this requirement of noble birth from the discourse of *honnêteté* is discussed below, p. 89.

107 See above, p. 40, and below, pp. 100—1.

108 Maurice Magendie, *La Politesse mondaine et les théories de l'honnêteté*, pp. 120—4; Stanton, *The Aristocrat as Art*, pp. 25—6; Fumaroli, pp. 658—60.

109 Lougee, p. 5; Antoine Adam, *Histoire de la littérature française au XVIIe siècle*, 5 vols., vol. I, p. 263.

Notes to pages 49–62

110 Norbert Elias, *The Civilizing Process*, 2 vols., vol. I, *The History of Manners*, pp. 201–2. The theme is more fully developed in vol. II, *State Formation and Civilization*: see, e.g., pp. 235–7, 258–82.

111 The importance of the system of governorships is discussed in David Parker, *The Making of French Absolutism*, pp. 26–7; the decline of magnate clienteles is dealt with on p. 102.

112 On the importance of this trend see Parker, *The Making of French Absolutism*, p. 103.

113 The importance of such norms is valuably emphasized by Strosetzski, pp. 71–6, 156.

114 Fumaroli, p. 521.

2. Defining 'goût': the dictionaries

1 Pierre Richelet, *Dictionnaire françois, Avertissement*.

2 Méré, *OC* III, 69.

3 Bernard Quemada, *Les Dictionnaires du français moderne, 1539–1863*, p. 59.

4 'J'ai fait un Dictionnaire François afin de rendre quelque service aux honnêtes gens qui aiment nôtre langue', says Richelet in his *Avertissement*. A specifies as its object 'la Langue commune, telle qu'elle est dans le commerce ordinaire des honnestes gens, & telle que les Orateurs & les Poëtes l'employent' (*Préface*).

5 Pomey, *Dictionaire royal, Advertissement*, section V.

6 *Recueil des factums d'Antoine Furetière de l'Académie Françoise contre quelques-uns de cette Académie*, edited by Charles Asselineau, 2 vols., vol. I, p. 20.

7 Georges Matoré, *Histoire des dictionnaires français*, p. 78.

8 Natalie Zemon Davis, *Society and Culture in Early Modern France*, pp. 245–6. See also Mornet, *Histoire de la littérature française classique*, p. 101.

9 Elias, *The Civilizing Process*, vol. I, p. 116.

10 Pascal, *Pensées*, 512 (*Œuvres complètes*, p. 576). For the distinction between the two *justesses*, see Méré, *OC* I, 14, 96, and Ch.-H. Boudhors, 'Divers propos du chevalier de Méré en 1674–1675', *RHL* 30 (1923), p. 82.

11 I give the full names of the authors, referred to in the original in abbreviated form. Incidentally, when Naves (*Le Goût de Voltaire*, p. 100, n. 3) names these authors as responsible for the most important definitions of *goût* quoted by early eighteenth-century dictionaries, he is presumably referring to these very passages. The sources of the quotations, where I have been able to discover them, are as follows: 2. is adapted from Bouhours, *La Manière de bien penser dans les ouvrages d'esprit*, pp. 516–17. 3. occurs in Saint-Evremond, *Œuvres meslées*, sixième partie (Paris, 1680), but its true author would appear to be Damien Mitton. (See Quentin M. Hope, *Saint-Evremond*, p. 78, and Henry A. Grubbs, Jr,

Damien Mitton (1618–1690), pp. 51–55.) In what follows, I have referred
to the author as 'Saint-Evremond', since contemporary readers would
presumably have taken the attribution at face value. 4. is taken from Méré,
Lettres, vol. I, pp. 218–19. 5. is La Rochefoucauld's maxim 258. I have
not been able to locate 1. in the works of Mlle de Scudéry, though it is
of course identical to the quotation from Anne Le Fèvre's preface to
Aristophanes's *Plutus* and *Clouds* discussed above in chapter 1 (pp.
13–15).

12 *L'Honnête Homme*, p. 84.
13 On 'geometric' ideas of taste, see Naves, pp. 10–35, 100–6.
14 See above, n. 10.
15 See La Bruyère, 'Des ouvrages de l'esprit', 11, which is discussed below,
   pp. 149–50.
16 Bouhours, *Les Entretiens d'Ariste et d'Eugène*, p. 151.
17 Jean Louis Guez de Balzac, *Les Entretiens (1657)*, edited by B. Beugnot,
   2 vols., vol. I, p. 118.
18 Bossuet, *Oraisons funèbres*, edited by J. Truchet, p. 140.
19 The two passages in question may be found, with slight variations, in Saint-
   Réal, *Œuvres*, 4 vols., vol. I, p. 36; and Nicole, *Essais de morale*, 15 vols.,
   vol. II, p. 251.
20 Based on *Les Caractères*, 'De la chaire', 23. F2 frequently modifies the
   passages it uses as illustrations.
21 Renée Kohn, *Le Goût de La Fontaine*, p. 15, following Cayrou, *Le
   Français classique*, s.v. *goût*.
22 The words in italics do not appear in F2.
23 See above, pp. 20–1.
24 It should be noted that Guez de Balzac frequently compares reading to
   eating, on a hedonic basis (see Brooks, 'Taste, Perfection and Delight',
   pp. 71, 74–8). But although he stresses Balzac's participation in a whole
   seventeenth-century critical tradition, Brooks opines that 'Balzac is surely
   exceptional in his readiness to exploit such metaphors' (p. 76). I think this
   is probably correct. Méré compares the arrangement of a piece of writing
   to a banquet, in which not only must the various dishes be good, but they
   must be served in the proper order (Boudhors, 'Divers propos (suite)',
   RHL 30 (1923), p. 87). But these instances do not invalidate the suggestion
   that the stress on the life-preserving role of taste is characteristic of religious
   discourse.
25 Louis Althusser, *Reading Capital*, p. 112.
26 The survival in seventeenth-century popular culture of the Charlemagne
   stories and other mediaeval heroic legends is noted by Robert Mandrou,
   De la culture populaire aux XVIIe et XVIIIe siècles, pp. 131–47.
27 See Renate Baader, 'La Polémique anti-baroque dans la doctrine
   classique'.
28 On the antiquarian Gaignières, see F. H. Taylor, *The Taste of Angels*,
   pp. 343–5.
29 On the quarrel between supporters of the pre-eminence of drawing over

colour and their opponents, see Anthony Blunt, *Art and Architecture in France, 1500–1700*, pp. 360–2.

30 Niels von Holst, *Creators, Collectors and Connoisseurs*, p. 159.
31 *The Taste of Angels*, p. 330; and see pp. 324–9.
32 Philippe Ariès, *L'Enfant et la vie familiale sous l'ancien régime*, p. 50.
33 Montchrétien, *Traité de l'œconomie politique*, p. 60.
34 Stanton, *The Aristocrat as Art*, pp. 127–30.
35 Alter, *Les Origines de la satire antibourgeoise*, vol. II, p. 106.
36 Mme de Sévigné, *Correspondance*, edited by Roger Duchêne, Bibliothèque de la Pléiade, 3 vols., vol. II, p. 20.
37 Marx, *Economic and Philosophical Manuscripts*, in *Early Writings*, p. 377.
38 The substitution of bourgeois for noble patronage is discussed by Blunt, p. 195; the patronage of individual artists and architects is dealt with on pp. 205 (Mansart), 222 (Le Vau), and 283 (Poussin).
39 Boileau, *Art poétique*, I. 151–2 (*OC*, 160).

3. Méré: taste and the ideology of *honnêteté*

1 *OC* I, 56. All subsequent references will be given in parentheses in the text, using the abbreviations *OC* for the *Œuvres complètes*; *L* for the *Lettres*; and *RHL*, followed by the number of the relevant issue, for the 'Divers propos du Chevalier de Méré en 1674–1675' published by Ch.-H. Boudhors in the *Revue d'histoire littéraire de la France*, nos. 29–32 (1922–5). Full details of these will be found in the Bibliography.
2 Jean-Claude Bonnet, 'La Table dans les civilités', in *La Qualité de la vie au XVIIe siècle* (p. 102).
3 Norbert Elias, *The Civilizing Process*, vol. I, p. 116.
4 John Lough, *Paris Theatre Audiences in the Seventeenth and Eighteenth Centuries*, pp. 58–72.
5 See also *OC* I, 96; and, for a rather different formulation, *RHL*, 30, p. 82.
6 *The Aristocrat as Art*, *passim*.
7 Marivaux, *Les Sincères*, sc. xii, in *Théâtre complet*, edited by Bernard Dort, p. 487.
8 For compliments to correspondents on their 'taste', see *L* I, 321, 350 and *L* II, 401, 403, 537. For the recorded compliment on Méré's own 'taste' (from Guez de Balzac, as it happens), see *L* I, 11.
9 He would have made better speeches than Cicero (*RHL* 30, p. 524); Pascal and Mitton would have known nothing but for him (*RHL* 30, p. 525); Pascal did well to start writing three months after meeting him, but should have gone on seeing him (*RHL* 32, p. 73); his secretary has learned more from him than he would have done in a lifetime at court (*RHL* 32, p. 435); he used to dazzle Voiture, and without him Mitton would have been a beggarly fellow all his life (*RHL* 32, p. 440); he is, or was, also something of a superstud, husbands trembling when he spoke to their wives (*RHL* 32, p. 434).
10 The Molière passage is of course ambiguous; it does not at all exclude

the idea of an elite whose pleasure is somehow more valuable than everyone else's. But the issue is left unresolved, whereas Méré makes his position quite clear.

11 See below, chapter 7.

12 It is true that Méré acknowledges that provided one has *discernement*, one can become *honnête* 'sans voir la Cour ny le monde' (*OC* II, 129), because *discernement* makes one aware of the proper way to behave in any given situation. Méré is contrasting this perception of the fundamental proprieties with the more superficial knowledge of fashion and custom that necessarily presupposes acquaintance with society. But *discernement* arguably presupposes some social experience, since it involves a knowledge of what is going on in people's minds (*OC* II, 126). In any case, the emphasis on acquiring 'taste' and *honnêteté* in the company of others is by far the more typical.

13 Raymond Williams, 'The Bloomsbury Fraction', in his *Problems in Materialism and Culture*, p. 150.

14 Erich Auerbach, 'La Cour et la Ville', p. 164.

15 Maurice Magendie, *La Politesse mondaine*, pp. 367–8, 389, 787.

16 Roger Lathuillère, *La Préciosité*, p. 563; Stanton, *The Aristocrat as Art*, pp. 80–1.

17 Compare Saint-Evremond, *Les Opéra*, edited by Robert Finch and Eugène Joliat, p. 64, where professional experts are enjoined to defer to the 'taste' of 'les Honnétes-gens de la Cour'.

18 Bernadette B. de Mendoza, 'L'Art de vivre de l'honnête homme: éthique ou esthétique', pp. 20–1.

19 Horace is criticized in *L* I, 95. Méré's attitude to Cicero is complex, but the general line is that, supreme in his profession (*RHL* 32, p. 75), he is sadly at fault outside it, defective in 'taste' (*RHL* 30, p. 381), and a pedant (*RHL* 30, p. 89; *RHL* 32, p. 77). He is admired as a statesman, none the less (*RHL* 32, p. 434), and his speeches 'servent pour le monde', which for Méré is really the only thing that matters (*RHL* 30, p. 521). Boileau is called a pedant in *RHL* 29, p. 214, and in *RHL* 32, p. 597 it is stated that he will never make it as an *honnête homme*. Socrates ties with Caesar as the greatest man of all time (*OC* III, 140). Méré claims to know the works of the 'divin Platon' by heart (*L* I, 355) and the letter to Pascal shows an indebtedness to Platonist thought and imagery (*L* I, 125).

20 Fumaroli, *L'Age de l'éloquence*, p. 692.

21 Maclean, *Woman Triumphant*, pp. 64–87; for the contradictions in seventeenth-century 'feminist' discourse, see, e.g., pp. 67–71, 250–1.

22 Four times out of five (*L* I, 321, 350, and *L* II, 403, 537); only in *L* II, 401 is the compliment addressed to a man.

23 'The system of the aristocratic self ... emits a continual chain of signs with no nonsignifying space in between', Stanton, *The Aristocrat as Art*, p. 117.

24 There is a mistake here in the pagination of the original, where there are two pages numbered 350. I have given what would be the correct number.

25 See, for instance, Pascal, *Pensées*, 586 (Brunschvicg, 33); Guez de Balzac, *Les Entretiens (1657)*, vol. I, p. 211; Boileau, *L'Art poétique*, II. 1–8 (*OC*, p. 163).

26 Michel Foucault, *Histoire de la sexualité*, vol. I: *La Volonté de savoir*, p. 133.

27 Pascal, *Pensées*, 90, 92 (Brunschvicg, 337, 335), and see *Trois Discours sur la condition des grands*, Second Discours, in *Œuvres complètes*, edited by Louis Lafuma, p. 367.

4. Saint-Evremond: taste and cultural hegemony

1 Saint-Evremond, *Lettres*, vol. II, p. 436. All subsequent references are given in parentheses in the text, using the abbreviation *L*, volume and page numbers.

2 Saint-Evremond, *Œuvres en prose*, vol. I, p. xl, n. 1. All subsequent references to this edition are given in parentheses in the text, using the abbreviation *OP*, volume and page numbers.

3 *Les Opéra*, p. 65.

4 Ternois points out that the reading 'Cohon' is probably a misprint for 'Coton', the name of a Jesuit preacher contemporary with Nervèze and Coëffeteau (*OP* III, 377, n. 3).

5 On the complexities of the various uses of 'culture', see Raymond Williams, *Keywords*, pp. 76–82, and *Marxism and Literature*, pp. 11–20.

6 Quentin M. Hope, *Saint-Evremond: the 'Honnête Homme' as Critic*, pp. 77–8.

5 La Rochefoucauld: tastes and their vicissitudes

1 In this chapter, the word 'taste' appears in the text without quotation marks when it denotes an inclination or preference that is not in some sense backed up by the discourse, and between quotation marks when implicitly defined by the discourse as a perception of objective value. The particular complexities of La Rochefoucauld's use of *goût* render this procedure necessary.

2 'Des coquettes et des vieillards' in *Maximes suivies des Réflexions diverses* ..., edited by J. Truchet, p. 215. All references are to this edition and will be given in parentheses in the text. Maxims are usually cited by their number alone. The abbreviations MS or MP followed by a number denote, as in Truchet, a 'maxime supprimée' or a 'maxime posthume'. The *Réflexions diverses* are referred to by a page number, and where the *réflexion* in question has not already been named in the text it is additionally designated by the letter R followed by its number.

3 De Mourgues, *Two French Moralists*, p. 90.

4 Malcolm Bowie, 'Jacques Lacan', in *Structuralism and Since*, edited by John Sturrock, p. 136.

5 Jean Starobinski, 'La Rochefoucauld et les morales substitutives', pp. 18–19.
6 Jonathan Culler, 'Paradox and the Language of Morals in La Rochefoucauld', pp. 34–9.
7 E.D. James, 'Scepticism and Positive Values in La Rochefoucauld', p. 353.
8 Starobinski, pp. 211–29. The word 'morality' is perhaps inappropriate here as Starobinski presents the code of social behaviour set out by La Rochefoucauld as aesthetic rather than moral in nature (p. 211). E.D. James has justly criticized Starobinski for the rigidity of his antithesis between aesthetic and moral values ('Scepticism and Positive Values in La Rochefoucauld', p. 355), and for the whole notion of a 'substitution' of one set of values for another – according to James, the positive values are there from the start. I am not concerned to defend the substitution-thesis, so much as to emphasize the distinction between two kinds of discourse in La Rochefoucauld, one typical of the *Maximes* and dealing for the most part with human beings in general, the other characteristic of the *Réflexions diverses* and bearing on the conduct towards one another of what James himself calls 'the privileged few' (p. 359).
9 Roland Mousnier, *Les Hiérarchies sociales*, p. 66.

6. La Bruyère: taste-discourse and the absent subject

1 I am grateful to Dr Terence Cave for his helpful comments on the importance of this text and 'De la cour', 74, in response to an earlier version of this chapter.
2 Subtitle of André Stegmann's useful study *Les Caractères de La Bruyère*. Stegmann's last sentence (p. 219), however, refers to 'cette singulière Bible de l'homme de bien', which is the more accurate description. La Bruyère himself distinguishes between the *honnête homme* and the *homme de bien* in 'Des jugements', 55.
3 'S'il n'y avoit quelque chose de délicat et d'honneste homme, en ce que je fais et en ce que je dis, cela ne me siéroit pas' (*RHL* 32, pp. 437–8).
4 For a condemnation of *viande noire* by a gourmet, see Saint-Evremond, *L* I, 258. Saint-Evremond is writing to the comte d'Olonne, whom one *clef* identifies with La Bruyère's Cliton (see p. 336, n. 3, of the Garapon edition of *Les Caractères*). Both Saint-Evremond and Olonne belonged to the *Coteaux*, a circle of aristocratic gourmets mentioned in 'Des grands', 24; see Saint-Evremond, *OP* I, xliii.
5 *Discours*, pp. 129–37.
6 *La Manière de bien penser*, pp. 460, 530, 532.
7 Saint-Evremond abjures belief in the cultural supremacy of the Augustan Age in *OP* II, 345, and asserts the superiority of the late Republic in the plainly oppositional context of the 'Dissertation sur le mot de Vaste' (*OP* III, 376). See above, pp. 109, 117.
8 Méré draws the distinction in *OC* II, 37–8, and *L* II, 528–30.

9 See above the discussion of this question in connexion with Saint-Evremond (pp. 116–17).

10 *Mémoires*, vol. IV, pp. 946, 1006.

11 *Two French Moralists*, p. 140.

12 For the connexions between *honnêteté* and the erotic, see Stanton, *The Aristocrat as Art*, pp. 135–9, and above, pp. 100–1.

13 Diderot, *Le Neveu de Rameau*, in *Œuvres romanesques*, pp. 430–2.

14 The 'good taste' of the *parterre* is of course defended in the *Critique de l'Ecole de Femmes*, scene v (Molière, *Œuvres complètes*, vol. I, pp. 653–4) Bénichou shrewdly observes that this position in no way impugns the prestige of the aristocracy as such: the aristocrats who go against the *parterre* are shown as a tiny minority; they are blamed precisely for giving an unfavourable and inaccurate picture of their class as a whole, and they are condemned from the point of view of the court idea of *honnêteté* (*Morales du grand siècle*, p. 299; I feel that I should have paid special tribute to this remarkable work above: it still ranks as a most powerful critique of a certain idealist interpretation of seventeenth-century French culture). Other assertions of the authority of the *parterre* are mentioned in Lough, *Paris Theatre Audiences*, pp. 104–6.

15 See p. 92, n. 4 of the Garapon edition, and De Mourgues, *Two French Moralists*, p. 140.

16 *La Critique de l'Ecole des Femmes*, scene vi (*Œuvres complètes*, vol. I, p. 505).

17 'Idéologie et appareils idéologiques d'Etat', pp. 124–5.

18 Pascal, *Pensées*, 764 (Brunschvicg, 11); Bossuet, *Maximes et réflexions sur la comédie*, in Ch. Urbain and E. Lévesque, *L'Eglise et le théâtre*, pp. 175–82.

19 Ferdinand Brunot, *Histoire de la langue française des origines à 1900*, 13 vols., vol. III (1909), p. 716.

20 See Taylor, *The Taste of Angels*, pp. 324–30; and above, pp. 77–8.

21 For instance, in 'Du mérite personnel', 15; 'Des femmes', 13; 'Des biens de fortune', 75; 'De la cour', 9.

22 See *L* II, 429, 458.

23 It is useless to urge the judgment of the public against La Bruyère's *Moderne* opponents: 'ils répliqueront avec confiance que le public a son goût, et qu'ils ont le leur: réponse qui ferme la bouche et qui termine tout différend' (*Discours de reception à l'Académie française*, *Préface* (in *Les Caractères*, edited by Garapon, p. 501).

24 On the *rentes* (a form of government bonds), see Parker, *The Making of French Absolutism*, p. xiv. La Bruyère's own father was *contrôleur général des rentes sur l'Hôtel de Ville* (*Les Caractères*, ed. Garapon, pp. i–ii).

7. Boileau: taste and the institution of 'literature'

1 Bray, pp. iii, 363–5; Mornet, pp. 75–6; Théodore A. Litman, *Le Sublime en France (1660–1714)*, pp. 94–5.

2 *Satire X*, line 449 (*OC*, p. 74). All future references will be given in the text in this form. *L'Art poétique* will be abbreviated as *AP*, followed by the number of the *chant*, and the line number.

3 The image of the heroic woman is discussed in Maclean's *Woman Triumphant*, pp. 64–87; as he points out (p. 269), such women tend to disappear, from life as from literature, after the Fronde. The marquis as a comic stereotype is mentioned in Molière, *L'Impromptu de Versailles*, scene ii: 'Le marquis est aujourd'hui le plaisant de la comédie; et comme dans toutes les comédies anciennes on voit toujours un valet bouffon qui fait rire les auditeurs, de même, dans toutes nos pièces de maintenant, il faut toujours un marquis ridicule qui divertisse la compagnie' (*Œuvres complètes*, vol. I, p. 524).

4 The social origins of *préciosité* are discussed in Lathuillère, *La Préciosité*, pp. 550–7, and Lougee, *Le Paradis des Femmes*, pp. 113–70.

5 The *précieuse* here was identified by contemporaries both as a Mlle du Pré, a friend of Perrault's, and as Mme Deshoulières (*OC*, p. 937, n. 54), the marquis as the comte de Fiesque, a friend of Boileau's (*OC*, p. 972, n. 11). But, irrespective of whether the author had someone particular in mind, the reader who interprets a fictional character as a portrait of a real one is always free to dispute its accuracy ('X isn't at all like that'). Even if he or she accepts that it is a true representation of X, this does not dissolve whatever substantive ideological disagreements he or she may have with the author who had decided to use X to illustrate a generalization.

6 For this particular topos, see *Discours au Roy*, lines 43–4 (*OC*, p. 10); *Satire IX*, lines 67–74 (*OC*, pp. 50–1); *Epistre X*, lines 57–64 (*OC*, p. 142); *AP* III. lines 331–2 (*OC*, p. 177).

7 Jules Brody, *Boileau and Longinus*, p. 104.

8 J.-B. Barrère, *L'Idée de goût de Pascal à Valéry*, p. 53, where Boileau's confidence in the consensual verdict of the centuries is branded a 'déviation dangereuse' and the beginnings of a 'gangrène sournoise'.

9 The connexion between the marketplace, popular language, and bodily appetites is brilliantly explored in Mikhail Bakhtin, *Rabelais and his World*, pp. 145–95.

10 This isn't quite literally true: the *parterre* was a socially composite body, noblemen rubbing shoulders with tradesmen, lawyers, writers, and lackeys. But the importance of this should not be exaggerated. First, the plebeian element in the *parterre* was probably small: this section of the audience was predominantly bourgeois, with a sprinkling of noblemen, these usually army officers or members of the household troops (Lough, *Paris Theatre Audiences*, pp. 81–99). In the early eighteenth century, lackeys in livery were actually banned from the Comédie-Française and the Théâtre des Italiens (pp. 77–8). Secondly, the types of seat available, and their prices, became more varied, thus tending to create a more stratified audience, even if seat-location and class-position never corresponded systematically. Thirdly, ladies

were never found in the *parterre*, and mixed groups from polite society would sit in the more expensive seats, away from the rest of the audience (pp. 107—9). In his ideal theatre, D'Aubignac envisaged seating arrangements that would clearly separate persons of rank from the common people (*Projet pour le rétablissement du théâtre françois*, in *La Pratique du théâtre*, p. 397).

11 The quotation comes from the *Avis au lecteur* to the second edition of the *Epistre I* (1672), which is omitted from the Pléiade *Œuvres complètes*, but included in Boileau, *Œuvres*, edited by Jérôme Vercruysse and Sylvain Menant, Garnier-Flammarion, 2 vols., vol. II, p. 33.

12 Martin, *Livre, pouvoirs et société*, vol. II, p. 914, n. 22.

13 Quoted in Martin, ibid., vol. II, p. 915; and see pp. 914—21.

14 See *OC*, p. 1003, n. 13.

15 Actually nobles could do very well out of war. Saint-Evremond set himself up for life by his profiteering during the Fronde, netting, by his own account, fifty thousand francs in two years and a half. See Silvestre's biography (*OP* I, xxvii).

16 This quotation comes from the *Dissertation sur Joconde*, of which Boileau's authorship is far from certain. After a close study of the evidence, Pierre Clarac suggests that it may be the result of a collaboration between Boileau and his elder brother Gilles, with the latter as senior partner (*Boileau*, pp. 48—57). See also Françoise Escal's notes in *OC*, pp. 1063—4. But in any case the attitude adopted in this passage tallies perfectly with Boileau's in works that are certainly his, such as the *Réflexions sur Longin*. Since Gilles himself was working on a translation of Longinus, it seems reasonable to suggest a connexion between the appeal to the verdict of 'tous les hommes' and an espousal of the notion of the sublime.

17 It may be worth comparing the attitudes pilloried by Boileau with those of Méré and Saint-Evremond. We have seen that Méré has severe reservations about Virgil (*L* I, 134—6; see also *RHL* 30, pp. 87—8), but his judgment of Virgil and of Terence is far more favourable in *RHL* 29, p. 216. Like Méré, Saint-Evremond criticizes Virgil's characterization of Aeneas (*OP* III, 105—15), and he finds Terence lacking in *galanterie*, passion and *honnêteté* (*OP* I, 178). The lovemaking of his characters is condemned as bourgeois (*L* I, 344). I am not of course identifying these two individuals as Boileau's specific targets but as representatives of an aristocratic-*mondain* culture where such iconoclasm was encouraged.

18 For the notion of 'relexicalization', see chapter 1, n. 97.

19 Rousseau, *Du contrat social*, I.7 (*Œuvres complètes*, edited by Bernard Gagnebin and Marcel Raymond, Bibliothèque de la Pléiade, 4 vols., vol. III, p. 364).

20 See Bussy's letter of 30th May, 1673, in *Correspondance* edited by Ludovic Lalanne, 6 vols., vol. II, p. 256.

21 Corneille, *Médée*, I.v. 320. There seems to be a discrepancy here between the text Boileau is quoting from, if he is not quoting from memory, and that of modern editions, which does not, however, affect the point at issue.

BIBLIOGRAPHY

I. **Works of antiquity, the Renaisance, and the seventeenth and eighteenth centuries**

Aristotle; Horace; Longinus, *Classical Literary Criticism*, ed. T.S. Dorsch (Harmondsworth, 1965)

Aubignac, François Hédelin, abbé d', *La Pratique du théâtre*, ed. Pierre Martino (Algiers and Paris, 1927)

Balzac, Jean Louis Guez de, *see* Guez de Balzac, Jean Louis de

Boileau-Despréaux, Nicolas, *Œuvres*, ed. Jérôme Vercruysse and Sylvain Menant, Garnier-Flammarion, 2 vols. (Paris, 1969)

  Œuvres complètes, ed. by Antoine Adam and Françoise Escal, Bibliothèque de la Pléiade (Paris, 1966)

Bossuet, Jacques-Bénigne, *Maximes et réflexions sur la comédie*, in Ch. Urbain and E. Lévesque, *L'Eglise et le théâtre* (Paris, 1930)

  Oraisons funèbres, ed. Jacques Truchet, Classiques Garnier (Paris, 1961)

Bouhours, Dominique, *Doutes sur la langue françoise* (Paris, 1674; repr. Brighton, 1971)

  Les Entretiens d'Ariste et d'Eugène, introduced by Ferdinand Brunot (Paris, 1962)

  La Manière de bien penser dans les ouvrages d'esprit, nouvelle édition (Paris, 1715; repr. Brighton, 1971)

  Pensées ingénieuses des anciens et des modernes, nouvelle édition augmentée (Paris, 1734; repr. Brighton, 1971)

Bussy, Roger de Rabutin, comte de, *Correspondance ... avec sa famille et ses amis (1666–1693)*, ed. Ludovic Lalanne, 6 vols. (Paris, 1858–9)

Callières, François de, *Des mots à la mode* and *Du bon et du mauvais usage dans les manières de s'exprimer* (1692 and 1693: repr. in one vol., Geneva, 1972)

Callières, Jacques de, *La Fortune des gens de qualité et des gentilshommes particuliers* (Paris, 1668)

Castiglione, Baldassare, *The Book of the Courtier*, trans. Sir Thomas Hoby (London, 1974)

Chapelain, Jean, *Lettres*, ed. Ph. Tamizey de Larroque, 2 vols. (Paris, 1880–3)

  Opuscules critiques, ed. A.C. Hunter (Paris, 1936)

Bibliography

Soixante-dix-sept lettres inédites à N. Heinsius, 1649–1658, ed. Bernard Bray, Archives internationales d'histoire des idées, 13 (The Hague, 1966)

Cicero, *Brutus, Orator*, with English trans. G.L. Hendrickson and H.M. Hubbell (London and Cambridge, Mass., 1952)

De oratore, with an English trans. E.W. Sutton and H. Rackham, 2 vols. (London and Cambridge, Mass., 1959–60)

Commentaires sur les Remarques de Vaugelas, by La Mothe Le Vayer and others, ed. Jeanne Streicher, 2 vols. (Paris, 1936)

Corneille, Pierre, *Œuvres complètes*, ed. André Stegmann (Paris, 1963)

Corneille, Thomas, *Dictionnaire des arts et des sciences*, 2 vols. (Paris, 1694)

Dacier, Mme, *Des causes de la corruption du goût* (Paris, 1714). *See also* Le Fèvre, Anne.

Descartes, René, *Discours de la méthode*, in vol. I of *Œuvres philosophiques*, ed. F. Alquié, Classiques Garnier, 3 vols. (Paris, 1963–73)

Dictionnaire de l'Académie françoise, 2 vols. (Paris, 1694)

Diderot, Denis, *Œuvres esthétiques*, ed. Paul Vernière, Classiques Garnier (Paris, 1965)

Œuvres romanesques, ed. Henri Bénac, revised by Lucette Perol, Classiques Garnier (Paris, 1981)

Faret, Nicolas, *L'Honneste Homme ou l'art de plaire à la court*, ed. Maurice Magendie (Paris, 1925)

Fontenelle, Bernard Le Bovier de, *Œuvres*, nouvelle édition, 10 vols. (Paris, 1758)

Frain du Tremblay, Jean, *Discours sur l'origine de la poésie, sur son usage et sur le bon goût* (Paris, 1713 (first published 1711): repr. Geneva, 1970)

Furetière, Antoine, *Dictionnaire universel* (The Hague and Rotterdam, 1690)

Dictionnaire universel, second ed., revised by H. Basnage de Bauval (The Hague and Rotterdam, 1701)

Recueil des factums d'Antoine Furetière de l'Académie Françoise contre quelques-uns de cette Académie, ed. Charles Asselineau, 2 vols. (Paris, 1859)

Le Roman bourgeois, in *Romanciers du XVIIe siècle*, ed. Antoine Adam, Bibliothèque de la Pléiade (Paris, 1958)

Guez de Balzac, Jean Louis, *Les Entretiens (1657)*, ed. B. Beugnot, 2 vols. (Paris, 1972)

Lettres, ed. Ph. Tamizey de Larroque, (Paris, 1873)

Œuvres, 2 vols. (Paris, 1665)

Les Premières Lettres, ed. H. Bibas and K.T. Butler, 2 vols. (Paris, 1933–4)

La Bruyère, Jean de, *Les Caractères ou les Mœurs de ce siècle*, ed. Robert Garapon, Classiques Garnier (Paris, 1962)

La Rochefoucauld, François VI, duc de, *Maximes suivies des Réflexions diverses* ..., ed. Jacques Truchet, Classiques Garnier (Paris, 1967)

Le Brun, Pierre, *Discours sur la comédie*, seconde édition augmentée (Paris, 1731)

210

Bibliography

Le Fèvre, Anne, *Le Plutus et les Nuées d'Aristophane: comédies grecques traduites en françois* (Paris, 1684). *See also* Dacier, Mme.

Loyseau, Charles, *Œuvres*, nouvelle édition (Paris, 1678)

Marivaux, *Théâtre complet*, ed. B. Dort (Paris, 1964)

Méré, Antoine Gombauld, chevalier de, *Lettres*, 2 vols. paginated as one (Paris, 1682)

    Œuvres complètes, ed. Charles-H. Boudhors, 3 vols. (Paris, 1930). *See also* Section II, under Boudhors.

Molière, *Œuvres complètes*, ed. Georges Couton, Bibliothèque de la Pléiade, 2 vols. (Paris, 1971)

Montchrétien, Antoyne de, *Traité de l'œconomie politique*, ed. Th. Funck-Brentano, Collection des Economistes et des Réformateurs Sociaux de la France, 14 (Paris, n.d.)

Morvan de Bellegarde, Jean-Baptiste, *Lettres curieuses de littérature et de morale*, second ed. (Amsterdam, 1707)

    Modèles de conversation pour les personnes polies, seconde édition augmentée (Paris, 1698)

    Réflexions sur ce qui peut plaire, ou déplaire dans le commerce du monde (Amsterdam, 1690)

    Réflexions sur la politesse des mœurs (Paris, 1700)

    Réflexions sur le ridicule, et sur les moyens de l'éviter, cinquième édition augmentée (Paris, 1701)

Nicole, Pierre, *Essais de morale*, 15 vols. (Paris, 1755)

    (attrib.), *Préface* to Jean de La Fontaine, *Recueil de poésies chrétiennes et diverses*, second ed., 3 vols. (Paris, 1679)

    'Traité de la vraie et de la fausse beauté dans les ouvrages d'esprit', trans. Pierre Richelet, in *Nouveau recueil des épigrammatistes françois, anciens et modernes*, ed. Antoine-Auguste Bruzen de la Martinière, 2 vols. in 1 (Amsterdam, 1720)

Pascal, Blaise, *Œuvres complètes*, ed. Louis Lafuma (Paris, 1963)

Perrot d'Ablancourt, Nicolas, *Lettres et préfaces critiques*, ed. Roger Zuber (Paris, 1972)

Pomey, François Antoine, *Le Dictionaire royal*, dernière édition (Lyons, 1677)

Quintilian, *Institutio oratoria*, with a trans. by H. E. Butler, 4 vols. (London and New York, 1920–2)

Rapin, René, *Les Réflexions sur la poétique de ce temps*, ed. E. T. Dubois (Geneva, 1970)

Renaudot, Theophraste, Isaac, and Eusèbe, *Recueil général des questions traictées ès conférences du bureau d'adresse*, 5 vols. in 4 (Paris, 1660)

Rhetorica ad Herennium, with an English trans. by Harry Caplan (London and Cambridge, Mass., 1954)

Richelet, Pierre, *Dictionnaire françois* (Geneva, 1680, repr. 1685)

Rousseau, Jean-Jacques, *Du contrat social*, in *Œuvres complètes*, ed. Bernard Gagnebin and Marcel Raymond, Bibliothèque de la Pléiade, 4 vols. (Paris, 1959–69), vol. III (1964)

Saint-Evremond, Charles Marguetel de Saint-Denis, seigneur de, *Lettres*, ed. René Ternois, 2 vols. (Paris, 1967–8)

Œuvres en prose, ed. René Ternois, 4 vols. (Paris, 1962–9)

Les Opéra, ed. Robert Finch and Eugene Joliat, Textes Littéraires Français, 266 (Geneva, 1979)

Sir Politick Would-be, ed. Robert Finch and Eugène Joliat, Textes Littéraires Français, 250 (Geneva, 1978)

Textes choisis, ed. Alain Niderst (Paris, 1970)

Saint-Evremond and the comte d'Etelan, *La Comédie des Académistes*, and Saint-Evremond, *Les Académiciens*, ed. Paolo Carile, with a preface by Enea Balmas (Milan and Paris, 1976)

Saint-Réal, César Vichard, abbé de, *Œuvres*, nouvelle édition augmentée, 4 vols. (Paris, 1724)

Saint-Simon, Louis de Rouvroy, duc de, *Mémoires*, ed. Gonzague Truc, Bibliothèque de la Pléiade, 7 vols. (Paris, 1948–61)

Sévigné, Marie de Rabutin-Chantal, marquise de, *Correspondance*, ed. Roger Duchêne, Bibliothèque de la Pléiade, 3 vols. (Paris, 1984)

Somaize, Antoine Baudeau de, *Le Dictionnaire des précieuses*, nouvelle édition, ed. Ch.-L. Livet, 2 vols. (Paris, 1856)

Tallemant des Réaux, *Historiettes*, ed. Antoine Adam, Bibliothèque de la Pléiade, 2 vols. (Paris, 1960–1)

Vaugelas, Claude Favre de, *Remarques sur la langue françoise*, ed. Jeanne Streicher (Paris, 1934)

Voiture, Vincent, *Œuvres*, ed. M.A. Ubicini, 2 vols. (Paris, 1855)

II. Works directly related to the seventeenth century

Adam, Antoine, *Grandeur and Illusion: French Literature and Society, 1600–1715*, trans. by Herbert Tint (Harmondsworth, 1974: first publ. 1972)

Histoire de la littérature française au XVIIe siècle, 5 vols. (Paris, 1948–56)

Adam, Antoine, Pierre Clarac and René Pomeau, *L'Age classique*, Littérature française, 6–8 (Paris, 1968–71)

Alter, Jean V., *Les Origines de la satire antibourgeoise en France*, 2 vols., vol. II: *L'Esprit antibourgeois sous l'ancien regime: littérature et tensions sociales aux XVIIe et XVIIIe siècles*, Histoire des idées et critique littéraire, 103 (Geneva, 1970)

Anderson, Perry, *Lineages of the Absolutist State* (London, 1974)

Angenot, Marc, *Les Champions des femmes: examen du discours sur la supériorité des femmes, 1400–1800* (Montreal, 1977)

Apostolidès, Jean-Marie, *Le Roi-Machine: spectacle et politique au temps de Louis XIV*, Arguments (Paris, 1981)

Ariès, Philippe, *L'Enfant et la vie familiale sous l'ancien régime* (Paris, 1960)

Atkins, J.W.H., *English Literary Criticism: the Medieval Phase* (Cambridge, 1943)

Bibliography

Auerbach, Erich, 'La Cour et la Ville', in *Scenes from the Drama of European Literature*, trans. Ralph Manheim, pp. 133–79 (New York, 1959)

Baader, Renate, 'La Polémique anti-baroque dans la doctrine classique', *Baroque*, 6 (1973), 133–48

Bakhtin, Mikhail, *Rabelais and his World*, trans. from the Russian by Helene Iswolsky (Cambridge, Mass., 1968)

Barnwell, H.T., *Les Idées morales et critiques de Saint-Evremond* (Paris, 1957)

Barrère, Jean-Bertrand, *L'Idée de goût de Pascal à Valéry*, Critères, 1 (Paris, 1972)

Barthes, Roland, 'La Bruyère', in his *Essais critiques* (Paris, 1964), pp. 221–37

Becq, Annie, 'Genèse de l'esthétique française moderne: de la raison classique à l'imagination créatrice, 1680–1814' (unpublished thesis, University of Paris, 1979)

Benay, Jacques G., 'L'Honnête Homme devant la nature, ou la philosophie du chevalier de Méré, *PMLA*, 79 (1964), 22–32

Bénichou, Paul, *Morales du grand siècle* (Paris, 1948)

Bernard, Leon, 'French Society and Popular Uprisings under Louis XIV', *French Historical Studies*, 3 (1964), 454–74

Bitton, Davis, *The French Nobility in Crisis, 1560–1640* (Stanford, Calif., 1969)

Bloch, Marc, *Les Caractères originaux de l'histoire rurale française*, second edn, 2 vols. (Paris, 1960–1: first publ. Oslo, 1931)

Blunt, Anthony, *Art and Architecture in France, 1500–1700*, fourth edn (Harmondsworth, 1980)

Bonnet, Jean-Claude, 'La Table dans les civilités', in *La Qualité de la vie au XVIIe siècle*, Actes du 7e Colloque de Marseille, in *Marseille*, 109 (1977), pp. 99–104

Borgerhoff, E.B.O., *The Freedom of French Classicism*, Princeton Publications in Modern Languages, 9 (Princeton, N.J., 1950)

Boudhors, Ch.-H., 'Divers propos du chevalier de Méré en 1674–1675', *RHL*, nos. 29 (1922), pp. 76–98, 214–24; 30 (1923), pp. 79–89, 380–3, 520–9; 31 (1924), pp. 490–6; 32 (1925), pp. 68–78, 432–56, 596–601

Bray, Bernard, 'Le Dialogue comme forme littéraire au XVIIe siècle', *CAIEF*, 24 (1972), 9–29

Bray, René, *La Formation de la doctrine classique en France* (Paris, 1927, repr. 1961)

Brenner, Robert, 'Agrarian Class Structure and Economic Development in Pre-Industrial Europe', *Past and Present*, 70 (1976), 30–75

Briggs, Robin, *Early Modern France 1560–1715* (Oxford, 1977)

Brody, Jules, *Boileau and Longinus* (Geneva, 1958)

'Images de l'homme chez La Bruyère', *L'Esprit Créateur*, 15 (1975), 164–88

'La Bruyère: le style d'un moraliste', *CAIEF*, 30 (1978), 139–53

'Platonisme et classicisme', *Saggi e ricerche di letteratura francese*, 2 (1961), 7–30

'Sur le style de La Bruyère', *L'Esprit Créateur*, 11, no. 2 (summer 1971), 154–68

Brooks, H. Frank, 'Taste, Perfection and Delight in Guez de Balzac's Criticism', *Studies in Philology*, 68 (1971), 70–87

Brunot, Ferdinand, *Histoire de la langue française des origines à 1900*, 13 vols. (Paris, 1905–53)

Burke, Peter, *Popular Culture in Early Modern Europe* (London, 1978)

Cassirer, Ernst, *The Philosophy of the Enlightenment*, trans. Fritz C. A. Koelln and James P. Pettegrove (Princeton, N.J., 1951)

Cayrou, Gaston, *Le Français classique: lexique de la langue du XVIIe siècle* (Paris, 1924)

Chamaillard, Edmond, *Le Chevalier de Méré: étude biographique et littéraire* (Niort, 1921)

Chaunu, Pierre, *La Civilisation de l'Europe classique*, Les Grandes Civilisations, 5 (Paris, 1966)

Chevalier, Jean-Claude, 'Les *Entretiens d'Ariste et d'Eugène* du père Bouhours, soit la littérature et l'idéologie', in *Langue et langages de Leibniz à l'Encyclopédie*, ed. Michèle Duchet and Michèle Jalley, pp. 25–43 (Paris, 1977)

Chouillet, Jacques, *L'Esthétique des Lumières*, Collection SUP, section Littératures modernes, 4 (Paris, 1974)

Clarac, Pierre, *Boileau* (Paris, 1964)

Couton, Georges, 'Effort publicitaire et organisation de la recherche: les gratifications aux gens de lettres sous Louis XIV', in *Le XVIIe siècle et la recherche*, Actes du sixième colloque de Marseille (janvier 1976) (Marseilles, 1977)

Croot, Patricia and David Parker, 'Agrarian Class Structure and Economic Development', *Past and Present*, 78 (1978), 37–47

Culler, Jonathan, 'Paradox and the Language of Morals in La Rochefoucauld', *MLR* 68 (1973), 28–39

Dainville, François de, 'Collèges et fréquentation scolaire au XVIIe siècle', *Population*, 12 (1957), 467–94

Davidson, Hugh M., *Audience, Words and Art: Studies in Seventeenth-Century French Rhetoric* (Columbus, Ohio, 1965)

'Perrault, Fontenelle and the Realignment of the Arts', in *Literature and History in the Age of Ideas: Essays on the French Enlightenment presented to George Remington Havens*, ed. Charles G. S. Williams (Columbus, Ohio, 1975), pp. 2–13

Davis, Natalie Zemon, *Society and Culture in Early Modern France* (London, 1975)

De Mourgues, Odette, *Metaphysical, Baroque and Précieux Poetry* (Oxford, 1953)

'Quelques paradoxes sur le classicisme', The Zaharoff Lecture for 1980–1 (Oxford, 1981)

Bibliography

Two French Moralists: La Rochefoucauld and La Bruyère, (Cambridge, 1978)

Dens, Jean-Pierre, '"Les Agréments qui ne lassent point": le chevalier de Méré et l'art de plaire', *L'Esprit Créateur*, 15 (1975), 221–7

'L'Art de la conversation au XVIIe siècle', *Les Lettres Romanes*, 27 (1973), 213–22

'*Beauté* et *grâce* au XVIIe siècle', *RHL*, 75 (1975), 795–9

'Le Chevalier de Méré et la critique mondaine', *XVIIe Siècle*, 101 (1973), 41–50

L'Honnête Homme et la critique du goût, French Forum Monographs, 28 (Lexington, Ky, 1981)

'L'Honnête Homme et l'esthétique du paraître', *PFSCL*, 6 (1976–7), 69–82

'Morale et société chez La Rochefoucauld', *L'Information littéraire*, 37 (1975), 55–7

'La Notion de bon goût au XVIIe siècle: Historique et définition', *RBPH*, 53 (1975), 726–9

Deyon, Pierre, 'A propos des rapports entre la noblesse française et la monarchie absolue pendant la première moitié du XVIIe siècle', *Revue historique*, 231 (1964), 341–56

Doubrovsky, Serge, 'Lecture de La Bruyère', *Poétique*, 2 (1970), 195–201

Duby, Georges, *Les Trois ordres ou l'imaginaire du féodalisme* (Paris, 1978)

Duby, Georges and Robert Mandrou, *Histoire de la civilisation française*, fifth edn, 2 vols. (Paris, 1968)

Dumonceaux, Pierre, *Langue et sensibilité au XVIIe siècle: l'évolution du vocabulaire affectif*, Publications romanes et françaises, 131 (Geneva, 1975)

Ehrard, Jean, *L'Idée de nature en France dans la première moitié du XVIIIe siècle*, Bibliothèque générale de l'Ecole Pratique des Hautes Etudes, VIe section, 2 vols. in one (Paris, 1963)

Elias, Norbert, *The Civilizing Process*, trans. Edmund Jephcott, 2 vols., vol. I: *The History of Manners*, vol. II: *State Formation and Civilization* (Oxford, 1978–82)

The Court Society, trans. Edmund Jephcott (Oxford, 1983)

Fagniez, G., *La Femme et la société française dans la première moitié du XVIIe siècle* (Paris, 1929)

Foucault, Michel, *Les Mots et les choses* (Paris, 1966)

France, Peter, *Racine: Andromaque*, Studies in French Literature, 32 (London, 1977)

Rhetoric and Truth in France: Descartes to Diderot (Oxford, 1972)

France, Peter, and Margaret McGowan, 'Louis XIV and the Arts' in *French Literature and its Background*, ed. John Cruickshank, vol. II: *The Seventeenth Century*, Oxford Paperbacks, 171 (London, 1969), pp. 82–98

France in Crisis, 1620–1675, ed. P. J. Coveney (London, 1977)

Fumaroli, Marc, *L'Age de l'éloquence: rhétorique et 'res literaria' de la*

Renaissance au seuil de l'époque classique, Hautes Etudes Médiévales et Modernes, 43 (Geneva, 1980)

Gaiffe, Félix, *L'Envers du Grand Siècle: étude historique et anecdotique* (Paris, 1924)

Garrity, Henry A., 'Taste and a Case for Understatement in Bouhours's *La Manière de bien penser*', *Romance Notes*, 14 (1972–3), 136–8

Gasté, Armand, *La Querelle du Cid: pièces et pamphlets publiés d'après les originaux* (Paris, 1898)

Godard de Domville, Louise, *Signification de la mode sous Louis XIII* (Aix-en-Provence, 1978)

Goldmann, Lucien, *Le Dieu caché: études sur la vision tragique dans les 'Pensées' de Pascal et dans le théâtre de Racine*, Collection Tel, 11 (Paris, 1979; first publ. 1959)

Goubert, Pierre, *L'Ancien Régime*, 2 vols. (Paris, 1969–73)
Louis XIV et vingt millions de Français (Paris, 1966)
See also: *Histoire économique et sociale de la France*

Grubbs, Henry A., Jr, *Damien Mitton, 1618–1690: 'Bourgeois Honnête Homme'*, Elliott Monographs in the Romance Languages and Literatures, 29 (Princeton, N.J., and Paris, 1932)

Guellouz, Suzanne, 'Le Père Bouhours et le *je ne sais quoi*', *Littératures*, 18 (1971), 3–14

Harth, Erica, 'Classical Disproportion: La Bruyère's *Caractères*', *L'Esprit Créateur*, 15 (1975), 189–210
'Classical Innateness', *Yale French Studies*, 49 (1973), 212–30
'Exorcising the Beast: Attempts at Rationality in French Classicism', *PMLA*, 88 (1973), 19–24
Ideology and Culture in Seventeenth-Century France (Ithaca, N.Y., 1983)

Hauser, Arnold, *The Social History of Art*, trans. in collaboration with the author by S. Goodman, 2 vols. (London, 1951)

Hazard, Paul, *La Crise de la conscience européenne (1680–1715)*, 3 vols. (Paris, 1935)

Hepp, Noémi, 'Esquisse du vocabulaire de la critique littéraire de la querelle du Cid à la querelle d'Homère', *Romanische Forschungen*, 69 (1957), 332–408
Homère en France au XVIIe siècle, Bibliothèque française et romane, série C, Etudes littéraires, 18 (Paris, 1969)

Hippeau, Louis, *Essai sur la morale de La Rochefoucauld* (Paris, 1967)

Histoire de la France rurale, ed. G. Duby and A. Wallon, L'Univers historique, 4 vols. (Paris, 1975–7), vol. II: *L'Age classique des paysans, 1340–1789*, by Hugues Neveux, Jean Jacquart, and Emmanuel Le Roy Ladurie, ed. Emmanuel Le Roy Ladurie (1975)

Histoire économique et sociale de la France, ed. Fernand Braudel and Ernest Labrousse, 4 vols. (Paris, 1970–80), vol. II: *Des derniers temps de l'âge seigneurial aux préludes de l'âge industriel*, by Ernest Labrousse and others (including Pierre Goubert and Pierre Léon) (1970)

Holst, Niels von, *Creators, Collectors and Connoisseurs: the Anatomy of*

Artistic Taste from Antiquity to the Present Day, with an introduction by Herbert Read, trans. from the German by B. Battershaw (London, 1967)

Hope, Quentin M., *Saint-Evremond: the 'Honnête Homme' as Critic*, Indiana University Humanities Series, 51 (Bloomington, Ind., 1962)

Huppert, George, *Les Bourgeois Gentilshommes* (Chicago and London, 1977)

Jacquart, Jean, *La Crise rurale en Ile-de-France, 1550–1670*, Publications de la Sorbonne, N.S. Recherches, 10 (Paris, 1974)

    See also: *Histoire de la France rurale*

James, E. D., 'Scepticism and Positive Values in La Rochefoucauld', *French Studies*, 23 (1969), 349–61

Jasinski, René, *Deux accès à La Bruyère* (Paris, 1971)

Jehasse, Jean, *Guez de Balzac et le génie romain* (Saint-Etienne, 1978)

    La Renaissance de la critique: l'essor de l'humanisme érudit de 1560 à 1614 (Saint-Etienne, 1976)

Kelso, Ruth, *Doctrine for the Lady of the Renaissance* (Urbana, Ill., 1964)

Kohn, Renée, *Le Goût de La Fontaine* (Paris, 1962)

Koppisch, Michael S., 'The Ambiguity of Social Status in La Bruyère's *Caractères*', *L'Esprit Créateur*, 15 (1975), 211–20

    The Dissolution of Character: Changing Perspectives in La Bruyère's 'Caractères', French Forum Monographs, 24 (Lexington, Ky, 1981)

Kristeller, Paul Oskar, 'The Modern System of the Arts', in *Renaissance Thought and the Arts: Collected Essays*, second edn (Princeton, 1980), pp. 163–227

Labatut, Jean-Pierre, *Les Ducs et pairs de France au XVIIe siècle* (Paris, 1972)

Lafond, Jean, 'La Rochefoucauld, d'une culture à l'autre', *CAIEF*, 30 (1978), 155–69

Lainé, Pascal, 'Art et politique sous Louis XIV', in *Qu'est-ce que la culture française?*, ed. J.-P. Aron, Collectif Médiations, 2 (Paris, 1975), pp. 211–21

Lathuillère, Roger, *La Préciosité: étude historique et linguistique*, vol. I: *Position du problème: les origines*, Publications romanes et françaises, 87 (Geneva, 1966)

Lévêque, André, ' "L'Honnête Homme" et "l'homme de bien" au XVIIe siècle', *PMLA*, 72 (1957), 620–32

Lewis, Philip E., *La Rochefoucauld: the Art of Abstraction* (Ithaca, N.Y., 1977)

Litman, Théodore A., *Le Sublime en France (1660–1714)* (Paris, 1971)

Lougee, Carolyn C., *Le Paradis des Femmes: Women, Salons and Social Stratification in Seventeenth-Century France* (Princeton, N.J., 1976)

Lough, John, *An Introduction to Seventeenth-Century France* (London, 1954)

    Paris Theatre Audiences in the Seventeenth and Eighteenth Centuries (London, 1957)

    Writer and Public in France: From the Middle Ages to the Present Day (Oxford, 1978)

Bibliography

Lublinskaya, A. D., 'The Contemporary Bourgeois Conception of Absolute Monarchy', *Economy and Society*, 1 (1972), 65–92
French Absolutism: the Crucial Phase, 1620–1629, trans. Brian Pearce (Cambridge, 1968)
'Popular Masses and the Social Relations of the Epoch of Absolutism', *Economy and Society*, 2 (1973), 343–75
Maclean, Ian, *Woman Triumphant: Feminism in French Literature, 1610–52* (Oxford, 1977)
Magendie, Maurice, *La Politesse mondaine et les théories de l'honnêteté, en France, au XVIIe siècle, de 1600 à 1660* (Paris, 1925)
Magne, Bernard, *Crise de la littérature française sous Louis XIV: humanisme et nationalisme*, 2 vols. (Lille, 1976)
Maland, David, *Culture and Society in Seventeenth-Century France* (London, 1970)
Malcovati, Enrica, *Madame Dacier: una gentildonna filologa del gran secolo* (Florence, 1952)
Mandrou, Robert, *Classes et luttes de classes en France au début du XVIIe siècle* (Messina and Florence, 1965)
De la culture populaire aux XVIIe et XVIIIe siècles: la Bibliothèque bleue de Troyes (Paris, 1964)
La France aux XVIIe et XVIIIe siècles, Nouvelle Clio, 33, second edn (Paris, 1970)
Introduction à la France moderne: essai de psychologie historique (1500–1640), L'Evolution de l'humanité, Bibliothèque de synthèse historique, 52 (Paris, 1961)
Marin, Louis, *La Critique du discours: sur la 'Logique de Port-Royal' et les 'Pensées' de Pascal* (Paris, 1975)
Martin, Henri-Jean, *Livre, pouvoirs et société à Paris au XVIIe siècle, 1598–1701*, Centre de Recherches d'Histoire et de la Philologie de la IVe Section de l'Ecole Pratique des Hautes Etudes, 6, Histoire et civilisation du livre, 3. 2 vols. paginated as one (Geneva, 1969)
Matoré, Georges, *Histoire des dictionnaires français* (Paris, 1968)
Mélèse, Pierre, *Le Théâtre et son public à Paris sous Louis XIV (1659–1715)* (Paris, 1934)
Mendoza, Bernadette B. de, 'L'Art de vivre de l'honnête homme: éthique ou esthétique', *PFSCL*, 1 (1973), 17–26
Meyer, Jean, *La Noblesse bretonne au XVIIIe siècle*, 2 vols. (Paris, 1966)
Michéa, R., 'Les Variations de la raison au XVIIe siècle', *Revue philosophique de la France et de l'étranger*, 126 (juillet-décembre 1938), 183–201
Mongrédien, Georges, *La Vie littéraire au XVIIe siècle*, Histoire de la vie littéraire (Paris, 1947)
La Vie quotidienne sous Louis XIV, La Vie quotidienne (Paris, 1948)
Moore, W. G., 'Le Goût de la cour', *CAIEF*, 9 (1957), 172–82
La Rochefoucauld: his Mind and Art (Oxford, 1969)
Mornet, Daniel, *Histoire de la littérature française classique, 1660–1700: ses caractères véritables, ses aspects inconnus*, second edn (Paris, 1942)

Bibliography

Mousnier, Roland, *Les Hiérarchies sociales de 1450 à nos jours*, Collection SUP, L'historien, 1 (Paris, 1969)

'Recherches sur les soulèvements populaires en France avant la Fronde', *Revue d'histoire moderne et contemporaine*, 5 (1958), 81–113

La Vénalité des offices sous Henri IV et Louis XIII, Collection Hier, second edn (Paris, 1971)

Navarro de Adriaensens, José M., *'Je ne sais quoi*: Bouhours – Feijoo – Montesquieu', *Romanistisches Jahrbuch*, 21 (1970), 107–15

Naves, Raymond, *Le Goût de Voltaire* (Paris, 1938)

Onze études sur l'image de la femme dans la littérature française du XVIIe siècle, ed. Wolfgang Leiner, Etudes litteraires françaises, 1 (Tubingen, 1978)

Papin, Claude, 'Le Sens de l'idéal de "l'honnête homme" au XVIIe siècle', *La Pensée*, 104 (juillet-août 1962), 52–83

Parker, David, *The Making of French Absolutism* (London, 1983)

'The Social Foundations of French Absolutism, 1610–30', *Past and Present*, 53 (1971), 67–89

Philips, J. Henry, *The Theatre and its Critics in Seventeenth-Century France* (Oxford, 1980)

Pintard, René, '1660: la littérature et le goût au seuil de l'époque classique', *XVIIe Siècle*, 50–1 (1961), 5–7

Pocock, Gordon, *Boileau and the Nature of Neo-Classicism* (Cambridge, 1980)

Porchnev, B.F., *Les Soulèvements populaires en France de 1623 à 1648*, trans. from the Russian by Mme Ranieta, with an introduction by Robert Mandrou, Ecole Pratique des Hautes Etudes, VIe section, Centre de recherches historiques, Œuvres étrangères, 4 (Paris, 1963)

Pottinger, D.T., *The French Book Trade in the Ancien Regime, 1500–1791* (Cambridge, Mass., 1958)

La Qualité de la vie au XVIIe siècle, Actes du 7e Colloque de Marseille, *Marseille*, 109 (1977)

Quemada, Bernard, *Les Dictionnaires du français moderne, 1539–1863: étude sur leur histoire, leurs types et leurs méthodes*, vol. I; Etudes lexicologiques, 1 (Paris, 1967)

Reiss, Timothy J., 'Cartesian Discourse and Classical Ideology', *Diacritics*, 6, no. 4 (winter 1976), 9–27

'Du système de la critique classique', *XVIIe Siècle*, 116 (1977), 3–16

'Sailing to Byzantium: Classical Discourse and its Self-Absorption', *Diacritics*, 8, no. 2 (summer 1978), 34–46

Reynier, Gustave, *La Femme au XVIIe siècle, ses ennemis et ses défenseurs* (Paris, 1929)

Rosset, Théodore, *Entretien, doutes, critique & remarques du Père Bouhours sur la langue française, 1671–1692* (Grenoble, 1908; repr. Geneva, 1968)

Saisselin, Rémy G., *The Rule of Reason and the Ruses of the Heart: a Philosophical Dictionary of Classical French Criticism, Critics, and Aesthetic Issues* (Cleveland, Ohio, 1970)

Bibliography

Taste in Eighteenth Century France: Critical Reflections on the Origins of Aesthetics, or An Apology for Amateurs (Syracuse, N.Y., 1965)

Salmon, J. H. M., 'Venality of Office and Popular Sedition in Seventeenth-Century France: a Review of a Controversy', *Past and Present*, 37 (1967), 21–43

Simon, P.-H., 'Le *je ne sais quoi* devant la raison classique', *CAIEF*, 11 (1959), 104–17

Snyders, Georges, *La Pédagogie en France aux XVIIe et XVIIIe siècles* (Paris, 1965)

Soreil, Arsène, *Introduction à l'histoire de l'esthétique française* (Brussels, 1966)

Soriano, Marc, *Le Dossier Perrault* (Paris, 1972)

Stanton, Domna C., *The Aristocrat as Art: a Study of the 'Honnête Homme' and the 'Dandy' in Seventeenth- and Nineteenth-Century French Literature* (New York, 1980)

'*L'Art de plaire* and the semiotics of *honnêteté*', *PFSCL*, 6 (1976–7), 11–22

'The Fiction of *Préciosité* and the Fear of Women', *Yale French Studies*, 62 (1981), 107–34

Starobinski, Jean, 'La Rochefoucauld et les morales substitutives', *Nouvelle Revue Française*, 163–4 (juillet-août 1966), 16–34, 211–29

Stegmann, André, *Les Caractères de La Bruyère: bible de l'honnête homme* (Paris, 1972)

Stone, Donald, *French Humanist Tragedy: a Reassessment* (Manchester, 1974)

Strosetzski, Christoph, *Rhétorique de la conversation: sa dimension littéraire et linguistique dans la société française du XVIIe siècle*, trans. from the German by Sabine Seubert, Biblio 17, 20 (Paris–Seattle–Tübingen, 1984)

Sutcliffe, F. E., *Guez de Balzac et son temps: littérature et politique* (Paris, 1959)

Tatarkiewicz, Ladislas, 'L'Esthétique du Grand Siècle', in *XVIIe Siècle*, 78 (1968), 21–35

Taylor, F. H., *The Taste of Angels: a History of Art Collection from Rameses to Napoleon* (London, 1948)

Thweatt, Vivien, *La Rochefoucauld and the Seventeenth-Century Concept of the Self*, Histoire des idées et critique littéraire, 188 (Geneva, 1980)

Tocanne, Bernard, *L'Idée de nature en France dans la seconde moitié du XVIIe siècle: contribution à l'histoire de la pensée classique*, Bibliothèque française et romane, série C, Etudes littéraires, 67 (Paris, 1978)

The Transition from Feudalism to Capitalism [by Paul Sweezy and others] with an introduction by Rodney Hilton (London, 1976)

Urbain, Ch., and E. Lévesque, *L'Eglise et le théâtre* (Paris, 1930)

Van Delft, Louis, 'Clarté et cartésianisme de La Bruyère', *French Review*, 44 (1970–1), 281–90

La Bruyère moraliste: quatre études sur les Caractères, Histoire des idées et critique littéraire, 117 (Geneva, 1971)

Bibliography

Le Moraliste classique: essai de définition et de typologie, Histoire des idées et critique littéraire, 202 (Geneva, 1982)

Van der Cruysse, D., 'L'Honnête Homme selon le duc de Saint-Simon', *RBPH*, 48 (1970), 775–83

Vogler, Frederick W., 'The Cult of Taste in Bouhours' *Pensées ingénieuses des anciens et des modernes*', in *Renaissance and other Studies in Honor of William Leon Wiley*, ed. George Bernard Daniel, Jr, University of North Carolina Studies in the Romance Languages and Literatures, 72 (Chapel Hill, N.C., 1968), pp. 241–8

Wellek, René, *The Rise of English Literary History* (Chapel Hill, N.C., 1941)

Zuber, Roger, *Les 'Belles Infidèles' et la formation du goût classique: Perrot d'Ablancourt et Guez de Balzac* (Paris, 1968)

III. General and theoretical works

Althusser, Louis, *For Marx*, trans. Ben Brewster (London, 1977; first publ. 1969)

'Idéologie et appareils idéologiques d'Etat (notes pour une recherche)', in *Positions* (Paris, 1976), pp. 79–137 (in English, trans. by Ben Brewster, in *Lenin and Philosophy* (New York and London, 1971), pp. 127–86)

Althusser, Louis, and Etienne Balibar, *Reading Capital*, trans. by Ben Brewster (London, 1970)

Barthes, Roland, *Critique et vérité* (Paris, 1966)

Le Degré zéro de l'écriture [1953], *suivi de Nouveaux essais critiques*, Collection Points, 35 (Paris, 1972)

Image – Music – Text, essays selected and trans. by Stephen Heath (London, 1977)

Leçon (Paris, 1978)

Mythologies (Paris, 1957)

Le Plaisir du texte (Paris, 1973)

Sur Racine (Paris, 1963)

S/Z (Paris, 1970)

Benjamin, Walter, 'Theses on the Philosophy of History', in *Illuminations*, ed. Hannah Arendt, trans. Harry Zohn (London, 1973), pp. 255–66

Bennett, Tony, *Formalism and Marxism* (London, 1979)

Benveniste, Emile, *Problèmes de linguistique générale*, vol. I, Collection Tel, 7 (Paris, 1982; first publ. 1966)

Bourdieu, Pierre, *La Distinction: critique sociale du jugement* (Paris, 1979)

Burke, Peter, *Sociology and History*, Controversies in Sociology, 10 (London, 1980)

Cohen, G. A., *Karl Marx's Theory of History: a Defence* (Oxford, 1978)

Critical Sociology: Selected Readings, ed. Paul Connerton (Harmondsworth, 1976)

Culler, Jonathan, *The Pursuit of Signs: Semiotics, Literature, Deconstruction* (London, 1981)

Bibliography

Structuralist Poetics: Structuralism, Linguistics and the Study of Literature (London, 1975)

Eagleton, Terry, *Criticism and Ideology: a Study in Marxist Literary Theory* (London, 1976)

Literary Theory: an Introduction (Oxford, 1983)

Escarpit, Robert, *Sociologie de la littérature*, Que sais-je?, 777 (Paris, 1964)

Foucault, Michel, *Histoire de la sexualité*, vol. I: *La Volonté de savoir* (Paris, 1976)

L'Ordre du discours (Paris, 1971)

Fowler, Roger, *Literature as Social Discourse* (London, 1981)

Gombrich, E. H., *Meditations on a Hobby-Horse* (London, 1971)

Gramsci, Antonio, *Selections from the Prison Notebooks*, ed. and trans. by Quintin Hoare and Geoffrey Nowell Smith (London, 1971)

Heath, Stephen, *The Sexual Fix* (London, 1982)

Hindess, Barry, and Paul Hirst, *Pre-Capitalist Modes of Production* (London, 1975)

Hobsbawm, Eric, 'Class-Consciousness in History', in *Aspects of History and Class-Consciousness*, ed. István Mészáros (London, 1971), pp. 5-21

Jakobson, Roman, 'Closing Statement: Linguistics and Poetics', in *Style in Language*, ed. Thomas A. Sebeok (Cambridge, Mass., 1960), pp. 350-77

Lukács, Georg, *History and Class Consciousness: Studies in Marxist Dialectics*, trans. by Rodney Livingstone (London, 1971)

MacCabe, Colin, 'On discourse', *Economy and Society*, 8 (1979), 279-307

Macdonell, Diane, *Theories of Discourse: an Introduction* (Oxford, 1986)

Macherey, Pierre, *Pour une théorie de la production littéraire*, Collection Théorie, 4 (Paris, 1980: first publ. 1966)

Marx, Karl, *Capital*, vol. I, introduced by Ernest Mandel, trans. by Ben Fowkes (Harmondsworth, 1976)

Capital, vol. III, with an introduction by Ernest Mandel, trans. by David Fernbach (Harmondsworth, 1981)

Economic and Philosophical Manuscripts, in *Early Writings*, introduced by Lucio Colletti, trans. Rodney Livingstone and Gregor Benton (Harmondsworth, 1975)

Grundrisse, trans. with a foreword by Martin Nicolaus (Harmondsworth, 1973)

Pre-Capitalist Economic Formations, trans. Jack Cohen, ed. Eric Hobsbawm (London, 1964)

Selected Writings, ed. David McLellan (Oxford, 1977)

Marx, Karl and Frederick Engels, *The German Ideology*, Part One, ed. C. J. Arthur (London, 1970)

On Literature and Art (Moscow, 1976)

Selected Works in one vol. (London, 1968)

Ste.-Croix, G. E. M. de, *The Class Struggle in the Ancient Greek World: from the Archaic Age to the Arab Conquests* (London, 1981)

Bibliography

Sontag, Susan, *A Susan Sontag Reader* (Harmondsworth, 1983)

Structuralism and Since, ed. John Sturrock (Oxford, 1979)

Thompson, E.P., 'Eighteenth-Century English Society: Class Struggle without Class?', *Social History*, 3 (1978), 133–65

Williams, Raymond, *Culture and Society 1780–1950* (Harmondsworth, 1963; first publ. 1958)

Keywords: a Vocabulary of Culture and Society (London, 1976)

The Long Revolution (London, 1961)

Marxism and Literature (Oxford, 1977)

Politics and Letters: Interviews with 'New Left Review' (London, 1979)

Problems in Materialism and Culture (London, 1980)

INDEX

Index

Boileau, Gilles 207
Boileau (Nicolas Boileau-Despréaux) 5,
    6, 7, 16, 17, 55, 64, 81, 87, 95,
    105, 156, 169, 171–88, 191, 194,
    195, 201, 202, 203, 205–8
Boisdauphin, marquis de 106
bon goût (distinguished from *goût*) 64
bon sens 12–13, 15, 138, 148, 149–50,
    166, 183
Bonnet, Jean-Claude 83, 200
Borgerhoff, E.B.O. 61, 105
Bossuet, Jacques-Bénigne 70–1, 158,
    186, 200, 205
Boudhors, Ch.-H. 96, 102
Bouhours, Dominique 10, 11, 13,
    18–20, 21, 55, 62, 64–6, 67, 68,
    72, 79, 147, 150, 171, 199
Bourdieu, Pierre 4
bourgeois, bourgeoisie 5, 33, 44, 45,
    78, 79, 84, 118, 170
Brébeuf, Georges de 122
Brody, Jules 173, 175, 183
Brossette, Claude 17
Buckingham, George Villiers, second
    duke of 116
bureaucrats 41–3, 48
burgundy 106
Burke, Peter 198
Bussy-Rabutin (Roger de Rabutin,
    comte de Bussy) 186, 207

Caesar, Gaius Julius 91, 153, 202
Callot, Jacques 162, 166
Cambert, Robert, composer 110
capitalism 26, 28–31, 32–3, 34, 35,
    37, 43, 153, 185, 187, 189, 197
Castiglione, Baldassare 39–40, 47, 89
Cayrou (*Le Français classique*) 72–3,
    200
champagne 106
Champaigne, Philippe de 77
Chapelain, Jean 171, 172, 184
Charlemagne 74
Chaulieu, abbé de 108
Christianity 20–1, 38–9, 111, 122,
    158, 167, 170
Church Fathers 38
Cicero 84, 95, 98, 108, 112, 181, 201,
    202
civil society 23, 40
class 2, 3, 11, 23, 24–38, 41–3, 46, 52,
    89, 98, 139–40, 164–5, 176–7,
    181, 189–92
    definitions of 25–6
    and order 32–5, 36, 42–3
class-consciousness 25–6

class struggle 3, 8, 23, 26
classicism 6, 20, 150, 170
Claude (Claude Gellée, *known as*
    Claude Lorrain) 77
Cleopatra 90–1
Clérambault, maréchal de 83
Clérambault, maréchale de 101
climatic determinism 110
clothing 5, 78
Coëffeteau, Nicolas 109
Cohen, G.A. 196
Cohon (Coton?) 109, 203
Colbert, Jean-Baptiste 52–3, 78
collecting 77–8, 79–81, 161–2
Comédie-Française 206
commerce 34
commercialization (of culture) 105,
    167, 169, 178–80, 186, 187, 188,
    191
Condé, Louis, prince de ('le grand
    Condé') 170, 178
consumption (of culture) 81, 111,
    113–14, 118, 148, 152
Conti, Armand, prince de 37
conversation 40, 85, 127–8, 153, 162
Corneille, Pierre 6, 112, 113, 148,
    156–9, 187, 208
    Attila 112
    Horace 157
    Médée 187, 208
    Rodogune 157
Corneille, Thomas 57
Costar, Pierre 86–7, 93
'*Coteaux*', les 106, 204
Cotin, Charles, abbé 172
Coton *see* Cohon
Coulanges, Philippe-Emmanuel de 79
court, courtier(s) 25, 35, 36, 37, 39, 40,
    46–51, 52, 90–3, 94, 96–7, 100,
    105, 109–10, 111, 113–19, 141,
    144, 151–2, 153, 166, 167, 168,
    176, 178, 187, 190–1, 202, 205
court culture 16, 39–40, 46, 170
culture 37–8, 52, 54, 82, 105, 106,
    110, 117, 118, 160, 141–3, 146–7,
    165–6, 169, 203
curiosité 161–3, 166, 169

Dacier, André 17
Dacier, Anne (Mme Dacier) *see* Le
    Fèvre, Anne
D'Aubignac: *see* Aubignac, abbé d'
délicatesse 109–10, 111, 114–17, 118
    and morality 111, 114–17
De Mourgues, Odette 120, 126, 129,
    153, 155, 195

Index

middle classes 168, 170, 178, 185, 187
Miremont, marquis de 108
misogyny 38–9; see also anti-feminism
Mitton, Damien, 66, 199–200, 201;
    see also 'Saint-Evremond'
Moderns, *Modernes* 16, 20, 156,
    159–60, 169, 186, 205
Molière 6, 33, 37, 46, 87, 155, 156,
    168, 184, 194, 201–2, 205
    La Critique de l'Ecole des femmes
    6, 194, 201–2, 205
    L'Ecole des femmes 33, 197
    Les Femmes savantes 138
    L'Impromptu de Versailles 206
    Le Misanthrope 37
monarchy, the 35–7, 77–8, 82, 92–3,
    96–7, 99, 104, 105, 118, 152, 153,
    179–80, 187
Monet, Philibert 55
Montausier, Charles de Sainte-Maure,
    duc de 37, 50
Montchrétien, Antoine de 5, 78, 194,
    201
Montespan, Françoise-Athénaïs de
    Rochechouart, marquise de 186
Montesquieu, Charles Louis de
    Secondat, baron de 142
Montmorency, Henri II, duc de 45
morality (and taste) 114–17, 120–2,
    128, 150, 158, 160–1, 165, 175–7,
    182, 186
    and *honnêteté* 114–17, 150, 158, 167
Mornet, Daniel 7, 9, 171
Morvan de Bellegarde, Jean-Baptiste
    55
music 106, 110, 148

nationalism (cultural) 20, 45, 149–51,
    166
naturalness, *naturel* 66, 94–5, 100
Naves, Raymond 3, 194, 199, 200
Nero 108, 110, 116, 117, 119
Nervèze, Antoine de 109
Nicole, Pierre 72–3
Nicot, Jean 55
nobility, noble, nobiliary 33, 36–7,
    41–3, 47–8, 49–52, 78, 79, 82,
    90, 91, 93, 98, 105, 114, 118–19,
    137, 139–40, 150, 152, 164, 167,
    168, 170, 172, 180, 185, 186,
    187–8, 189–91
noble birth, whether required for
    honnêteté 89, 118, 163–4, 194
noblesse d'épée 35, 36–7, 41, 43, 45,
    49, 80, 90, 114, 118, 191
noblesse de robe 35, 36

Oedipus 112
office-holders, officials, *officiers*
    33–4, 43, 80, 96, 170, 187
Olonne, comte d' 106, 107, 204
order (social category) 27
    in relation to class 32–5, 36, 42–3
Ossat, cardinal d' 155
Ovid 147

painting (and taste) 59, 76–7, 79–82
Paris 176, 177; see also *ville, la*
parlements, parlementaires 39, 80, 114
parterre, the 154, 205, 206–7
partisans 36–7
Pascal, Blaise 61–2, 103–4, 133, 158,
    199, 201, 202, 203, 205
passion, the passions 121, 123, 142
patronage
    in literature 179–80, 187, 188
    in the visual arts 80–1, 201
'pedant', 'pedantry' 23, 44, 96, 100,
    155, 167, 172, 183–4, 191
Pellisson, Paul 186
'people/persons of taste' 86–8, 93–4,
    106–8, 111, 154, 168
Perrault, Charles 169, 176, 181, 183,
    184, 188, 206
Petronius 106, 108, 110, 116, 117, 119
peuple, popular 16, 58, 84–5, 87–8,
    96–7, 99, 151, 154, 165–6,
    167–9, 177–80, 190, 192
Pindar 181
plaire 6, 7, 50
Plato 91, 95, 120, 181, 202
Plautus 20
Pléiade, the 75
Plutarch 88, 116
poetry 111, 182–3
Pomey, Père 55, 56
Pontchartrain 186
Poussin, Nicolas 76–7, 80, 201
précieuses, préciosité 41, 44, 45–6,
    171–2, 184, 206
pride 121–2, 124, 130
production (of culture) 81, 111,
    113–14, 118, 148, 152
professions, professionals 92, 98–9,
    110, 111, 113–14, 118, 185, 187
proverbs 58
provinces, the 50, 74, 176, 177
public, the 14, 15, 16, 45, 84, 105,
    150, 154, 168, 170, 172–8, 185–8,
    191

querelle des femmes 46

228

Index

Racine 6, 10, 74, 151, 153, 156–9, 160, 167, 179, 194
   Athalie 160
   Bajazet 157
   Bérénice 6, 194
   Iphigénie 74
   Mithridate 157
raison 15, 62, 63–4, 65, 68, 74, 138, 150, 183
Rambouillet, Angélique-Clarisse d'Angennes, Mlle de 50
Rambouillet, Catherine de Vivonne, marquise de 48
Rambouillet, Hôtel de 37, 48–9, 50–1, 53, 162
Rapin, René 10, 55, 186
Régnier, Mathurin 184
relexicalization 44, 184, 198, 207
religion
   and taste-discourse 20–1, 70–3, 116–17, 121–2, 146, 152, 160, 167
   and *honnêteté* 114–17
Renaissance, the 44, 51, 55, 76, 155
rentes 170
rentes constituées 31, 34
rentiers 35, 36, 98, 187
Richelet, Pierre 54, 55, 199
   his *Dictionnaire* 55, 56, 57, 59, 65, 74, 81, 149, 199
Richelieu, Armand du Plessis, cardinal de 36, 52–3, 77, 117, 137, 155, 162
Roannez, Artus Gouffier, duc de 133
robe, robins 35, 36, 39, 43, 45, 48, 51–2, 69, 98, 99, 111, 114, 118, 191; see also *noblesse de robe*
Ronsard, Pierre de 75, 76, 147, 171
roturiers 5, 33–4, 99
Rousseau, Jean-Jacques 185
Rubens 76–7
rules in matters of taste 93, 127, 130, 156, 171, 181, 183

Saint-Evremond, Charles Marguetel de Saint-Denis, seigneur de 7, 11, 38, 55, 105, 106–19, 143, 145, 147, 154, 172, 173, 174, 177, 180, 182, 190, 197, 199, 202, 203, 204, 205, 207
   Les Opéra 106, 110, 113
'Saint-Evremond' (Damien Mitton) 62, 63, 64, 66, 68, 200
Saint-Réal, César Vichard, abbé de 72–3
Saint-Simon, Louis de Rouvroy, duc de 35, 152

Ste.-Croix, G. E. M. de 26
salons 17–18, 39, 41–9, 66, 90, 154, 186, 190–1
Sarrasin (Sarasin), Jean-François 108
Saussure, Ferdinand de 54
savants 77, 110, 111–13, 155
Scaliger 86–7
scholars, scholarship 93, 95–6, 111–13, 118, 141–2, 155, 166, 167, 172, 188
Schurman, Anna Maria van 44
Scudéry, Madeleine de 44, 62, 63, 69, 172, 200
   Clélie 181
Séguier, Pierre 33–4
Seignelay, Jean-Baptiste Colbert the younger, marquis de 176
seigneuries, seigneurial 27–8, 29, 30, 33, 34, 35, 36, 43, 82, 99, 140, 197
seigneurial dues 27–8, 30, 32–3, 197
Seneca 97, 109–10, 116, 117
sentiment 62, 63, 65, 66, 68, 74, 86, 90, 145, 163
sentiment, plaisir (definition of *goût*) 69–71
Séraphin, Père 152
Sévigné, Marie de Rabutin-Chantal, marquise de 79
Silver Age (of Latin literature) 19, 147
social relations 24–53
Socrates 91, 95, 99, 153, 202
Somaize, Antoine Baudeau de 41, 44
sovereign courts 33, 41–3, 114; see also *parlements*
Spanish literature, attitudes to 19, 45, 147, 149–50
Stanton, Domna C. 25, 46, 48, 78, 86, 89, 91, 101, 202, 205
Starobinski, Jean 121, 128, 204
state, the 35–7, 40, 49–50, 52–3, 189
state apparatus 41–2; *see also* ideological state apparatuses
Stoics, the 121
study, value of 93–4
subject, the 6, 9, 12, 21–4, 60–1, 63–5, 67, 68–9, 70, 74, 82, 85, 86, 106, 118, 120–1, 124, 125–6, 129–40, 146, 147, 148–9, 151, 156, 157–8, 163, 166–7, 168, 169, 184, 194
sublime, the 171, 181, 185, 186–7, 207
surplus labour, extraction of 26–8, 35, 43, 189

taille, the 33
Tallemant, abbé 17

229

Cambridge Studies in French

General editor: MALCOLM BOWIE

Also in the series

STIRLING HAIG
Flaubert and the Gift of Speech: Dialogue and Discourse in Four 'Modern' Novels

NATHANIEL WING
The Limits of Narrative: Essays on Baudelaire, Flaubert, Rimbaud and Mallarme

MITCHELL GREENBERG
Corneille, Classicism, and the Ruses of Symmetry

HOWARD DAVIES
Sartre and 'Les Temps Modernes'

ROBERT GREER COHN
Mallarmé's Prose Poems: A Critical Study

CELIA BRITTON
Claude Simon: Writing the Visible

DAVID SCOTT
Pictorialist Poetics: Poetry and the Visual Arts in Nineteenth-Century France

ANN JEFFERSON
Reading Realism in Stendhal

DALIA JUDOVITZ
Subjectivity and Representation in Descartes: The Origins of Modernity

RICHARD D. E. BURTON
Baudelaire in 1859: A Study in the Sources of Poetic Creativity

232